Personal Branding FOR DUMMIES®

by Susan Chritton

WILEY-INDIA

Personal Branding For Dummies®

Authorised reprint by Wiley India Pvt. Ltd., 4436/7, Ansari Road, Daryaganj, New Delhi-110002.

Published by John Wiley & Sons, Inc., Hoboken, New Jeney

Reprint: 2023

Printed at: Nice Printing Press

ISBN: 978-81-265-3873-7

About the Author

Career and Personal Brand Master Strategist, **Susan Chritton, M.Ed.**, brings direction, creativity, and renewed enthusiasm to the careers of professionals. Susan excels at guiding her clients toward a more authentic and meaningful career using personal branding strategies that make the most of who they are, not just what they can do.

Susan serves as a speaker and media resource on the topic of personal branding and capitalizing on one's strengths. An advocate of creative life planning, Susan's methods integrate work, family, and other life pursuits.

Susan holds a Master of Education degree in Career Education from St. Mary's College, a Post-Master's Certificate in Career Development from John F. Kennedy University, and a coaching certificate from The Hudson Institute. Susan's professional certifications are numerous and current and include Master Career Counselor (MCC), Professional Certified Coach (PCC), National Certified Career Counselor (NCCC), Master Personal Branding Strategist, Board Certified Coach (BCC), Career Management Fellow Practitioner (CMF), Career Development Facilitator Instructor (CDFI), and Certified in Family and Consumer Sciences (CFCS).

In her work with individuals and organizations, Susan has designed career solutions for enhanced success and fulfillment. She serves as a Personal Brand Strategist and Executive Coach to partners in a Big 4 accounting firm and has been an Adjunct Professor of Career Counseling at the University of San Francisco. She has managed career centers guiding more than a thousand people through career transition.

Actively embodying the principles of work/life balance, Susan raised four children with her husband in Lafayette, California, where she both participates in and leads nonprofit organizations that support her community. Susan spends her free time traveling the world, partaking in book clubs, and riding her red Vespa. Find her at `http://susanchritton.com`.

Dedication

I dedicate this book to my parents for giving me such a different set of talents to live by: my mother for modeling her crazy uniqueness and pioneering independence and my father and stepmother who gave me a strong work ethic and solid approach to life. And to my husband, Rand, who seems to still like those opposing qualities in me. I am lucky to have amazing people in my life who have contributed to the wisdom that shows up in this book.

Author's Acknowledgments

I believe the best things in life are accomplished when we collaborate with others. I want to thank the following contributors for sharing their personal branding expertise with you. I am lucky to be a member of the Reach Personal Branding Community where most of the experts who have contributed to this book belong.

Winnie Anderson works with service business owners to express their brand and clearly communicate the value they offer their Ideal Clients. Together they create Client-Focused organizations and marketing strategies that don't sell — they help people buy. Get her free e-course, information, resources, and special offers at `http://ClientFocusedMarketing.com/blog/personal-branding-for-dummies`.

William Arruda is credited with turning the concept of personal branding into a global industry. William is a sought-after public speaker, bestselling author, and Founder and President of Reach — the world's leading personal branding company. William's clients include 20 percent of Fortune 100 companies and many international brands. Learn more at `www.williamarruda.com`.

Paula Asinof, Wharton MBA, CCM, MCD, and Career Thought Leaders Associate, is an authority on bios, resumes, professional positioning, and executive visibility. Drawing on years of "real-world" leadership experience in corporations and executive search recruiting, she helps clients become more focused, articulate, and energized. Find her at `www.yellowbrickpath.com`.

Mina Brown has been an Executive Coach and Career Consultant for 15 years. A Certified NLP Coach, BCC, Vanderbilt MBA, and former CFO and Operations Executive, Mina defines career strategies, creates career plans, and executes successful job searches. Find Mina at `www.minabrown.com`.

Randi Bussin is a Career Reinvention and Personal Branding Coach and Strategist. She partners with executives and business owners guiding them to a "renewed" sense of professional direction and to an actionable career reinvention and personal branding plan. Learn more about Randi and her career reinvention resources at www.aspireforsuccess.com/reinventionfree-ebook.

Dr. Sarah David is the Founder and Chief Empowerment Officer of NICE: The National Institute for Career Empowerment. Visit her at www.nicealliance.com for free tools on "Do What You Love 365!"

Kirsten Dixson is the Personal Branding expert for positive influencers who want to profit from their ideas and coauthor of *Career Distinction: Stand Out by Building Your Brand* (Wiley). She's been a TODAY show guest and quoted in national media about online reputation management. Learn more at www.kirstendixson.com.

Maren Finzer helps people over 40 attract their ideal career opportunities. Following a step-by-step process, she teaches you how to build a wildly irresistible personal brand and become the only choice in your niche. For access to her free resources, go to www.marenfinzer.com/personal-branding-for-dummies.

Megan Fitzgerald, expatriate and international career coach, helps forward-thinking expats become highly visible, sought-after experts and leaders and succeed abroad. With 20 years experience in 40-plus countries, she's been named a top personal branding consultant and featured in Fortune Magazine, CNN Money, and WSJ Online. For free resources, visit www.careerbychoice.com/personalbrandingfordummies.

Robin S. Fox is a San Francisco Bay Area Social Media Coach, Corporate Trainer, and Workshop Leader. Robin helps clients leverage online tools to raise brand awareness, generate leads and support word of mouth referrals. Learn more at www.robinsfox.com.

Rachel Gogos, brandiD founder, aims to help everyone from seasoned entrepreneurs to authors turn the Internet into the secret to their success by making the web a more personal place. With over 20 years marketing experience, Rachel can help put you on the digital map. Go to www.thebrandiD.com.

Susan Guarneri, the Career Assessment Goddess and a certified career counselor and coach, is a Master Personal Branding Strategist, one of only nine in the world. Find her at www.assessmentgoddess.com.

Meg Guiseppi is a C-level Executive Branding and Job Search Strategist. She partners with her clients to differentiate their unique value proposition and strategically positions them to land their next great gig. To learn more and access free executive job search resources, go to `www.executivecareerbrand.com`.

Kristen Jacoway, founder of Career Design Coach (`www.careerdesigncoach.com`), provides professional speaking and training on job searching with social media as well as consultation focused on career marketing services. She authored *I'm in a Job Search-Now What???* (Happy About).

Diana Jennings helps professionals nonverbally communicate the quality of their personal brand. Her clients emerge from her coaching with the image, skills, and confidence to attract the best opportunities. For more information, see `www.BrandYouImage.com/personal-branding-for-dummies`.

Tara Kachaturoff is an online business and project manager, a radio show producer/consultant for entrepreneurs, and a professional interviewer. She's the creator, producer, and host of Michigan Entrepreneur TV, a weekly television talk show and Teach Me Law, a radio show focusing on legal topics for the lay person. See `www.radioshowproducer.com` for details.

Bernadette Martin, a Career Transition Brand Strategist, is Founder of Visibility Branding, LLC where she offers career development services for individuals. Bernadette resides in Paris. You can reach her at `http://visibilitybranding.fr`.

Tripper Ortman and **Rand Chritton** are attorneys by day and sports aficionados always. Thank you for your contributions to Chapter 3.

Valerie Sokolosky, author and executive coach, has a passion for developing talent through building a strong professional presence and leadership brand. She is an expert in the field of professionalism and has authored eight books on the subject. Check out her books and client reviews at `www.valerieandcompany.com`.

Wendy Terwelp, `http://rockyournetwork.com`, is a coach and speaker who's helped thousands of execs and entrepreneurs get hired faster and be rock stars at work since 1989. Dubbed "LinkedIn Guru" by *The Washington Post* and author of *Rock Your Network*, Wendy is the go-to person on how to network.

Kelly Welch, MHRM, is a certified personal branding strategist. She coaches high achievers to understand their brand, apply it strategically, and achieve next level career wins. Certified as a professional resume writer and online identity strategist, Kelly's strengths lie in communicating the brand messages of her clients for clarity and impact of message. Learn more at `www.yescareerservices.com`.

The Team at Wiley & Sons: Words cannot express how much I appreciate Joan Friedman, my guardian angel (and amazing editor), for not only making me sound better but for her personal support. Without her, this book would have been an overwhelming adventure. I was wise to make Joan my partner from the beginning and cannot thank her enough for all that she did.

To Erin Calligan Mooney who contacted me out of the blue to write this book — thank for you having faith that I was the right person for the job. Thank you to Kelly Ewing, my terrific project editor, for all your sage advice. Thank you to the entire Wiley staff that has helped bring this book to fruition. You are a great publisher to work with, and I see why you have such an outstanding brand.

Publisher's Acknowledgments

We're proud of this book; please send us your comments at `http://dummies.custhelp.com`. For other comments, please contact our Customer Care Department within the U.S. at 877-762-2974, outside the U.S. at 317-572-3993, or fax 317-572-4002.

Some of the people who helped bring this book to market include the following:

Acquisitions, Editorial, and Vertical Websites

Project Editor: Kelly Ewing

Acquisitions Editor: Erin Calligan Mooney

Assistant Editor: David Lutton

Editorial Program Coordinator: Joe Niesen

General Reviewer: Myriam-Rose Kohn

Editorial Supervisor and Reprint Editor: Carmen Krikorian

Editorial Assistant: Alexa Koschier

Art Coordinator: Alicia B. South

Cover Photos: © iStockphoto.com/Sirgunhik

Cartoons: Rich Tennant (`www.the5thwave.com`)

Composition Services

Project Coordinator: Nikki Gee

Layout and Graphics: Jennifer Creasey, Cheryl Grubbs, Joyce Haughey, Corrie Niehaus

Proofreaders: Lindsay Amones, Toni Settle

Indexer: Steve Rath

Publishing and Editorial for Consumer Dummies

Kathleen Nebenhaus, Vice President and Executive Publisher

Kristin Ferguson-Wagstaffe, Product Development Director

Ensley Eikenburg, Associate Publisher, Travel

Kelly Regan, Editorial Director, Travel

Publishing for Technology Dummies

Andy Cummings, Vice President and Publisher

Composition Services

Debbie Stailey, Director of Composition Services

Contents at a Glance

Table of Contents

Introduction

Imagine that you can step outside your own body and observe yourself. Picture yourself walking into a job interview and shaking hands with people you're meeting for the first time. How do you look? Are you smiling confidently and making eye contact, or are your eyes darting nervously around the room? Does your handshake seem firm or limp? Is your clothing neatly pressed and closely fitted, or is it a bit rumpled and frumpy? Do you look like you're in control of the situation, or do you seem overwhelmed?

Now picture yourself walking into your neighborhood grocery store. Are you dressed in a way that shows you pay attention to yourself, or have you thrown on stained sweats and an oversized t-shirt? Are you interacting with the store workers or avoiding eye contact? If you run into a neighbor or coworker, do you seem excited to see this person or anxious to get away from her?

One more: Picture yourself at your computer, checking your Facebook page. A friend has sent you an off-color joke. How do you respond? Do you type a raunchy response and send it immediately with the hope of making someone laugh? Or do you opt not to respond in case someone would take offense?

Many people would say that they pull themselves together nicely for a job interview but don't pay much attention to how they look and act at the grocery store or how their social media comments come across. After all, who are you trying to impress in the produce section? And the people who interact with you on Facebook are your *friends,* right? Shouldn't they accept you for who you are — raunchy jokes and all?

But here's the rub: People who are the most successful in this world — in business and otherwise — know that impressions matter in every circumstance. They know the importance of being consistent with their actions, words, and appearances so that every person they interact with carries away a similar impression.

About This Book

This is a how-to book. It's action-oriented. I suppose you could read it without taking any of the steps I encourage, but I'm not sure doing so would prove very helpful! I hope that you interact with the information in this book by taking notes, doing the exercises, and thinking seriously about how you can benefit from each step of the personal branding process. You don't necessarily have to tackle each step in order (I've written each chapter so that it makes sense on its own), but you may find that working this program from start to finish creates the best results.

In this book, I show you how to create a consistent, targeted impression that can help you achieve your personal and professional goals. First, I help you focus on determining who you really are — what you enjoy, what you do well, and what you want from life. Then, I walk you through a series of thoughtful steps you can take to bring every aspect of your world into alignment with your true self. The goal of this book is to help you break down self-imposed barriers to success and show the world your best authentic self.

The term *personal branding* is a marketing phrase. Corporations have been branding themselves for a long time in order to reach their target audiences and sell more stuff. Corporate branding efforts often involve displaying a company or product name, a tagline, specific colors, a logo, and/or other images in every marketing tool about that company or product. Consistency is key to getting potential buyers to recognize, trust, purchase, and repurchase a product, for example.

Does it seem crass to think in marketing terms when considering your own self and your personal goals? It shouldn't. I don't ask you to think of yourself as a product. Instead, this book is dedicated to helping you figure out who you are as a human being and what sets you apart from every other person on this planet. My hope is that, armed with the information you get in this book, you figure out how to soar in your chosen profession or whatever field of action you pursue. No matter what your goals are, making a consistent, positive impression on people will help you achieve them.

Conventions Used in This Book

To help you navigate this text, I use the following conventions:

- When I introduce a new term, it appears in *italic* and I provide a definition or explanation nearby.
- Sometimes I share interesting information that isn't crucial to your understanding of the topic at hand. I place that information in a *sidebar,* which is a gray box set apart from the rest of the text.
- All website addresses appear in `monofont` so they're easy to pick out if you need to go back and find them. Keep in mind that when this book was printed, some web addresses may have needed to break across two lines of text. If that happened, rest assured that I haven't put in any extra characters (such as hyphens) to indicate the break. So, when using one of these web addresses, just type exactly what you see in this book, pretending as though the line break doesn't exist.

Foolish Assumptions

My biggest assumption about you is that you're going through a change in your life — or hoping to create a change — that may feel somewhat intimidating. Perhaps one of these descriptions comes close to describing your circumstance:

- You're graduating from college soon and are facing the prospect of looking for work in a tight job market. You want to set yourself apart from your peers and have heard that personal branding can help you do so.
- You're a young professional in your first or second job and feel like you've got greater potential than your coworkers or managers realize. You want to figure out how to show them what you're worth.
- You're an executive facing a transition — either self-imposed or prompted by changes at your company. You know you've got what it takes to succeed, but you want to focus your remaining work years on activities that are truly meaningful for you. You want to think outside the paycheck with your next move.
- You're an entrepreneur getting ready to embark on a new venture, and you've heard that branding is key to your success. You don't think of yourself as a corporation, so studying corporate branding techniques doesn't quite make sense. You know that your own interactions with potential customers are crucial to building your business, and you need help to make sure that those interactions generate business.
- You've been out of the workforce for a while and are uncertain how to start the process of getting back in. Maybe you've been raising children or serving in the military. Maybe you retired early and now realize that you need or want to return to work. You need to determine how to market yourself to employers.

I know I'm biased, but I believe everyone can benefit from the information in this book. Even if your aspirations don't relate to business, knowing yourself, setting goals, and taking steps to achieve them can improve your life.

How This Book Is Organized

I've divided this book into five parts. Here, I explain what you find in each.

Part I: Why Is Personal Branding Important?

Crafting your own personal brand allows you to show the world your best true self. It helps you align every part of your life with your characteristics, strengths, values, and goals. By doing so, you create a meaningful, lasting impression on everyone you meet. That impression can translate into success on the job, in a new business, and in every aspect of your life.

Before jumping in to the action steps involved in creating a personal brand, I use this part to demonstrate the power of the branding process. I show you what corporations and celebrities know about how to use branding to position themselves for success, and I get you primed for action.

Part II: Knowing Your Brand

What do you want people to know about you? Are you a consummate professional who is thorough and exact? Are you a creative spirit who thrives when you're given the freedom to approach projects independently? What is your expertise? And what are you hoping to accomplish?

The first action step in crafting a brand is figuring out what that brand should be. The process starts with spelling out your values, loves, strengths, and skills — the many things that define you. Your next challenge is determining who else is important to your brand. Who is your target audience, and what do they need from you? Who are your competitors, and how do you differ from them?

To pull together everything you discover about yourself, your target audience, and how you stand out from the crowd, you need to write a personal brand profile. This document spells out your *unique promise of value:* the promise you make to your target audience that your brand can fulfill. You circle back to this promise at every subsequent step of the personal branding process, so I encourage you not to bypass the chapters in this part — especially Chapter 7.

Part III: Communicating Your Brand with the World

I suppose that you could develop your personal brand for your own purposes — just for the sake of knowing yourself better. But I suspect your goals require interacting with people outside your home, which means you need to know how to announce your brand to the world.

A terrific first step to take is to write the story of *you.* At the heart of that story you'll discover a message that you can polish and use as your own personal commercial — an elevator pitch that lets you present your unique promise of value in 30 seconds or less.

Next, if you're in a job search, I illustrate how to get your resume, cover letter, bio, and other communication tools to reflect your brand. Then I devote a chapter to ensuring that your online presence — on both professional and social media sites — helps you achieve your goals (and doesn't send up red flags to potential employers or customers).

Finally, I help you craft an overall communications plan so that you can spend your time and money wisely and maximize your results. I show you how to figure out the best ways to communicate with your target audience, boost your reputation as an expert, and achieve the three Cs of communication (clarity, consistency, and constancy).

Part IV: Controlling Your Brand Ecosystem

Your *brand ecosystem* refers to every part of your world that your target audience may encounter. It includes your appearance, body language, marketing materials, office space, website, blog, professional network, and more. (Your broom closet and bathroom are off the hook.)

In this part, I help you get every aspect of your ecosystem as on-brand as possible. First, I discuss how to dress the part of your personal brand. (Not everyone needs to wear a suit and tie, but everyone needs to consider how clothes make an impression.) Then I focus on developing marketing materials that boast consistent and appropriate fonts, colors, and images.

Your brand ecosystem depends on who you are and what stage of life you're in, so I devote a chapter here to discussing specific populations (such as young professionals, entrepreneurs, and women). I also show you how to tailor your brand to fit a new culture when your career takes you overseas.

I then focus on helping you build and nurture your professional network, which is a strong reflection of your brand. And finally, I demonstrate how you can promote your personal brand within your workplace.

Part V: The Part of Tens

In this part, I give you four short chapters featuring quick tips. First, I note the benefits of developing your personal brand, and I warn you against actions that can undermine your personal brand. I offer hints for how best to demonstrate your brand, and finally I suggest steps you can take to build your brand after all its fundamental elements are in place.

Icons Used in This Book

Throughout the book, I place icons in the margins that call your attention to certain types of text. Here's what each icon means:

This icon points out stories that show you how certain branding ideas have played out for real people in the real world.

This whole book is full of action-oriented, how-to material. But this icon denotes paragraphs that contain especially useful how-to's for developing your brand.

When you see this icon, pay close attention. The point I'm making is something that's worth recalling long after you read the words.

This icon highlights potential missteps that I want to help you avoid.

Throughout this book, you will find contributions from experts in the field of personal branding. When you see this icon, one of these experts has contributed his expertise.

Where to Go from Here

I wrote this book so that each chapter makes sense no matter where you begin reading, so feel free to check out the table of contents or index and search for a subject of particular interest. For example, if you're mostly concerned about how to improve your online presence, Chapter 10 may be your first stop. If you've already got a job and need ideas for how to promote yourself within your existing position, Chapter 16 can help. If you're curious why everyone in your professional circle is talking about personal branding, start with the chapters in Part I.

Note: If you're committed to developing your personal brand, I consider the chapters in Part II must-reads — especially Chapters 4 and 7. Be sure to spend time with them whenever you're ready to start the branding process in earnest.

Part I

Why Is Personal Branding Important?

The 5th Wave By Rich Tennant

"From the front of your shirt I'd say your personal brand is a combination of Burger King, Taco Bell, and Pizza Hut."

In this part . . .

Personal branding is an ongoing, conscientious effort to show the world your best authentic self (not an inflated version of yourself that can't be maintained). It's the process of bringing every aspect of your life into alignment with your characteristics, strengths, values, and goals so that you can make an instant and lasting impression on the people you meet.

In this part, I focus on the why's of creating your personal brand so that you can recognize what's at stake — and what rewards you can reap — when you begin the work of crafting your brand.

Chapter 1

Showing the World Who You Are

In This Chapter

- Defining the personal branding process
- Revealing your true self and your mission
- Considering your target market and competition
- Sharing your brand in every form of communication
- Ensuring that your entire environment is on-brand

> *It's a new brand world. You're branded, branded, branded. We are CEOs of our own companies: Me Inc. To be in business today, our most important job is to be head marketer for the brand called YOU.*
>
> — Tom Peters

The greatest success stories inevitably involve people who stand out from the crowd — people who may or may not have extraordinary talents but who most definitely know how to represent their capabilities in everything they do.

This chapter is your preview of how you can distinguish yourself by creating an image and reputation that set you apart; build trust among the people you want to serve; and represent the true, authentic you. This process — the process of creating your own personal brand — can serve you well whether you're searching for a first job, exploring a change in career, looking to be more viable and successful in your current workplace, or hoping to serve your community as a volunteer or leader.

Crafting a personal brand can be exciting and a bit intimidating. To do it right, you have to spend time up front studying yourself and figuring out what really makes you tick. Only with a strong sense of yourself in mind can you undertake the steps that follow, which include identifying your target market, setting yourself apart from your competitors, communicating your brand to the people who need to know you, and aligning every visible aspect of your life with your brand. In this chapter, I outline the whole process so you know what to expect from the rest of the book. Your own success story is waiting to be written!

Discovering Personal Branding

Personal branding caught fire when *Fast Company* magazine ran a cover article called "The Brand Called You" by Tom Peters in 1997. Soon, books like Daniel H. Pink's *Free Agent Nation* (Business Plus) and William Bridges' *Creating You & Co.: Learn To Think Like The CEO Of Your Own Career* (Da Capo Press) joined in to support the idea that you direct your own career path. Being self-reliant means that you are responsible for the direction of your career and the impression that people have of you. The time has come to take control of your personal brand.

So what exactly is *personal branding?* Your personal brand is your reputation, which is defined by your character. Your personal brand is also your legacy; it's the way others remember you through your actions, your expertise, and the emotional connections that you make. Your personal brand shows your authenticity from the inside out.

You have a personal brand whether you know it or not:

- "She is so smart."
- "He is such a slob."
- "I can always count on him to finish what he starts."

REMEMBER

Personal branding is about expressing your authentic self by allowing you to be the person you are meant to be. But it isn't just some feel-good, self-help mumbo jumbo: It's a strategic process that makes you an active partner in creating the direction of your life. Through personal branding, you find out how to bring more value to your work and to the target market that you serve. You discover how to identify and communicate your unique promise of value.

Your personal brand acts as a filter that helps you make decisions that are congruent with who you are and what you stand for. It identifies what makes you unique and clearly communicates your individuality to the people who need to know about you.

Having a personal brand sounds like a great idea, but how do you get one? If you're serious about developing your personal brand, a very clear road map can get you there. This book guides you through every stop along that map. The following section, in brief, walks you through what you need to do.

Know your brand

Knowing your brand sounds easy enough, but how do you figure out what your brand is?

1. **Define who you are.**

   The beginning of any branding process is being able to clearly define that brand. In personal branding, the product is you! You must take time to get to know yourself and what is important to you. That's what Chapter 4 is all about.

2. **Spot your target audience.**

   Are you interacting with and trying to promote yourself to the right people? In Chapter 5, I help you determine who needs to know about your personal brand.

3. **Get to know your competitors.**

   Who are you competing with? In order to have a strong brand, you need to understand who your competitors are and which market niche works for you. Chapter 6 gives you the tools to accomplish this step.

4. **Craft a personal brand profile.**

   This all-important tool, which I discuss in detail in Chapter 7, gathers all the data that you collect about yourself, your target audience, and your competitors into one defining document. This profile helps you pinpoint your unique promise of value and write a statement that succinctly expresses your brand.

Communicate your brand

After you get to know your brand, your next challenge is to communicate it clearly, concisely, and consistently to the people who need to know about it. Here's how:

1. **Write your story.**

   Chapter 8 is a lesson on how to make your story appealing to others. You need to be able to tell others about yourself and to develop a personal commercial (or *elevator pitch*).

2. **Brand your traditional communication tools.**

   You want to express your personal brand in your letters, resume, professional biography, and presentations — and, if you have the opportunity, on television. Chapter 9 shows you how.

3. **Communicate your brand online.**

   Chapter 10 demonstrates how to merge the world of social media with your personal brand.

4. **Create a communications plan.**

   You need a communications plan so that you're sharing your brand on your own terms — not leaving anything to chance. Chapter 11 gives you the inside scoop on how to craft a communications plan.

Control your brand ecosystem

The phrase *brand ecosystem* may sound intimidating, but it's just shorthand for "every element of your life, from your clothes to your professional colleagues, that influences how your target audience perceives you and whether it wants to learn more about the product or service you're offering." Phew! You can see why I opted for the shorthand. Here are some of the elements of your ecosystem that you want to control:

- **Your image:** Whether you like it or not, what you look like on the outside does matter. Fashioning your image to match your personal brand helps you communicate something authentic about yourself at first glance, and Chapter 12 shows you how.
- **The appearance of your branded materials:** From business cards to your website, you want to create a consistent visual image for your brand that makes the right impression on your target audience. Chapter 13 explains how to select images, colors, and fonts that create the visual effect you want.
- **Your unique career path:** Your target audience — and the way you interact with it — is determined by where you are in your career. In Chapter 14, I discuss special considerations to keep in mind if you're just out of college, if you're midstream in your career and trying to switch jobs, if you're an executive, if you're an entrepreneur, and more.
- **Your network:** The people you associate with are very important; they factor into the impression you make on your target audience, as well as your ability to make connections with future employers. Chapter 15 is full of tips for finding people who can support your goals and connecting with them in meaningful ways.
- **Your performance in your current workplace:** Personal branding is not just for job seekers. If you're already employed, Chapter 16 offers lots of ideas for developing your personal brand in the context of your current workplace.

Figuring Out Who You Really Are

Today you are You, that is truer than true. There is no one alive who is Youer than You.

— Dr.Seuss

In the previous section, I note that the first step in developing a personal brand is knowing yourself. You need to look at the expectations others have of you and how they influence how you want to be seen. In this process, you ask questions of yourself to discover your authenticity and understand what you need in order to live your mission through your personal brand. Here, I help you start thinking about what that process involves.

Shedding others' ideas and expectations

Becoming an authentic human being means that you accept yourself for who you are. Everyone has different approaches to life, likes and dislikes, and skills and talents.

Most likely, when you were in junior high, standing out was deadly. At that age, nothing is more important than fitting in. But fitting in can carry you only so far. At some point, if you truly want to succeed and shine, you have to figure out how to differentiate yourself from the crowd.

I'm not saying that you need to stop caring about what other people think or to stop listening to what your loved ones think is good for you. Instead, in this book I ask you to make an honest assessment of what you want and who you are. You can't build a personal brand based on someone else's ideals. If you did, you'd be a fake.

REMEMBER

Taking an honest assessment about who you are and what you want means looking at what you do well and owning it, as well as knowing what you don't do well and recognizing those limitations. You definitely should seek input from others during this process. However, you can't let them determine who you will be. Personal branding is about you being you in the most authentic way.

Getting to know the authentic you

In the 1960s, a cartoon character named Tooter the Turtle was never satisfied with his life and was always looking to be someone else. He wanted to experiment with what it would be like to live another's life. He would visit Mr. Wizard, who would cast his spell on Tooter, allowing him to explore living someone else's life.

Poor Tooter the Turtle always got himself into trouble trying to be someone he was not. Just when the mess would become too much to handle, Tooter would yell, "Help, Mr. Wizard." Mr. Wizard would say the magic words, "drizzle, drazzle, druzzle, drome — time for this one to come home." Tooter came home as himself, the only self he could ever really be. Mr. Wizard would say upon Tooter's return that "he is what he is — not what he is not."

The personal branding process helps you own who you are, quirks and all, so that you don't waste your life wishing to be someone else. In this process, you need to take a realistic look at yourself to understand all the factors that make you who you are. Getting to know yourself is truly the toughest part of crafting your personal brand. But the end goal — to live and thrive as an authentic human being — is absolutely worth the effort.

Knowing what you need

To determine what matters to you, you first need to identify what you need. A *need* is something that is necessary for you to live a healthy life. Needs can be as basic as food and shelter or as complex as contributing your talents to the world. Needs develop as you grow up and become a central part of your character. In order to brand yourself, you must know what you need.

Do you stop yourself from trying something new or taking risks for fear of putting your basic needs in jeopardy? Motivation is directly tied to needs. Maslow's Hierarchy of Needs, which I explain in Chapter 4, states that people are motivated by their unsatisfied needs. When you have an unmet need, you are motivated to do something to change that. Needs direct your feelings and influence your values. Determining what you need will help you understand what you value and where you need to set your goals.

Shaping your identity

Branding guru Robin Fisher Roffer believes that personal branding helps you "to know who you are and be valued for it, to attract what you want, to become more attractive to others, to inspire confidence, to walk your path with integrity, and to distinguish yourself in whatever field you've chosen."

Shaping your identity begins with self-awareness. When you know who you are, you can find purpose in your work. I know you must have a high IQ because you are reading this book, and I'm hoping you also have a high EQ: emotional intelligence quotient. That's because in order to make the changes necessary to reshape your identity, you must be self-reflective. Self-awareness occurs when you are able to observe yourself as others see you.

The most important ingredient as you embark on the personal branding path is self-acceptance. You need to be able to look closely at yourself, be able to listen to what others think about you, and be willing to grow and change.

Through this process, you'll discover your uniqueness and discover how to leverage it in the marketplace. As you get clarity about your vision, values, passions, purpose, and goals, you'll be able to demonstrate your authenticity knowing that you are coming from a place of strength rather than trying to practice the chameleon life. This clarity helps you live more consistently, which is vital to living a successful life.

Considering your life circumstances

Whether you're fresh out of school or a young professional or reconsidering your mid-career options or preparing for what comes after retirement, you can use your personal brand to help you enjoy each stage that you are experiencing. The beauty of a personal brand is that it is not static.

Throughout your lifetime, certain things about you (like your sense of humor or your intelligence) will be enduring. But as you gain experience and expertise, your brand will evolve to showcase these new aspects of who you are. Your personal brand grows with you.

Heeding your call

If figuring out who you really are seems a bit scary, I'd like to reassure you that it doesn't have to be difficult. You already have an inner voice that can guide you toward your true identity. It's the voice that tells you "Yes, go for it" or "Stop, this is a big mistake." I believe you know your own best answers if you pause to listen to that wise inner voice.

It is freeing to let your guard down and open up to the authentic you, the one where your true strengths, talent, and personality lie. As you work your way through the personal branding process, you want to pay extra attention to your inner voice so that you can know your calling, determine where your life's mission and your abilities intersect, and move forward in a purposeful way.

Living your "why"

Dr. Sarah David, Founder and Chief Empowerment Officer of NICE: The National Institute for Career Empowerment, offers seven strategies that she uses in her coaching programs to help others gain clarity in discovering their "why" — their purpose or mission. These steps can help you identify your strengths and translate your unique gifts into a dream career and personal brand that is fulfilling. Here are Dr. David's strategies, in her words:

- **Identify your mission in life.** Whether your mission is to start your own business, work for someone else, or volunteer for a worthy cause, the work around identification is very important to the process. Whether you have known your mission since you were a child or you are still trying to discover it, do the self-reflection needed to understand your mission in life.
- **Follow your heart.** In counseling and coaching others, I have found that many people have delayed their dreams. They put them on a shelf. They have other careers that may not be fulfilling but pursue them because they are more popular, they pay more, or someone else thinks they're

a good idea. There is nothing wrong with doing what is practical, but I have found that people always circle back around to their original dreams somewhere down the path. Find a way to incorporate what you love into your career.

- **Trust your outrageous ideas.** What makes your idea different from other ideas that are out there? One thing I have learned is that there are no new ideas. The difference between you and anyone else is how you take an idea and build on it to make it even better. You may also be thinking that your idea has already been done, so perhaps it's tired and not useful. But you can make it unique and different by bringing your special skills, talents, and personality to bear. What extra twist, service, or benefit can you add to a concept? How can you take it to a level that's truly new and different?
- **Know what you don't know and get the help with what you need to move forward.** The old saying "knowledge is power" is true, but knowing what to do with that power is key. You can't be an expert at everything, but you can ask other people for support with tasks that don't come easily to you. Do your research and know the options available when you can't tackle something alone.
- **Identify your strengths, values, passions, and goals.** Understand how these foundation steps are critical to identifying your business or career of choice. First, identify what you do well. There are several ways you can identify your calling. Some people already know what their calling is because it was a seed that was planted early in life. It may be the one thing that you knew you wanted to be or do when you grew up. For others, your calling may be something that you've been mentored to do your entire life, such as run a family business or continue with a craft.
- **Find your cheerleaders and identify your tribe.** Finding the support you need to excel will help you live your why. I highly recommend joining a support group of like-minded people. A coach can also serve as one of your biggest cheerleaders. Identify who you will follow and who you will lead.
- **Invest in yourself.** If you don't, who will? I will forever be a lifelong learner. There are many things that I am excited to continue to learn throughout my entrepreneurial career. Many years ago, I realized the importance of education. I have invested in myself both formally and informally in addition to obtaining the wise counsel of trusted business advisors, mentors, coaches, and consultants.

REMEMBER

Taking time out to identify your "why" is a very important step in identifying your personal brand. With a firm sense of your mission in mind, you can begin to create the type of business or career that provides meaning and fulfillment in your life.

Finding your sweet spot

Your *sweet spot* is a market niche that is uniquely yours. It exists at the intersection of various pieces of your life:

- **Your "why":** Your purpose or mission in life (see preceding section)
- **Your identity:** Your skills, talents, and personality
- **Your target market:** The people you want to work with
- **What you offer:** The ideas you have to share

Finding your sweet spot allows you to stay true to yourself, and it gives you direction to form a strategy for developing your niche. Chapter 6 offers details about how to determine your own sweet spot.

Your sweet spot applies whether you're an entrepreneur or working in a company. Your sweet spot in the workplace can be something that you are uniquely known for.

Owning the Business of You

Having a personal brand is a little like having your own business. As the owner of You & Co., you need to figure out who will benefit most from what you have to offer, as well as how you compare to people doing similar work. This part of the branding process, which I outline in Chapters 5 and 6, is essential whether you're an independent professional or employed in a workplace.

You also need to develop the personal equivalent of a business plan: your brand profile. While I offer all the details about your brand profile in Chapter 7, I help you start thinking about it here as well.

Spotting your target audience

It's not enough to just have a strong personal brand; you also need to communicate it to the right people. William Arruda of Reach Communications is a personal branding guru, and one of my favorite quotes from him is this:

> *"Personal branding is not about being famous; it's about being selectively famous." In looking for your target market, you're identifying your audience: the people who will help you reach your goals.*

Your target market consists of your customers, but depending on your life circumstances, your customers may or may not be people purchasing products or services from you in a retail setting. If you're an entrepreneur setting up a home computer repair service, you'll think about customers in a traditional way: They're the specific group of people you think will most likely pay for the unique services you offer. But if you're a salaried employee in a nonretail setting, your customers may be your employer, your manager, your coworkers, or your project team. If you're a community volunteer, your customers may be corporate, foundation, or individual donors who underwrite expenses for a nonprofit organization you support.

In other words, your target audience is the people who need to know about you. You want to market your personal brand to these people so that your brand has a direction.

Identifying your competitors

One of the key steps when working on your personal brand is to understand where you fit, who does the same type of work you do, and how you can better identify your uniqueness. You can only find the answers by looking at your competition.

You first want to study how your competition communicates its value to its target audience. With that information in hand, you can begin to identify what makes you different than your competition. You can find ways to articulate your brand in a way that is unique — and completely authentic.

Understanding your competition helps you live your personal brand by allowing you to find a place where what you offer stands out. Your goal is to create a less competitive space in which you can thrive. You can achieve your goal by owning your market niche — by creating a mini-kingdom where you are the king or queen. When people think of that niche, they think of you. You can minimize or eliminate the competition when you own a niche.

Synthesizing what you stand for

Your personal brand profile is where you combine what you know about yourself and what you know about your target market and competition. This document pulls together the various pieces of your personal brand puzzle, allowing you to see the whole picture of who you really are.

Working on the personal brand profile is validating, and you'll walk away having a clear sense of what motivates you and who you want to know about your brand. In doing so, you bring to light your unique promise of value, which allows you to then write a personal brand statement and develop a strategy for using your brand.

Your personal brand statement is extremely important to your branding success. Although it may be only a few words long (you want it to be concise), this statement expresses what you stand for, and it guides you in making decisions that are "on-brand" for you so that you never veer off into activities that are "off-brand." Your brand statement keeps you energized and focused on meeting your goals. It's the heart and soul of who you are and what motivates you.

Communicating Your Brand

When you know your personal brand, you want to communicate it in everything you do. That means not only making sure that your written communications reflect your brand, but also paying attention to your actions, your clothing, your body language . . . every facet of your communication.

When I was asked to write this book, I thought about what some of my brand characteristics were that I wanted to carry into the book. I am known for being collaborative in my work and in my community, and I thought that I would communicate that same quality in this book. You'll notice that I include articles written by contributing authors throughout the book. These are my personal branding colleagues from both the United States and Europe. I felt it was important to show my collaborative spirit through the contributions of the authors. You benefit from their expertise and this collaboration.

Similarly, you can figure out ways to communicate your brand in everything you do. In this section, I get you started.

Telling your story

You are the author of your own life. Personal branding gives you clarity to create your story, live your story, and then tell that story to the right audience. Stories are personal, and nothing builds your brand like a good story. Stories bring out your humanness and connect you emotionally with your audience. With your story in hand, you can craft a winning biography and be prepared to offer an engaging response whenever someone says, "Tell me about yourself."

Business leaders and politicians are often master storytellers. They're able to connect with their audience on every level, inspiring people to follow them. A good story influences the listener to action or motivates change. Stories are told in every culture to connect people to each other and teach cultural values.

To tell a good story, you need to have a good story. Telling a story is a way to build trust, and every brand wants you to trust what it stands for. When you tell a story to your target audience — whether it be a business colleague, a child, your partner, or a friend — you're creating a bond with that person. A story lets your listeners decide for themselves whether they'll trust you and the brand you're presenting.

The telling of a story is always personal. Whatever walk of life you come from, your stories define you. Your story becomes your personal brand, and you need to think about which stories you tell to others to illustrate who you are. Your story is an expression of your life, so put some thought into what you tell (and don't tell) others. For specific ideas about how to start the storytelling process, be sure to read Chapter 8.

Putting your identity in writing

When you're crafting a personal brand, consistency is your ally. You want every marketing item, every letter, every e-mail — every form of written communication — to highlight your brand. Your goal is to tell your brand's story with clarity so that you can engage your audience with your personality and your skills.

You want to manage your personal branding documents by following these basic principles:

- Communicate your message clearly, consistently, and constantly.
- Feature the same viewpoints, descriptors, taglines, and attributes throughout your documents.
- Use brand attributes that are visible in everything you do. All your written materials (as well as your spoken communication) should tie back to your personal brand attributes (which I discuss in Chapter 4).
- Leave off details that don't support or promote your brand.
- Practice writing and talking about your brand attributes and strengths when talking about your work or discussing a future plan.
- Look for similar words that show consistency in branding without being overly repetitive.
- Seek to understand the problems that your target market faces and offer solutions that highlight your brand.
- Identify your target audience carefully and understand what compels them (see Chapter 5). Then, reflect that information in your unique promise of value (defined in Chapter 7) that speaks to your audience with relevance.

Chapter 9 offers a quick course on how to brand your traditional communication tools: your letters, resume, bio, and cover letter.

Tapping in to social media

Google yourself for fun and see what you find. If you have a common name, you may find that so little information about you exists online that only your Facebook page shows up — on page 5 of the search results.

If you care about your personal brand, you *must* pay attention to what your online presence says about you. If you ignore your online presence or if you assume that you don't even have one, you run the risk of letting other people create your image for you. Get proactive about how you present yourself online.

Your message online needs to be based on what you have learned about yourself while putting together your personal brand. As with all written communications, your online message should highlight your unique promise of value: the promise that you make to your target market that your brand will fulfill.

Your online message should also describe your essential professional qualities. You want to show your knowledge and expertise and let your personality show through. Your message should exhibit your personal qualities, your professional characteristics, and your style in how you apply those qualities to your work life.

Social media is incredibly popular in part because your impressions can be even more personal than your written communication tools. That's because your online presence usually includes visual elements, including pictures and/or video of you. Keep in mind that your visual message needs to align with what you write or say. (The most winning words about your professional aplomb will be worthless if your picture screams "party girl!")

A *profile hub* is a central source online — such as a website, blog site, or personal web page — that guides people who are interested in your services to the multiple paths in which you communicate. Using a profile hub allows you to influence the impression that people have about you when they search for your name. You can set the look and feel of your brand, and the hub acts as a portal for the information seeker to find out about you. Here are some of the best-known examples:

- **LinkedIn:** If you're just beginning to think about using online tools to showcase your personal brand, begin with LinkedIn. LinkedIn has earned the respect of the business community and has become the number one tool to find a business colleague. Success with business networking comes at the intersection of sharing the right information to the right people at the right time and on the right social media platform.

- **Facebook:** Facebook is designed to share words, photos, video, website links, and more to help tell your story in ways that inform and entertain. Facebook allows you to navigate the balance of being social while also sharing enough of your personal brand to offer a taste of what others experience when they meet you in person. Be careful, though: Sharing the wrong information to the wrong people in the wrong way can impact how people feel about your personal brand.
- **Twitter:** Twitter is a social networking and micro-blogging online service that allows its users to send and read text-based messages of up to 140 characters, known as *tweets.* Twitter allows you to become a content expert without years of schooling and a prestigious job title. If you're consistent and build followers who are interested in what you have to say, you can rise to the status of content expert quickly.
- **Video:** Video is the next best communication tool to communicating in person. Video bios are a great tool for telling your story in a very personal way, as well as for introducing the viewer to your business. A well-done video bio lets you connect with your audience, establish trust and a connection, and build your credibility and expertise in your particular subject matter. Your personal brand and persona simply cannot be expressed only in the written word.

Thriving in Your Brand Ecosystem

Your brand ecosystem is everything that surrounds you, and your challenge is to make sure that it's "on brand." In other words, you want your clothing, your professional network, your behavior in the workplace, and every other visible aspect of your life to represent who you really are and what you're capable of doing. That way, your target audience is crystal clear about what you represent and what you can accomplish for them.

Polishing your personal image

Your personal image is the totality of what you say, how you say it, and how you appear while you're saying it. It's all the ways in which you present yourself. Chapter 12 is your primer on polishing your personal image.

Successful people recognize that all aspects of their appearance — their clothing, grooming, and body language — are nonverbal tools they can control to help them achieve their goals. Your outer appearance can create the message that you want to send, which allows your target market to feel trust in you at first sight.

A key goal — and challenge — is to dress in order to make an on-brand impression. To be clear, that won't necessarily mean wearing a suit every day. If you run a surf shop in Virginia Beach, your target audience doesn't want to see you in a suit — it'll make them scratch their heads and wonder what, exactly, your brand represents. But if you're aiming for corporate success, in Chapter 12 I offer a full rundown of the details you need to consider every time you get dressed.

REMEMBER

Having a personal brand means that you know who you are and what you stand for. As I say throughout this book, your brand must be authentic because pretending to be someone else can be painful and exhausting. When it comes to creating a style that boosts your personal brand image, your goal is to wear clothes that you feel good in and that help you visually express the real you. When your style matches your brand, your best self can shine through.

Like the clothes you wear, your grooming is a complex form of visual, nonverbal communication. Grooming includes keeping your body clean, as well as maintaining your teeth, breath, hair, hands, and nails.

The impression that you make extends to other aspects of your life as well. Having good phone manners, for example, can boost your personal brand score. Let your natural enthusiasm come through in your phone voice and try not to sound flat and monotone. If you're nervous before you make a call, practice what you are going to say. Be confident and practice good pitch, pace, enunciation, and volume to let your brand ring through.

Connecting with your network

Having a strong personal brand demands being connected to a network of resources for mutual development and growth. Your target audience pays close attention to your business partners and other alliances because the people you associate with say a lot about who you are. But how do you develop a network that's on-brand?

Give more than you get!

This is the golden rule in networking. A confident networker knows that to build his network and create a web of relationships, he must genuinely enjoy learning about the people he interacts with. You can confidently build a network that strengthens your personal brand by encouraging two-way relationships with people whom you want to be part of your circle. Grow your contacts by sharing information and introducing people to each other.

Growing a strong network is smart brand management. Your network is a powerful extension of your brand; it communicates volumes to your target audience about who values you and your business. See Chapter 15 for lots more tips on how to become a successful networker.

Living your brand at work

In the book, *The Coming Jobs War* by Jim Clifton (Gallup Press), the Gallup organization conducted a survey questioning the level of engagement in the workplace. The survey found that 28 percent of Americans are "engaged," 53 percent are "not engaged," and 19 percent are "actively disengaged." The 53 percent of not engaged workers are not hostile or disruptive but are just killing time and collecting a paycheck. The 19 percent of actively disengaged people are there to stir up trouble and destroy their workplaces.

Only the 28 percent of engaged employees are trying to do their best work and build their careers while serving the organizations that they work for. I may assume that you belong in the 28 percent because you're reading this book to further your own professional development. If you aren't part of that 28 percent, I can at least assume that you want to be.

Striving for a vocation

When you embark on creating a personal brand, you develop a different awareness about your relationship to your work. Sometimes you may do work just for the money, and that's fine if you know why you're doing what you're doing. But ultimately, moving into your authentic self and using all of who you are takes you past the point of working only for a paycheck.

Following is a list of the four types of relationships that people have to their work:

- **Job:** This word indicates the place where you work and the task you're doing; it's work based on material rewards (a paycheck).
- **Career:** This is the sequence of occupations in which you engage, which includes school, your work life, and retirement. Career work requires personal initiative but needs collective approval.
- **Occupation:** Work involving greater meaning, but dominated by outer activity, in an occupation. This is a definable work activity that occurs in many different settings.
- **Vocation:** From the Latin *vocare* (which means "call"), this word implies practicing the work that best fulfills your dreams and utilizes your unique talents. An intrinsic calling, vocation work is directed in service of a greater good and is said to be connected to the soul.

REMEMBER

Your goal with personal branding is to achieve a *vocation,* which is tied to a mission — not just a job title.

Adopting the personal branding mindset in the workplace

As I explain in Chapter 16, the personal branding mindset is about standing out from the crowd and closely resembles how an entrepreneur looks at his work. To be successful in the quickly changing business world means that you must move toward this mindset. By being proactive in the self-management of your career, you can charge forward with opportunity. You need to

- Have a distinct personal identity
- Seek employability security (the ability to find work)
- Look for the next career opportunity and be open to alternate paths
- Focus on loyalty to a project, to your profession, to your coworkers, and to yourself
- Aim for work/life balance (holistic life success)
- Understand how you and your personal brand fit with your company's work culture
- Practice lifelong learning
- Showcase your competencies
- Embrace fluid, gig (project-based) employment
- Know you'll have multiple positions in your work life
- Gauge success based on your own personal career strategy
- Build relationships on trust and authenticity
- Label yourself with an ever-evolving personal brand
- Understand the complex web of ever-changing reporting relationships
- Take personal ownership of everything you do

Chapter 2

Appreciating the Power of Branding

In This Chapter

- Figuring out why companies are brand-happy
- Focusing on some key brand elements
- Studying the emotional side of some famous brands
- Resolving to brand yourself

I could probably write an entire chapter consisting only of definitions of the words *brand* and *branding*. For example, "A brand is a promise about who you are and what you do that is strengthened every time people connect with you or your business" and "Branding is the process of building a positive set of experiences for the people who need to know about you."

But defining terms is one thing; showing you how those definitions play out in the real world is another. My purpose in this chapter is to get you thinking about how brands actually work in everyday life.

For most people, the initiation into branding comes from two sources: corporations and celebrities. I devote Chapter 3 to case studies of celebrities (media moguls, entertainers, famous entrepreneurs, and so on) who have tapped in to the power of personal branding. In this chapter, my focus is on corporations.

Successful companies all have brands that distinguish them from their competition. I can list certain company names (McDonald's, Apple, Disney, or Coca-Cola, for example), and chances are you can immediately recall some elements of their brands, such as colors, logos, and characters. Your goal when creating a personal brand is to emulate the success of these companies so that your own target audience recalls elements of your brand whenever your name comes up. But a brand — whether corporate or personal — involves more than colors and logos. In this chapter, I explain why corporations focus so strongly on branding, and then I illustrate how their brands work.

Eyeing Corporations: Your Initiation into the Purpose of Branding

A brand is a person's gut feeling about a product, service, or company.

— Marty Neumeier, Director of Transformation, Liquid Agency

Corporations must build and maintain their brand image in order to stay in business. *Brand equity* is the value of a brand based on the quality of the product or service, its reputation, and customer loyalty toward that product or service. When a company has a poor reputation from an inferior product or deficient customer service, its brand becomes tarnished, and staying in business becomes difficult. (Its brand equity loses value.) A company with a tarnished brand certainly doesn't grow. Brands are fragile, and all aspects of the business a customer encounters need to be consistent with the promised brand message.

In this section, I focus on the *why* of corporate branding, explaining the importance of developing a brand in order to set a product or service apart in the marketplace and connect in meaningful, lasting ways with potential customers.

Realizing why companies invest so heavily in branding

A successful brand is the result of the experiences a company creates with its customers, employees, vendors, and communities — and the emotional feelings that arise as a result of those experiences. Companies invest in branding because it sets them apart and increases sales.

REMEMBER

A brand is the total representation of a variety of characteristics, including

- The product or service itself
- Its reputation
- The price of the product or service
- Its logo and/or slogan
- The customer service that supports the product or service
- The brand's promise (meaning what will be delivered and how)
- Customers' feelings about the product or service

The personality of a brand is a combination of its sensorial appeal (the way it looks, feels, sounds, smells, and tastes), rational appeal (the way it performs and how cost efficient it is), and emotional appeal (the emotions that it induces and the associations it brings to mind). Successful brands are memorable and meaningful, and they appeal to the target audience that the product or service is intended for.

In other words, a brand isn't just a logo or sound bite; it's what people feel about the company, product, or service in question. According to Marty Neumeier, Director of Transformation at Liquid Agency, branding has become critical in the business world because

- People have too many choices and too little time.
- Most offerings have similar quality and features.
- People tend to base buying choices on trust.

Consider an example: When you think of Volvo, you think safety. If Volvo didn't deliver on that promise, it would lose its credibility. Because Volvo's brand is built on safety, the company makes sure that its cars are among the safest built. Volvo capitalizes on its safety record through advertising that solidifies the brand in the minds of consumers. This example brings up a crucial point: Brands must be built on what is true, or they cannot maintain their reputation.

Crafting a positive, unique brand image

> *Brands are built on what people are saying about you, not what you're saying about yourself.*
>
> — Guy Kawasaki

A *brand image* is the complete personality of a brand. Essentially, it's the accumulation of all customer experiences with the brand or product, and a company does everything within its power to make sure that image is positive, as well as unique in the market. A positive brand image is developed over time by consistently delivering on a brand promise.

In his book *The Brand Gap* (New Riders), Marty Neumeier writes that all leading companies do five things to brand themselves well:

- **Differentiate:** Stand out from the crowd. People are hardwired to notice what is different.
- **Collaborate:** Bring the best people together to build the brand.
- **Innovate:** Think creatively and strategically. They come up with ideas that make people nervous.

- **Validate:** Bring the target audience into the branding process to see whether they like it.
- **Cultivate:** Look at the brand as a pattern of behavior. A good brand should evolve over time.

Sometimes even successful companies get tripped up when their practices aren't aligned with their brand reputation. For example, a clothing company can create a product line that develops a stellar reputation for quality and fit, but if customers discover that the company uses child labor in another country for the clothing's manufacture, the company has a problem. The brand image and the company policies are out of alignment, and the company must close the gap between them in order for the brand image to remain positive.

Differentiating from competitors

In the list in the previous section, the first tactic that successful companies use when branding themselves is to differentiate. It's first on the list for a reason: Differentiation is crucial to branding success. But what, exactly, does differentiation mean?

If a brand looks like every other brand on the market, it's a *commodity:* a product or service that looks the same to the customer as every other option available. If the customer discerns nothing special about the product or service, she can just as easily buy it from someone else.

A company *differentiates* — it distinguishes itself — in two important ways:

- **By figuring out what makes its product or service distinctive:** Here are some questions a business asks itself in order to identify its uniqueness:
  - What is different about the services or products that we offer?
  - What do our current customers or clients have in common?
  - How do we differ from our competition?
  - What is special about what we bring to the market?
- **By marketing its products to a certain niche:** In some cases, companies concentrate all their marketing efforts on a small but well-defined segment of the population. Businesses can create niches by identifying needs, wants, and requirements that are being addressed poorly or not at all by other companies and by delivering products or services to fulfill them. Niche marketing allows the company to be a big fish in a small pond.

From a personal branding perspective, Chapters 5 and 6 address how you can identify your target market and get to know your competitors.

Connecting with customers emotionally

Successful brands make strong emotional connections between the product or service and the target market. A strong emotional connection increases customer loyalty, which translates into higher sales and the ability to charge a premium price. (Companies that manufacture luxury goods are especially skilled at tapping in to how you feel when you buy an item, whether you can afford it or not.) Successful brands know that connecting emotionally with the customer transforms that customer from someone making a purchase into someone who will become a loyal follower.

Businesses evoke emotions by injecting human characteristics into products. (It's not just cat food; it's cat food that cares about keeping your pet happy and healthy for as many years as possible!) In doing so, they link the hearts of the customers to the essence of the brand. (In the upcoming section "Examining How a Few Famous Brands Create Connections," I demonstrate how emotional connections are at the heart of some of the world's most successful brands.)

Behavioral economics is a relatively new field, and it involves the analytical tracking of what a person thinks before doing or buying something. Behavioral economics is the science of consumer choice. (*Classic economics,* by contrast, analyzes after-the-fact decisions.) If this sort of thing interests you, keep an eye out for articles about this field. As behavioral economics refines its methods of gathering data, it will surely impact brand buying decisions as marketers hone in on the psychology of choice.

Considering Elements of the Most Successful Corporate Brands

Clever corporate branding experts use a variety of mediums to build memorable brands. They use visual elements like logos, characters, colors, and fonts. They use verbal elements, such as slogans. And they use auditory elements, such as commercial jingles. In this section, I quickly walk you through how businesses use such elements for maximum impact, and I note how each type of element may come into play when you begin your personal branding efforts.

Visual elements: Logos, colors, and fonts

Visual images create strong impressions, and entire brand strategies have been built around logos, colors, and fonts:

- **Logos:** Branding is about making connections, and the logo used by a successful brand is designed to connect with the target audience. People recognize images more often than they remember text, so a well-crafted logo (or character) can create a memorable company or product identity.

  TIP

  Consider the *For Dummies* man who adorns the book you're reading right now. When you see him, you know you're looking at an easy-to-digest how-to book, right? You don't get sweaty palms because you think the book will be beyond your comprehension. Instead, you probably feel pretty comfortable when he's around because you know the product he adorns will be informative, helpful, and not stress-inducing.

- **Colors:** Corporate brands rely heavily on color. You identify company logos and most things that you purchase by the brand color. Starbucks is green. Shell gasoline is yellow. Facebook is blue. Ikea is blue and yellow. *For Dummies* books are yellow and black. These colors don't change when the company starts a new ad campaign; they remain consistent through the years because customers identify the products so closely with these colors.
- **Fonts:** Fonts are chosen to show mood and emotion. Rounded fonts send a more casual message than angular fonts. Fonts with narrow lines send a lighter message than do ones with heavy, bold stems. One of the gifts that Apple computers brought to the world was beautiful fonts that the general public (and not just professional printers) could use.

One of my favorite logos is the Google Doodle. Although its appearance has an underlying consistency, it changes frequently to represent what's happening in the world on any given day. This logo was first created in honor of the founders' attendance of the Burning Man Festival. (Burning Man is an annual festival held in the Nevada desert that began in 1986. Attendees are there to experience radical self-expression and self-reliance.)

The logo always spells Google but consistently sends the message of creativity and change. I recently celebrated my birthday and learned that the Google Doodle personalized to me by honoring my birthday with a birthday logo. Google now has my brand loyalty.

Language elements: Slogans and taglines

A *tagline* is a short phrase that encapsulates the brand promise of a product or service. A *slogan* is a short phrase that's used in advertising campaigns for a product or service. A tagline usually sticks around for the life of the brand, while a slogan may change from campaign to campaign. You can use both in all media (print, TV, radio, online) to help build a brand.

Table 2-1 show some well-known taglines and slogans. Note how they represent the brand promise made by the company to the target audience. For example, "You're in good hands with Allstate" encapsulates the brand promise that this insurance company will protect you and help you when times get tough.

Table 2-1 Famous Company Slogans and Taglines

Brand Name	***Company Slogan or Tagline***
Allstate	You're in good hands with Allstate.
American Express	Don't leave home without it.
Apple	Think outside the box.
Calgon Toiletries	Calgon, take me away.
Clairol	If I've only one life, let me live it as a blonde.
FTD Florist	Say it with flowers.
KFC – Kentucky Fried Chicken	Finger-lickin' good!
M&M's	Melt in your mouth, not in your hands.
Greyhound	Leave the driving to us.
Playtex	Lifts and separates.
Target	Expect more. Pay less.

TIP

In Chapter 7, I show you how to write your own tagline. As you develop your personal brand, you'll find lots of opportunities for using your tagline to remind your target audience about your own brand promise.

Auditory elements: Songs and sounds that stick in your memory

The most obvious example of a memorable auditory element is the commercial jingle. Writing one is truly an art because it has to be catchy and solidify the product message in the customer's brain. Table 2-2 gives examples of just a few jingles from yesteryear that were so memorable they've become part of popular culture.

Table 2-2 Company Jingles

Brand Name	*Company Jingle*
Alka Seltzer	Plop plop, fizz fizz, oh what a relief it is.
Band-Aids	I am stuck on Band-Aid brand 'cause Band-Aid's stuck on me.
Folger's Coffee	The best part of waking up is Folger's in your cup.
Oscar Mayer	Oh I'd love to be an Oscar Mayer weiner . . .
State Farm Insurance	Like a good neighbor, State Farm is there.

TIP

When it comes to personal branding, I don't necessarily expect you to hire a jingle writer to come up with a catchy tune. However, I do want you to realize that sound may be important depending on the nature of the work you're doing and the brand you're promoting. When you design a website, you may want to make music part of the online experience for your target audience. (If you're a massage therapist, for example, you may want soothing instrumentals to play while someone browses your website.) Or you may find that using a certain sound on your website or in any videos you create (see Chapter 10) is effective.

Not sure what I mean? Think about the infamous two-note sound that introduces every episode of every branch of the *Law and Order* brand on TV. That sound is as much a part of the brand as the music that plays during the opening credits, and it's just two little notes!

Examining How a Few Famous Brands Create Connections

REMEMBER

Successful brands personalize their products. In this section, I discuss just a few of the best-known brands in the world — brands I suspect you may be familiar with — and how they connect emotionally with their target audiences.

The emotional connection is what sells!

Disney princesses

Disney is a brand known for wholesome family entertainment and fun. The promise of a magical experience sets the Disney brand apart from all others. Here, I focus on a Disney sub-brand, the Disney princesses, to demonstrate how multiple characters connect with segments of the target audience — all while maintaining the broader Disney brand.

One of the common traits of the Disney princesses (adapted primarily from fairy tales) is that they are all either orphans or are being raised by their father. Most have a wicked stepmother or some other evil person in their inner circle. All of them need to gather their resources and solve a problem.

As the princesses evolved over time, Disney injected issues of race, prejudice, and feminism into the roles, which encouraged audiences to think about their own (and society's) values.

In the sections that follow, I describe each princess so that you can see how Disney has created multiple unique characters that each serve the brand's larger promise. No matter what a young girl's personality or interests may be, she's likely to resonate with at least one of these characters.

Belle (Beauty and the Beast)

Belle is smart — a bookworm. She has her head in the clouds and thinks about moving beyond the small town she lives in. She is self-confident and doesn't care what other people think of her. She accepts all kinds of people and sticks to her values. Belle solves her problems by outsmarting her foes and won't settle for just a handsome man. Belle bucks convention. Even her yellow dress sends the message of intelligence, creativity, and independence. (In Chapter 13, I show you what various colors communicate to audiences.)

Cinderella

Cinderella is an optimist and always believes life will be better. She is also the overworked stepchild who must clean and serve others. She transforms when someone gives her a chance to be her real self and becomes the most beautiful woman at the ball. She is humble, gracious, and cheerful and follows the rules. She is the perfect woman in the eyes of the prince.

Ariel (The Little Mermaid)

Ariel longs to be someone else. She has a vision of wanting to be human. She collects human things for a long time, persevering in her vision. She knows that in order to lose her tail and get human legs, she must make sacrifices. She is endearing as she adjusts to her changes and knows that she must make difficult choices to have what she wants.

Snow White

Snow White doesn't realize that she is beautiful. She clears away the dust and exposes resources available to her. She is able to use her resources (the seven dwarfs) by appreciating each of their unique qualities and pulling them together to create a working team. Her beauty shines both inside and out as she loves each dwarf for who he is. In turn, they will do anything for her.

Mulan

Mulan is the warrior princess who dresses like a man and becomes a warrior out of loyalty and the desire to protect her father. (Her character is inspired by Hua Mulan from the Chinese poem *The Ballad of Mulan.)* She is brave, cunning, and a capable warrior. Mulan is not afraid to fight for what she believes.

Pocahontas

Pocahontas, based on an historical figure (the daughter of a Native American chief), is a noble, independent, feisty, and spiritually connected princess. She is wise beyond her years and kind to those around her. She loves adventure and is able to connect with nature, talk to spirits, understand animals, and comprehend other languages. She brings cultures together.

Apple

Apple is a brand that inspires strong emotional connections. In the beginning, Apple users owned Macintosh computers. Most of them would not even consider switching to a PC because they had such strong brand loyalty. Even when forced to use a PC in the workplace, they would come home to their Macs at night. As Apple's product line grew, the brand loyalty extended to iPods, iPads, and iPhones.

Apple is synonymous with the concept of innovation, which is summarized by its famous ad campaign slogan "Think different." People who align with the Apple brand see themselves as innovative, creative, and just outside of convention. They own an Apple product not just to have a functional product but to reflect their lifestyle. (Read more about Steve Jobs, cofounder of Apple, in Chapter 3.)

Trader Joe's

Trader Joe's customers *love* Trader Joe's. The company has cultivated huge customer loyalty because people feel strongly that the company is giving them high-quality, interesting food at decent prices. Shopping at Trader Joe's is an adventure as well because the stores carry innovative, hard-to-find, great-tasting foods that you don't find in the average grocery store.

Customers also love the value concept: This chain offers low everyday prices on all its products — no sales, no gimmicks, no clubs to join, no special cards to swipe. Trader Joe's buys direct from suppliers and then passes the savings on to its customers.

Customers are so committed to the Trader Joe's brand that more than 30 Trader Joe's cookbooks show up on Amazon.com. A recently published cookbook, *Livin' Lean with Trader Joe's* (Resolve Publishing) by Jamie Davidson, shows how you can lose weight using the convenient foods offered at this chain. Trader Joe's is unique and memorable, and customers love it.

Starbucks

Starbucks has mastered the art of consistency. Starbucks has the same look and feel whether you are in a Starbucks in Vancouver or in New York. You know that if you ask for a double nonfat no foam vanilla latte, it will be the same quality no matter what location you have bought it from.

Starbucks has made having a cup of coffee an experience for the customer. That's why their customers will pay premium prices for a cup of coffee. Starbucks changed the view of coffee from a commodity into a differentiated brand that people seek out.

Target

I prefer the French pronunciation *Tar-jea* when I think of Target stores. It's my family's pronunciation, and it makes me chuckle as I take my shopping trips to one of my favorite stores. Target has found a way to distinguish itself from its competitors, such as Walmart and KMart. It is cheap chic.

Target offers the promise of well-designed clothing and household goods at modest prices. Its prices are good, and its items have some flair, which connects especially well with young women and female heads of household.

Target lives its corporate mission, which is "to make Target the preferred shopping destination for our guests by delivering outstanding value, continuous innovation and an exceptional guest experience by consistently fulfilling our Expect More. Pay Less. brand promise." Living that mission consistently creates a loyal and satisfied customer.

Embracing the Idea of Marketing Yourself

At this point, after thinking about products and corporate brands, you may be having a reaction that I often witness when I talk about personal branding. You possibly feel offended by the idea that you, as a person, could be branded much like a car or a cleaning product.

I offer an overview of corporate branding because many of the concepts connect to personal branding. You'll follow some of the same methodology used in corporate branding to brand yourself. But when the product is you, the branding process doesn't need to be overtly commercial; you don't necessarily have to think in terms of maximizing your profit potential (although that may be one of your goals). Because you are a complex human being, you'll spend much of your effort in defining who you are. You are more complicated than a product, and you'll explore what that means as you work your way through the personal branding process.

Feeling confident that you can set yourself apart

The most exhausting thing you can be is inauthentic.

— Anne Morrow Lindbergh

You've probably learned by now that no one is going to manage your personal brand except you. Personal branding is all about you taking charge of your own future and learning how to manage your own identity. You are a unique individual with a set of talents, and it's time to use your gifts to the fullest capacity.

I was once the president of a women's philanthropic organization. A different president served each chapter across the country. It always amazed me to notice how different each president was when I attended the conferences. Being chapter president was the same job, and yet each president was so different. Each successful president knew her strengths and used what she was best at to make her chapter work. An unsuccessful president, in contrast, tried to overcompensate for her weaknesses and ended up not being a good leader. The presidents who embraced their strengths and uniqueness and then delegated their weaknesses most often made the best leaders. These women also became the most memorable because they fully let their personalities shine.

Personal branding sets you apart because you identify your differences and then learn to use those differences to make yourself memorable. Having a brand distinguishes you from the crowd by celebrating your individuality and drawing on your unique strengths to offer value to the people you serve.

Seeing your market potential

Personal branding helps you identify the personality of your brand by examining your *sensorial attributes* (how you look and what you sound like), your *rational appeal* (your skills, education, and work experience), and your *emotional appeal* (how you make people feel when they are around you). Your successful personal brand will be memorable, meaningful, and appealing to your target audience (whom you can define in Chapter 5).

Personal branding guru William Arruda says, "Know that you offer something unique and valuable. You have an ingredient to contribute that's not available from anyone else. Once you know what that ingredient is, let it guide your career decisions and use it to stand out and attract what you need to reach your goals."

Investing up front to reap benefits down the road

Personal branding is about deciding to take an active role in the direction of your life. You begin to self-manage your life and stop depending on others to do it for you. You discover how to make the most of what you've got to offer. Personal branding gives you permission to be yourself so that you can create the destiny you're meant to fulfill.

Personal branding is a strategic process that originated in business and has been adapted to the individual. Each part of the process is important. Here are just some of the benefits the branding process can offer:

- **Self-understanding:** One of the key benefits of personal branding is that you do a lot of introspection, considering who you are, what you are capable of, and what talents you bring to the table. Through this process, you increase your self-awareness.
- **Self-esteem:** You feel better about yourself knowing that you are living an authentic life and that you can accept who you are.
- **Presence:** By examining how you appear to others, you better understand what it means to have a presence.
- **Visibility:** You increase your visibility by learning how to make yourself stand out using techniques that work for you.
- **Differentiation:** You identify what makes you different from others who do what you do. Personal branding embraces that difference instead of hiding it to fit in.
- **Control:** Having a personal brand puts you in control of your career. It's about taking control of who you are and what you need to do — not doing what you think others want you to do.
- **Prosperity:** Strong brands are paid more than commodities. Through the personal branding process, you learn to avoid being seen as just a commodity.
- **Achievement:** You increase your achievement and professional fulfillment because you are aligning who you are with what you do and how you do it. You can achieve more when you are a congruent human being and are able to use all that you have to offer.

Chapter 3

Case Studies in Personal Branding Success

In This Chapter

- Emulating media and business moguls
- Seeing how sports stars and entertainers can brand themselves
- Putting politicians and other public figures in the spotlight
- Eyeing the branding efforts of executives
- Heeding lessons from broken personal brands

You can easily see the power of a personal brand by considering public figures who have created and maintained (or destroyed) their own personal brands.

To drive home the power of a personal brand, this chapter offers examples of people who have used branding tools with maximum success. Each short case study shows how that person used his talents and passions to become known for something special and to build a distinct personal brand. I discuss people from various walks of life to show how a personal brand can look through the lens of a chosen career path. Though each person I discuss here has a unique story, almost all of them have stayed true to their core values, which is crucial to building a strong brand.

I say *almost* because I dedicate the final section in this chapter to people whose personal brands have fallen from grace because they violated their own principles and disregarded the people they were serving. Their stories illustrate how someone can spend years building a brand only to have it shattered (and their reputation dishonored) by their own actions. A tarnished brand doesn't mean a personal brand can never be rehabilitated, but doing so can be a long, difficult process.

I hope these short stories inspire you to think about your own brand. You, too, can take your best self out into the world.

Measuring the Brands of Media and Business Moguls

The three case studies that I feature in this section highlight people who are truly in touch with their personal brands and have used their names to build empires. I attempt, in just a few short paragraphs each, to help you recognize what lies at the core of each person's personal brand.

Oprah Winfrey

Oprah Winfrey was born into poverty in the rural south and has overcome adversity that most people never know. She has built a personal brand as a caring, authentic, sincere, inspiring, and spiritual person who strives for meaning in all that she pursues. Her talent and authenticity have brought her not only wealth, but also fame and power. She uses her power of influence to make the world a better place. Her philanthropic work has become legendary, and her spiritual influence is such that in 2002, *Christianity Today* wrote about "The Church of O."

She continues to be true to her brand and lead her life based on her deep values to serve humanity. Oprah has been called the most influential woman and the most influential black person of her generation. Her brand is so powerful that her influence is called the *Oprah Effect.* Much like a halo effect, everything she endorses or believes immediately becomes popular among her millions of loyal followers.

Oprah consistently lives her brand by emotionally connecting to her audience and making values-based choices. She has triumphed adversity and exudes the strength of the human spirit. Her greatest gift is that she leads by example and encourages others to live their best selves.

Howard Stern

When you think *shock jock,* you think Howard Stern. A native of New York and son of Jewish immigrants, he began working in radio in 1977 and has worked consistently in the business ever since. His radio and television shows, media appearances, books, and movies all add up to validate his self-proclaimed title of "King of All Media."

Stern's style is his brand. He is outspoken and controversial, and many people find him obnoxious. The fact that his shows have been the most-fined radio programs by the Federal Communications Commission (FCC) doesn't detract from his brand, but promotes it.

Stern's personal brand is meant to push the boundaries of acceptability. His adherence to his brand, and his use of Sirius radio to promote the Howard Stern label, mean that when you tune in to his show, you can expect to get a point of view outside the mainstream. He stays true to his shock-jock brand and has a large following that supports it.

Kathy Ireland

Forbes magazine published an article on Kathy Ireland in 2008 in which it dubbed her a supermodel turned super mogul. Hers is a brand worth mentioning because she has been able to transform her strong brand as a *Sports Illustrated* supermodel into the brand of an entrepreneurial CEO of a $1.5 billion business, Kathy Ireland Worldwide. She is proof that a personal brand can grow and change and still be authentic and successful.

Kathy was discovered when she was 17 and later appeared on the 25th anniversary cover of *Sports Illustrated's* swimsuit edition. She appeared in the *SI* swimsuit edition for 13 consecutive years, three times on the cover. She was known to all as the stunning model with beautiful green eyes and flowing brown hair. And yes, she looked great in a swimsuit.

But what Kathy really loved was business. She had been an entrepreneur from an early age with her paper delivery routes and had always worked hard. When she left the modeling field, she tried her hand at several businesses but failed due to the wrong partnerships. She used the failures as lessons about business and didn't give up. She is self-determined, independent, and much smarter than the public generally perceives a model to be.

Her vision was to build a powerful brand that had longevity and to be involved in every aspect of the business. Her first success was when she partnered with Moretz Sports to brand a line of socks that she went out and sold herself. She has turned that business into the 23rd most licensed business in the world, according to the 2008 issue of *Global License* magazine.

Kathy lives her trademarked brand of "making time for families, especially busy moms." She is a mother of three and believes in giving back to the communities she serves. She is a devout Christian who follows the principles that she believes in and exhibits her beliefs in the way that she conducts her business. She recently was awarded the Kennedy Laureate Award for her outstanding achievements and personal commitment to community service. Her brand built on poise, devotion, independence, and determined focus has consistently served her in each of her entrepreneurial ventures.

Simon Cowell

For many a would-be singer, the mention of Simon Cowell may cause cringing and an urge to run for the exit. Cowell has taken his skills as an artist and repertoire executive (a talent scout and developer), television producer, and entrepreneur to fashion a personal brand that demands excellence. He is known for his straight-shooting evaluation of talent.

Cowell's personal brand is his business brand — one built on direct feedback and honesty with a critical eye for talent. His brand strengthened in the United States during his first season as a judge on *American Idol.* "I don't mean to be rude, but . . ." became his signature phrase that indicated he was about to tell a contestant that he or she did not measure up to his standards.

Cowell has used his brand to expand his influence by developing other television shows both in the United States and abroad. His brand has almost become a caricature, with other reality contestant judges doing their best Simon Cowell imitation.

Studying How Sports Figures Brand Themselves

Volumes have been written on sports figures and how they have played a significant role in the games at which they excel. Here, I highlight just three people who have distinctive brands — people who have evolved beyond the sports they're known for and have continued their legacies elsewhere.

Tony LaRussa

Integrity, intelligence, and loyalty are key elements of Tony LaRussa's personal brand. Best known as a manager for three major league baseball teams (winning six league championships and three World Series titles), he has gone on to evolve his brand beyond baseball.

LaRussa and his wife, Elaine, founded the Animal Rescue Foundation in Northern California. His love of animals fueled the creation of this organization, which saves abandoned and injured animals and also runs programs to bring dog and cat visits to abused children, hospital patients, seniors, and shut-ins. LaRussa is also a vegetarian. Helping animals is one way that he makes a difference in the world.

He reinforces his brand through his commitments. LaRussa is known for keeping his word and for his loyalty to others, whether in baseball or in philanthropy.

Cal Ripkin

This section was written by Tripper Ortman, sports aficionado and attorney.

Since breaking Lou Gehrig's "unbreakable" consecutive-games-played streak in 1995, Cal Ripken Jr., baseball's Iron Man, has built on his family's baseball legacy through thoughtful development of the Ripken Baseball brand.

Ripken was a 19-time All-Star and a first-ballot Hall of Famer, and he is best known for playing in 2,632 consecutive games at shortstop and third base. Perhaps more importantly for branding purposes, Ripken spent his entire career with one team: the Baltimore Orioles. And for the better part of 12 years, he was coached and then managed by his father, Cal Ripken Sr., who himself had been a catcher in the Orioles organization. Ripken Jr. also spent five years playing shortstop with his brother Billy at second base, a rare brotherly double-play combination.

Before retiring in 2001, Ripken Jr. earned a reputation as a family man and, in a world of pampered athletes, earned respect from sports fans as a regular guy who showed up and worked hard every day. Capitalizing on his family history and his reputation as a hard worker, since 2001 Ripken has coauthored several best-selling books about coaching and playing baseball, about business, and even about parenting young athletes *The Ripken Way.*

Today, Ripken Jr. serves as the CEO of Ripken Baseball, Inc., a multimillion dollar business and philanthropy conglomerate consisting of Ripken youth baseball schools and camps, a baseball management and design arm, and ownership of several minor league baseball teams. By staying focused on traits valued by most Americans — dedication, loyalty, and family — Ripken Jr. has established himself as a trusted advisor to parents and sports fans nationwide.

Shaquille O'Neal

You know someone has been successful in establishing a personal brand when that person is known by only one name. The name Shaq immediately brings to mind the almost cartoon-like image of Shaquille O'Neal, standing 7'1" tall and weighing 325 pounds. He played basketball professionally for 19 years.

Shaq works diligently to maintain his brand — that of the biggest and the best in all that he does. He has taken his celebrity status beyond basketball to create four rap albums, the first of which went platinum. He has starred in numerous films and reality shows, inevitably being featured as the larger-than-life Goliath whose personality has you rooting for him. Shaq has carefully tailored his brand to reflect his success, emphasizing his cheerful outlook and contributions to both sports and entertainment.

Creating an Entertaining Brand

Entertainers fill the tabloids with their crazy stories and quest for media attention. I've chosen to highlight just two very famous people here, but I've selected them because the brands are so very different. I want you to consider how a young star has created herself and how a star with longevity has maintained her brand.

Lady Gaga

Lady Gaga appears in outrageous outfits, performs sexually charged songs, and has earned the reputation of giving the audience something unexpected. She has taken over a role that Madonna played for many years, building a brand that always surprises. Whether she's on stage or just walking down the street, she entertains.

"I'm star-struck over Lady Gaga right now," Tony Bennett said on a recent episode of VH1's *Big Morning Buzz Live.* "She's fabulous. I think she's going to be America's Picasso. She changes every day, and she has unlimited energy. And each thing she does is wilder and greater than the thing she does the day before."

In an interview with Barbara Walters, Lady Gaga said the biggest misconception people have of her is that she is artificial and simply seeks attention. "Every bit of me is devoted to love and art, and I aspire to be a teacher to my younger fans," she said. "I want to liberate them from their fears and help them create their own space in the world." Lady Gaga's is a personal brand that she feels is authentic artistic expression, but others have interpreted it as artificial and attention getting. Personal brands blend both what you think about yourself and what others think of you.

Love her or hate her, you can't deny that she is a brilliant, creative artist who redefines her look with each new act or public appearance. She *always* surprises.

Meryl Streep

Meryl Streep is one of the greatest actors of our time. For more than three decades, she has been known for her chameleon-like ability to play a diversity of characters with intense humanness. Her deep study of the characters she plays shows in the perfection of each performance, including her uncanny ability to master almost any accent.

Her brand is one of excellence at her craft. When you see one of her movies, you know that the acting will be superb. Her trademarks are quality, perfection, and mastery, and she has gained the respect of the people she works with and the people she entertains.

Streep's brand has paid dividends. She was a Kennedy Center Honoree in 2011 and has won three Academy Awards and seven Golden Globes. She has been nominated more often than any other actor in the history of either the Academy Awards (17 nominations) or the Golden Globes (26 nominations).

Streep describes herself as being able to see and feel the world through another's eyes. "The thing that makes me feel good is when I have said something for a soul," she said at the Kennedy Center Awards in 2011.

Putting Public Figures in the Spotlight

This section looks at three people who occupy a prominent spot on the world stage and considers how they have branded themselves to maximize their impact.

Kate Middleton, the humble princess

In 2011, Kate Middleton wowed the world when she married Prince William. She went from being a commoner to being a celebrated new royal and fashion icon. She is admired for her elegant conservatism and is gaining a reputation as sensible, levelheaded, and down-to-earth. She is the first royal bride to have earned a college degree, and her subjects love her.

Middleton is winning rave reviews for her ladylike intelligence, her elegant sense of style, her charming personality, and her easy connection with people from all walks of life. Whatever she wears becomes the latest style.

This brand is making waves across the world, and it will be fun to watch Middleton grow and evolve as she settles into her royal role.

Jimmy Carter

You'd think that being the 39th President of the United States would be sufficient enough to establish a lasting personal brand. But Jimmy Carter's personal brand as a man of character and compassion, with a deep belief in peace, has been more firmly established since he left the Presidency in 1981.

In 2009, the *Independent* in London wrote that "Mr. Carter is widely considered a better man than he was a President." He is the only President to have received the Nobel Peace Prize after leaving the Presidency. This prize was awarded to him for his work with the foundation that he created, The Carter Center in Atlanta.

Through the creation of The Carter Center, he has strengthened his brand as a peacemaker. This NGO (nongovernment organization) works to resolve international conflicts, support human rights, monitor elections, and improve health conditions in other countries.

Being true to his brand does not mean that Mr. Carter is subservient to U.S. politicians. His concern and deep commitment to his principles have led him to criticize both Republican and Democratic presidents whose actions he felt were not in accord with the higher standards that he holds as a humanitarian and advocate of world peace.

Barack Obama

Regardless of your political persuasion, you must acknowledge the power of Barack Obama's personal brand. He broke huge barriers by becoming the first African-American U.S. President. He rose to his position as a relatively young man known for his intellect, his public speaking prowess, and his persistence in the face of what other people considered to be impossible. His brand was founded on hope, change, and progress.

In 2009, President Obama won the Nobel Peace Prize for his extraordinary efforts to strengthen international diplomacy and cooperation between people. The world celebrated his brand: that of a man who brings the hope of change and peace.

Brands are always evolving, especially in the political arena. For presidents who run for a second term, their brand will need to progress with the nation's changes.

BigLeague Executives: Mirroring a Corporate Brand with a Personal Brand

This section showcases three entrepreneurs who wouldn't give up on their ideas. They were true to themselves and their passions, and they created companies that have reshaped the global business landscape. You'll notice that very little separates what these individuals stand for in their personal brand and what the companies they created stand for. Their personal brands and their companies' corporate brands are virtually the same.

Steve Jobs's commencement speech

Steve Jobs addressed the 2005 graduating class of Stanford in what has become his most famous speech. He expressed the importance of being true to yourself and living authentically throughout your career. He talked about dropping out of college, being fired from Apple, and being diagnosed with cancer. His speech epitomized his personal brand. Here are some of the highlights:

- Jobs noted that as difficult as it was for him to be fired from Apple, it turned out to be a pivotal moment in his life. "The heaviness of being successful was replaced by the lightness of being a beginner again, less sure about everything," he said. "It freed me to enter one of the most creative periods of my life."
- Finding a career based on your passions was a central theme of the speech. Jobs urged the Stanford graduates to figure out what they love and not to settle for anything less because they were going to spend such a large part of their lives focused on work. He said that "the only way to be truly satisfied is to do what you believe is great work. And the only way to do great work is to love what you do."
- Jobs also spoke about how short our lives are and how crucial it is to live your own life — not anyone else's. He urged the graduates to think for themselves and listen to their own inner voices. "And most important, have the courage to follow your heart and intuition," he said. "They somehow already know what you truly want to become."

You can view the whole speech on YouTube at `www.youtube.com/watch?v=UF8uR6Z6KLc`. You may find it truly inspirational as you begin to develop your own personal brand.

Steve Jobs: "Think different"

Just after his passing in 2011, Jobs was dubbed an American Icon by *Time* magazine. At the time of his death, Apple was the most valuable company on earth. When you think of Apple, you think of Steve Jobs.

Jobs is difficult to summarize in a few paragraphs because he did such amazing things in his life. His motto and key ad campaign was "Think Different," and that he did. Jobs was both an artist and an engineer. He was able to bring simplicity to the complex with artful design that appealed to anyone who wanted to be cool. (Apple's sales numbers would indicate that means just about everyone.)

Jobs's career has been well-chronicled, but here are some highlights: He started Apple on April Fool's Day in 1976 with two other founders. He developed the Apple and Macintosh computers, was fired from Apple, and then returned to introduce the world to iMacs, iPods, iTunes, iPads, and a revolution of communication ideas. Between leaving Apple in 1985 and returning in 1997,

Jobs founded NeXT (another computer company) and Pixar, which used image-processing computers to develop animated films such as *Toy Story* and to change the movie industry.

His personal brand is reflected in a quote concerning Apple in 2001, at a time when the company was still trying to recover from the Job-less administration. He said, "The way we're going to survive is to innovate our way out of this."

Time summed up his legacy this way: "He has revolutionized six industries — personal computers, animated movies, music, phones, tablet computing, and digital publishing." He also reimagined retailing with the Apple stores.

Jobs lived his brand of innovation in everything that he did. Through his ideas, he truly did change the world.

Spontaneous Smiley

She may not be as famous as the other people I profile in this chapter, but Ruth Kaiser is a personal branding success worth knowing about.

Kaiser is an artist, teacher, author, and mother of three. She runs on high creative energy and an entrepreneurial spirit. When her children were young, she noticed that not many options existed for parents who required childcare on an as-needed basis. She conceived Tot Drop, where a parent can take a child to childcare for up to four hours on any given day. The kids are met with quality preschool teachers and lots of fun projects. Her little project grew to multiple centers.

In 2008, Kaiser began a project on Facebook called Spontaneous Smiley. It hosted pictures that she took of objects that looked like smiley faces. The project followed her theme of choosing to live a happier life and sharing that feeling with the world. This art project lives on the Internet and involves thousands of people all over the world sharing their photographs of smiley faces appearing in everyday objects.

Kaiser created this project based on her love of life and her philosophy of choosing to soak life up in the most positive way. Her little project took off, and within a year of its launch, the site hit more than 10 million page requests.

Now, Kaiser is sharing her spontaneous smiles worldwide. She was asked to give a TEDx talk on her special project and has written a children's book of optimism called A Smiley Book of Colors (Random House: `http://tinyURL.com/3c2qyd6`). She has also partnered with the nonprofit Operation Smile raising funds for facial surgeries one Smiley upload at a time. You can find more about the project at `www.spontaneoussmiley.com`.

Kaiser has always had the brand of a free-spirited, community-minded artist and mom. She is both goofy and solid and always expresses her one-of-a-kind self. Everything she does, including her musical holiday CD gifts, exude her brand. She is consistent in living her brand whether she is at work, giving to the community, enjoying her hobbies, or sharing with her family. She has found a way to make her quirkiness succeed, and the world is better because of it.

Mark Zuckerberg

Mark Zuckerberg — whose brand may be summed up as *brilliant, change agent, visionary* — changed the way people communicate. He used his visionary timing and brilliant computer skills to cofound Facebook in 2004. As I write these words, Facebook has grown to have more than 800 million users, half of whom log in to the site every day.

Zuckerberg envisioned that in this fast-paced world, people would communicate differently. He was named *Time* magazine's Person of the Year in 2010 for his ability to wire together the world the way no one else had done. *Time* stated that "Facebook has merged with the social fabric of American life, and not just American but human life: nearly half of all Americans have a Facebook account, but 70% of Facebook users live outside the U.S. It's a permanent fact of our global social reality. We have entered the Facebook age, and Mark Zuckerberg is the man who brought us here."

As one of the wealthiest men on earth, Zuckerberg has signed the "Giving Pledge," promising to donate at least 50 percent of his wealth to charity over the course of his lifetime. Perhaps he will become known as one of the great philanthropists as his brand evolves.

Zuckerberg's vision may ultimately help people realize that what happens to one person, happens to us all. Who could have predicted that Facebook would be a catalyst for the 2011 revolution in Egypt?

Watching Famous Personal Brands Take a Dive (and Sometimes Rebound)

A personal brand is your reputation. In a moment, choices that run contrary to the brand you've built can erase years of work and dedication. While you can reclaim and resurrect a personal brand, the key to a strong personal brand is to remain consistently true to your values, core beliefs, and passions.

It's pretty easy to think of examples of personal brands gone awry. Here, I offer just a few short case studies of individuals who have damaged their brands — two of them quite seriously, and two in ways that have left the door open for brand resurrection.

Joe Paterno

Joe Paterno, or *Joe Pa* as he was known in Happy Valley, Pennsylvania, was the famed football coach at Penn State for 46 years. He was the revered patriarch of a football program known not just for its winning program but also for quality, values, and standing up for what was right.

Unfortunately, Coach Paterno won't be remembered only for all the good things that represented his brand. Instead, his legacy will forever be tied to the scandal involving Jerry Sandusky and the apparent coverup of alleged sexual molestation. Instead of retiring with the benefit of a personal brand that reflected integrity, wholesomeness, and caring for the players, Coach Paterno was fired in 2011, leaving his and the university's brand severely tarnished.

Anthony Weiner

Anthony Weiner was elected to the U.S. House of Representatives in 1999 at age 35 and held that seat until 2011. The recipient of a number of awards and viewed as an up-and-coming young Democrat, Wiener's personal brand was one of integrity and authenticity.

In May 2011, Weiner sent a link on Twitter to a woman in Texas with a sexually suggestive image of himself. Although he denied the claims for days, more suggestive photos and communications surfaced. Weiner's personal brand was destroyed to such an extent that he resigned from office in June 2011.

Magic Johnson

Earvin "Magic" Johnson was a star player for the Los Angeles Lakers starting in 1979. His basketball skills were matched by his outgoing enthusiasm for life. He was known for his exceptional athletic ability and his feel-good wholesomeness. But Magic's personal brand was impacted dramatically in 1991 when he announced that he tested positive for HIV. This announcement led to his retirement from basketball.

Johnson went on to resurrect his brand through his philanthropic and business activities and his HIV/AIDS activism. He became a champion for people with AIDS and helped the general population understand more about the virus. Through his proactive efforts, he was able to put his brand back on track.

Martha Stewart

Martha Stewart built an empire as America's goddess of domestic perfection, the queen of all things having to do with the home: cooking, decorating, and entertaining. She is known for the books that she has created, as well as her media empire in television and magazines. Martha made "It's a good thing" a well-known catch phrase.

In 2004, her world turned upside down when she was convicted of securities fraud and obstruction of justice and served five months in federal prison. No one believed that she could make a comeback, but upon her release in 2005, she was able to return her company to profitability within the year.

She has gone on to regain the throne as America's goddess of domestic perfection through her business savvy and resilient spirit. She launched an upscale home line for Macy's, which was the largest brand launch in the department store's history. Martha once again says, "It's a good thing."

Part II
Knowing Your Brand

The 5th Wave By Rich Tennant

"Think about it: you live in the forest, swing on a vine, and spend a lot of time in the trees. It's obvious; you're 'Tarzan, King of the Squirrels.'"

In this part . . .

Before you can put your personal brand into action, you have to define it for yourself. And that process begins by defining who you are — your values, passions, strengths, skills, and more — which is why I devote a chapter to increasing your self-knowledge.

I also show you how to identify other people who are important to your sense of self, especially in a business setting — your target audience and your competitors.

In addition, I walk you through the process of drafting a personal brand profile. This document pulls together your key ideas about yourself and highlights your *unique promise of value:* the promise you make to your target audience that your brand can fulfill. This promise lies at the heart of who you are and what you can accomplish, which means you can't fully tap into the power of personal branding without it. (In other words, Chapter 7 is a must-read!)

Chapter 4

Defining Who You Are

In This Chapter

- Figuring out your needs, values, and interests
- Defining your mission and vision
- Spotting your strengths and unique characteristics
- Bringing personality, education, and other traits into focus
- Looking at yourself from all angles
- Setting goals so that you can move forward

Defining who you are is the foundation of branding. Without this discovery, you are merely marketing something that isn't really you. Personal branding is all about authenticity, and you need to define yourself before you can market yourself authentically. This chapter contains the tools you need to define yourself.

To get the most out of this chapter, take the time to think about each piece of information that you need to gather about yourself. Enjoy taking a look at yourself and discovering your uniqueness. Also, do each exercise that I suggest; write your responses and hold on to them. In Chapter 7, I show you how to put your defining pieces together into a personal branding profile.

Identifying What Matters to You

Identifying what matters to you sounds like an easy task, but most people don't think very much about it. You probably go about your daily life making split-second choices (often subconsciously) rather than trying to make each decision based on whether it jibes with what's important to you. Developing a personal brand requires being more aware of yourself and your choices. In this section, I walk you through a variety of ways that you can heighten your awareness of the things that really matter to you.

Knowing your needs

To look at what matters to you, you first need to identify what you need. Needs develop unconsciously as you grow up and become a central part of your character. In order to brand yourself, examining your needs is crucial.

Abraham Maslow developed a theory called *Maslow's Hierarchy of Needs* that states that you must have your basic needs met before you can examine your higher-level needs. Figure 4-1 illustrates Maslow's hierarchy. Starting at the bottom, each level of need must be met in order for someone to be able to consider — and work toward — meeting the next higher level.

Maslow's theory illustrates that if you have *physiological* needs — you are hungry, tired, cold, or hot, for example — you won't be able to concentrate on much else. If your physiological needs are met but you have *safety* needs — you don't feel safe in your environment — you can't worry much about fulfilling your need for belonging and love.

REMEMBER

If all three of the lower levels of need are fulfilled, you can start to focus on esteem, which is where personal branding can really start to take place. This level of need involves being able to feel that you do your job well, respect yourself and others, and align the work you do with your sense of self. This alignment is absolutely necessary in order to authentically build your personal brand.

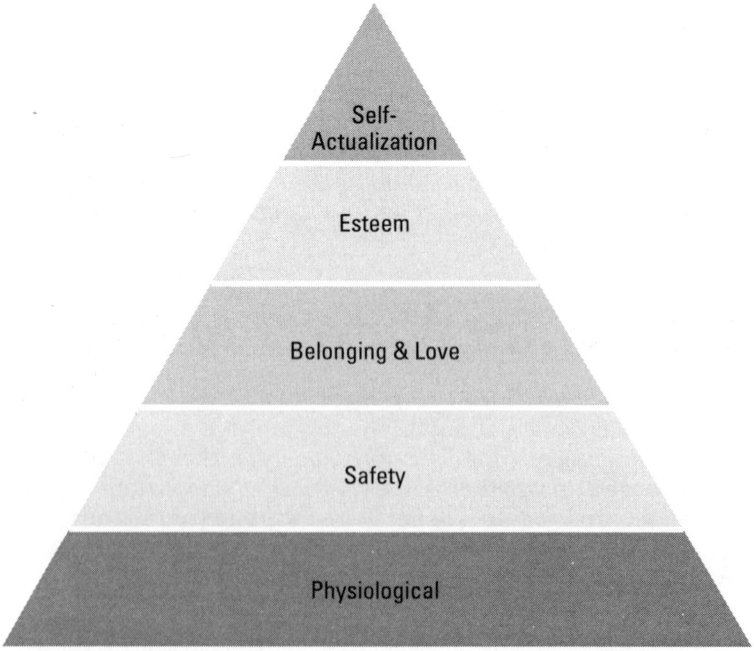

Figure 4-1: Maslow's Hierarchy of Needs.

The highest level of need is *self-actualization.* Maslow described self-actualization as becoming everything that you're capable of becoming. Striving toward fulfilling self-actualization is the goal of personal branding. If you achieve that goal, you get to be who you really are, and you'll shine brightly.

To help connect the hierarchy of needs with what happens in your workplace, I've created Table 4-1, which spells out what needs fall into each of Maslow's categories and then looks at the hierarchy through a work-specific lens.

Table 4-1 Considering Your Workplace Needs

Maslow's Hierarchy of Needs	*Hierarchy of Career Needs*
Physiological: Food, shelter, sleep, water, oxygen, sex, freedom of movement, and a moderate temperature	**Career Physiological Needs:** A paycheck, breaks to eat or rest, and work hours that provide time to go home and rest
Safety: Security, stability, safety of body and family, freedom from violence, and rituals and routines	**Career Safety:** Job security and no threat of layoffs; workplace safety including a workplace free of violence, psychological abuse, and hazardous toxic exposure; property safety; and regular and predictable work hours
Belonging and Love: Friendships, family, sexual intimacy, and community	**Career Belonging:** Having positive relationships with coworkers, boss, and customers; cultural fit; and an affinity to the mission of the organization
Self-Esteem: Self-confidence, mutual respect of and for others, achievement, and recognition	**Career Esteem:** Kudos such as "Wow, you did such a great job!", promotions, titles, new levels of responsibility, pay raises, respect for fellow employees, a feeling of being respected, and alignment of work with sense of self
Self-Actualization: Knowledge, understanding, peace, self-fulfillment, life mission, pursuit of inner talents, and creativity, beauty	**Career Mastery:** Fully using your talents in your work, contributing to the greater good, knowing your purpose in life, finding meaning in your work, and having a sense of mastery

Needs are important to consider because people commonly stop themselves from trying something new or taking risks for fear of putting their basic needs in jeopardy. For example, you may wonder, "Can I try this and not get fired from my work?" or "If I develop my personal brand, will everyone laugh at me?"

Needs direct your feelings and influence your values. They influence your motivation. Determining what you need will help you understand what you value and where you need to set your goals. Before you go any further with this chapter, I encourage you to take some time to answer these two questions (in writing):

- What needs of mine are met?
- What needs of mine are not met?

Defining your values

Values are the emotional currency of your life. They are the core principles that give meaning to your life and are defined as a set of standards that determine your attitudes, choices, and actions. Values change as you change; they reflect what's important to you at any given moment. For example, I would think if you value your frankness and your partner does, too, but doesn't have tact, you might then change and start valuing diplomacy more.

Values help you establish your sense of purpose and direction. They act as guideposts that assist you in evaluating choices in your life.

TIP

The quickest way to determine whether a value has been violated is to notice what things have ever made you feel angry. Think about a time when something felt wrong to you. Did someone cross an important line for you that did not mesh with something you value?

Your deepest values, and the ones that often stay with you the longest, are your *intrinsic* values. Intrinsic values are ends in themselves, such as happiness or integrity. They are the guiding principles by which you lead your life.

Values drive you and help you commit to your life. Often, the reason people are unhappy at work is because their values no longer align with their work. When you're crafting a personal brand, you must understand your core values because they are the heart of who you are.

TIP

The following list of values can help you think about what is important to you. Here's an exercise I play with my classes: Each person writes his top ten values on ten separate pieces of paper. During each round of the game, each player must throw away one piece of paper by considering which values are the greatest priorities. In the end, each player is left with just one piece of paper: that person's most important value. This exercise is very impactful, so if you're in the mood, find a friend or two to do this with.

Even if you don't do the exercise with anyone else, take the time to identify your top ten values from the list below. Start by identifying all the values that feel like they belong to you. Then select the ten that are the most important. Make note of your values because you will use them when you are building your mission statement in this chapter and the personal brand statement in Chapter 7.

abundance	acceptance	accomplishment
accuracy	achievement	acknowledgment
activeness	adaptability	adventure
affection	affluence	agility
altruism	ambition	appreciation
assertiveness	attractiveness	availability
awareness	balance	beauty
being the best	belonging	boldness
bravery	brilliance	calmness
challenge	charity	charm
clarity	cleanliness	comfort
commitment	compassion	completion
composure	concentration	congruency
connection	consciousness	consistency
contentment	contribution	control
coolness	cooperation	correctness
courage	creativity	credibility
curiosity	daring	decisiveness
dependability	determination	devotion
dignity	diligence	diplomacy
discipline	discovery	diversity
drive	duty	education
effectiveness	efficiency	elegance
empathy	endurance	energy
enjoyment	enthusiasm	excellence
excitement	experience	expertise
expressiveness	extroversion	fairness
faith	fame	family
fearlessness	fidelity	financial independence
fitness	flexibility	focus
freedom	friendliness	frugality
fun	generosity	giving
grace	gratitude	growth
happiness	harmony	health
helpfulness	heroism	honesty
humility	humor	hygiene
imagination	independence	insightfulness
inspiration	integrity	intelligence
intimacy	introversion	intuition
joy	justice	kindness
knowledge	leadership	learning
liberty	logic	love

loyalty
mindfulness
obedience
organization
peace
philanthropy
pleasure
power
precision
professionalism
reason
relaxation
resourcefulness
sacrifice
self-control
serenity
silence
skillfulness
spontaneity
success
synergy
traditionalism
trustworthiness
uniqueness
virtue
wisdom
making a difference
motivation
open-mindedness
originality
perfection
playfulness
polish
practicality
preparedness
prosperity
recognition
reliability
respect
satisfaction
selflessness
service
simplicity
solitude
stability
support
teamwork
timeliness
truth
variety
vision
mastery
neatness
optimism
passion
perseverance
pleasantness
popularity
pragmatism
privacy
realism
recreation
resilience
restraint
security
self-reliance
significance
sincerity
spirituality
strength
sympathy
temperance
tranquility
understanding
victory
warmth

Focusing on the things you love to do

Your interests or passions are things that intrigue you and motivate you to devote energy to them. They determine how you want to spend your time. Your interests often develop early in life, but not every interest is supported by a talent or ability, so your level of engagement may depend on your level of skill.

I often hear people explain that they just "fell into" their work. If that describes you, I encourage you to ask yourself what you like about your job and, more importantly, why you stay. If you think back to jobs you did in high school or college, you'll realize that even those jobs were likely ones that you chose to apply for. Shouldn't your grown-up job also be one of your choosing?

Of course, making a choice based on your interests (and steering clear of your disinterests) requires knowing what they are. You can start by asking yourself these questions:

- What do you like about your current job?
- What kinds of volunteer work do you enjoy doing?
- What hobbies do you spend the most time on?
- What are the activities you really *don't* enjoy doing?

Taking an interest inventory

Table 4-2 helps you put words to your interest areas. It outlines various categories of work or skills and the types of activities they entail. I encourage you to circle the specific activities in each line that have the greatest interest to you.

Table 4-2 Interest Inventory

Category	*Activities*
Researching	Research, observe, investigate, study, perceive, sense, measure, test, inspect, and examine
Analyzing	Analyze, compare, extract, correlate, derive, evaluate, differentiate, and identify
Interpreting	Interpret, explain, understand, portray, and advise
Problem-solving	Solve, troubleshoot, improve, critique, re-direct, redesign, and restructure
Systematizing	Systematize, coordinate, organize, and develop procedures
Planning	Plan short-term, plan long-term, forecast, strategize, and set goals
Managing	Manage, supervise, control, direct, budget, administer, and delegate
Leading	Lead, show the way, govern, inspire, motivate, assert, decide, and advise
Decision-making	Decide, judge, select, decide under pressure, and arbitrate
Following through	Persist, persevere, show tenacity, tie up all loose ends, and bring to closure
Mentoring	Mentor, teach, coach, counsel constructively, and help others to grow professionally and personally
Innovating	Innovate, invent, change, develop, devise, and break with convention
Imagining	Imagine, visualize, conceptualize, and fantasize
Visioning	Envision the future clearly, ask "what if?" or "why not?" and then act to find the answer
Synthesizing	Synthesize, adapt, and bring together with imagination

(continued)

Table 4-2 *(continued)*

Category	***Activities***
Creating	Create, draw, sketch, sculpt, and perform with originality
Counseling	Empathize, understand needs/feelings of others, relate to issues and concerns of others, comfort, offer kindness, help others, and be friendly and attentive
Listening	Listen actively and understand the message others are delivering
Communicating in writing	Write clearly, concisely, and effectively, spot grammatical errors, and use editorial ability
Communicating verbally	Speak clearly, concisely and effectively and use the spoken word to get results
Persuading verbally	Persuade, convince, influence, overcome opposition, and sell
Negotiating	Mediate, negotiate, intervene, resolve differences, and arbitrate
Initiating	Take the initiative, be among the first to do or try, and get things started
Changing dynamics	Be flexible, adapt easily to change, be aware, and go with the flow
Working on a team	Work well with a team and be a team player
Assembling	Assemble, build, prepare, fabricate, rebuild, and fashion
Installing	Install, fit, tailor, customize, and test
Operating	Operate, run, maintain, fix, and set up

Passions exercise: Past, present, and future questions

Another exercise to help you think about your key interests is to ask yourself these past, present, and future questions to explore what you love to do:

Past: Think about a time when you lost track of time. What were you doing?

Present: Cocktail party — you hear a great conversation next to you. What are they talking about?

Future: You have won $50 million in the lottery. What would you do?

Used with permission of William Arruda (`www.reachpersonalbranding.com`*).*

Another creative way that I like to play with interests and passions is through collage. You take a stack of magazines and rip out pictures that appeal to you. When you have a nice stack of pictures, take a large piece of paper (perhaps 11-x-17 inch) or a poster board, glue, and scissors and create your collage. Pictures will convey messages that words often don't. Step back and see what you notice. Did a surprise passion show up in your collage?

Figuring out whether your interests are general or specific

Interests vary widely from person to person. Some people have *wide interest patterns,* meaning that they like a lot of things and are often happy doing many types of work. For someone like that, the following factors determine whether a job is the right fit:

- Do I like the people I'll be working with?
- Do I like the work environment, including the work hours, commute, and physical surroundings?
- Does this work align with my values?

I have found that extroverted people tend to fall into the generalist category more than introverted people. If you're a generalist and are entering the branding process, you need to find other criteria to highlight for your brand rather than your expertise in a single subject.

Other people have far fewer interests, which run deeper. For them, the kind of work they do really matters, and the other factors (coworkers, environment, and values) play a lesser role. These people are subject matter experts and have a much easier time branding themselves because their area of expertise is more defined.

Determining your place in the world

One of my favorite books on the subject of mission and vision is Laurie Beth Jones' *The Path* (Hyperion). She identifies a *mission statement* as a written-down reason for being and believes it is the key to finding your path in life. A mission statement is focused on the practice of what you need to be doing.

Defining your mission

There are several definitions for mission in every dictionary. Here are two that apply to your personal branding work:

- A *mission* is a specific task that a person is sent to perform.
- A *mission* is an allotted or self-imposed duty or task; a calling; one's mission in life.

Missions themselves are simple statements that clarify what you are all about and what you want to do in life. Figuring out your mission sounds simple, but it's often hard. Often, the greater the mission, the more simply it can be stated. Your mission needs to include your enthusiasms for life. If you have no passion for your mission, then it isn't really your mission.

A personal mission statement or personal philosophy is what you feel you would like to become in your life. It is an internal process and needs to come from the core of who you are. There are no right or wrong answers; defining your mission statement is just a way to put your purpose or calling into words.

I used to teach a course called Gateway, and it was the first course a person took in a career transition series. In that class, the participants had to come up with mission statements. Here are some of the most memorable:

- To make cool stuff (computer engineer)
- To bring order from chaos (quality control manager)
- To live a life of service to others (human resources manager)

Ideally, a mission statement should encompass most aspects of your life, not just your work. A sense of mission can become a foundation piece of your personal brand.

A key practical use of a mission statement is that it becomes a filter for you in deciding whether opportunities are the right ones for you. As you incorporate your mission into your brand, you'll be able to ask, "Is this on brand for me?" After you have your mission, decisions become much clearer to make.

Writing your mission statement

Before you try to write your mission statement, be sure to look at your needs, values, and interests first. One strategy I recommend is to put keywords on sticky notes and think about them for a few days. Sometimes messages like your mission statement just come to you while driving or in the shower. Make sure to write your ideas down when you get a flash of insight.

I worked for weeks on my mission. I spent many hours playing with the words that had meaning to me. I finally wrote this:

I act as a guide to educate and empower others to use their gifts in the world.

Here are some steps you can take to help you craft your mission statement:

1. **Think of nouns that describe you.**

   Examples are *teacher, learner, strategist, farmer* — any word that applies to you.

2. **Add verbs of how you like to be in the world.**

   For example, maybe you like to *educate, inspire, sell,* or *run.*

3. **Add your picture of what a perfect world would look like.**

   This picture can be derived from your vision statement, which I explain in the next section. Examples can be "I picture a world in which all people are able to use their talents in meaningful work" or "I hope for a world in which no one is hungry" or "A place where everyone has enough money."

4. **Combine these three elements.**

   You have your mission statement.

You must have a strong sense of being before you can embark on your personal brand; otherwise, you may try to sound like someone else. Lewis Carroll wrote, "If you don't know where you are going, any road will get you there." You don't want that to be you. With the help of this book, you will find your road and your mission.

Outlining your vision: Taking your mission out into the world

As you establish your mission, you want to consider how your mission will look after you have done it in the world. Having a vision means imagining your ideal version of how you will use your mission. It is an external process and describes what you see as possible in the world.

A successful vision contains several elements:

- It's written down and is in the present tense as if you've already accomplished it.
- It contains strong descriptors to create a vivid picture, making it feel possible to achieve.
- Your vision is often bigger than what you individually can accomplish but includes the role you will take to contribute to the vision. An example of a large vision is to *live in a world where everyone has enough food.* Chances are, you can't accomplish that goal on your own, but you can volunteer at the local food bank and give money to a world hunger organization.
- It is clear and powerful, and it engages you to want to accomplish your vision. A well-written vision statement helps you consciously create and move from what currently is to what could be.

Here are some questions to ask yourself to outline your vision:

- When you think of the best version of yourself, what are you doing for work?

- What would you do if you weren't afraid to fail?
- What would your ideal picture of yourself be doing if you could do exactly what you wanted to?

Consider a specific mission statement and see how it would expand into a vision:

- **Mission:** "To bring order from chaos."
- **Vision:** "I work for a biotech company that takes me no more than 30 minutes to get to each day. I manage a department overseeing a cancer drug where we provide the highest level of quality control for the products that we produce. I know that I am contributing to a vital medicine that heals cancer patients and gives people more time on earth with their friends and family. I spend my weekends organizing food at the local food bank. I use my gifts of organizing to serve others."

I find one of the most powerful reasons to create a vision statement is that it takes you from focusing on your daily tasks and elevates you to a larger place in the world. It provides consideration that your work is in service to a larger purpose and carries you through times of uncertainty. Just think if everyone wanted to be part of something bigger than themselves — perhaps world hunger would end or everyone would at least see that they're all connected in the larger world.

Realizing What You're Naturally Good At: Your Strengths and Uniqueness

The earlier sections in this chapter look at the things that are important to you. This section shifts your focus to the things that you are naturally good at. I want to start by defining a few terms:

- **Talent:** When you have a talent, you're able to do something without even thinking about it. Talents are innate and non-teachable.
- **Knowledge and skills:** These are things you can learn. *Knowledge* can be facts that you learn or an understanding that you gain about how something works. *Skills* are the how-to's of a job and often involve the steps of an activity.
- **Strength:** When you combine your innate talent with your added knowledge and the skills that you've developed, you have a *strength.* Strengths are patterns of interests and abilities that consistently produce a positive outcome in a specific task.

In this section, you get a chance to consider your strengths, as well as your weaknesses, and to think about what makes you stand out from the crowd.

Studying your strengths

Whenever someone is gathering the building blocks of his personal brand, strengths are always a major component. The strengths movement is a trend focusing on a person's strengths instead of her weaknesses, and it is based on positive psychology, a psychology of positive human functioning instead of the study of what is wrong with a person. If you aren't certain how to identify your strengths, you can tap in to the results of a decades-long research project conducted by the Gallup Organization. The study focused on functions that people perform, and Gallup developed a list of 34 strengths based on that research.

Following is a summary of the 34 strengths, which Gallup refers to as *StrengthsFinder qualities.* I encourage you to review this list and note which ones sound like you:

- **Achiever:** You have a constant need for achievement and are known for your stamina and ability to work hard.
- **Activator:** You make things happen by turning thoughts into action.
- **Adaptability:** You discover your future one choice at a time. You are a flexible person who can stay productive when the demands of work are pulling you in different directions at once.
- **Analytical:** You see yourself as objective and dispassionate. You like data because it is value free. Others see you as logical and rigorous.
- **Arranger:** You enjoy managing all the variables, realigning them until you have found the most productive configuration possible. You are a great example of effective flexibility.
- **Belief:** You have certain core values that are unchanging. From these values, you form a defined purpose in your life.
- **Command:** You take charge. You can easily express your opinion with others. You have presence. You have command of a situation and enjoy aligning others with your goals.
- **Communication:** You like to explain, describe, speak in public, and write. You feel a need to bring your ideas to life and communicate them.
- **Competition:** You measure your achievements by finding a high-achieving person to compare yourself with. Competition invigorates you.
- **Connectedness:** You believe that things happen for a reason. You know that everyone is connected and part of something larger. You are aware that there is purpose beyond your everyday life.
- **Consistency:** Balance is important to you. You are keenly aware of the need to treat people the same, no matter what their station in life. You value fairness for all people.
- **Context:** You look back because that is where the answers lie. You look back to understand the present.

- **Deliberative:** You are careful, vigilant, and private. You identify, assess, and reduce risks. You have naturally good judgment and can provide advice and counsel.
- **Developer:** You see the potential in others and view individuals as a work in progress, alive with possibilities. Your goal is to help others experience success.
- **Discipline:** Your world needs to be predictable, and you like it ordered and planned. You set up routines and add structure to your world. You like to control the messiness of the world.
- **Empathy:** You can sense the emotions of those around you and can understand their perspective even if you don't agree. Your instinctive ability to understand is powerful.
- **Focus:** You need a clear destination. You like to set goals and work toward them.
- **Futuristic:** You love to peer over the horizon. You are a dreamer who sees visions of what could be.
- **Harmony:** You look for areas of agreement and look for the common ground when views differ. You steer away from confrontation and move others toward harmony.
- **Ideation:** You are fascinated by ideas and are able to make connections between seemingly disparate phenomena.
- **Includer:** You want to include people and make them feel part of the group. You are an instinctively accepting person and hate the sight of someone feeling like an outsider in the group.
- **Individualization:** You are intrigued by the unique qualities of each person. You focus on the differences between individuals. You find the right person to play the best part.
- **Input:** You are inquisitive and love to collect information. You find many things interesting and enjoy acquiring knowledge that you may use someday. You love keeping your mind fresh with new information.
- **Intellection:** You like mental activity and enjoy exercising the muscles in your brain. You are introspective and enjoy time alone to think. Your mental hum is a constant in your life.
- **Learner:** You are energized by the journey from ignorance to competence. You thrill at the growing confidence of a skill mastered.
- **Maximizer:** You focus on strengths as a way to stimulate personal and group excellence. You seek to transform something strong into something superb.
- **Positivity:** You always look for the positive in the situation. Your enthusiasm is contagious. You are able to keep your sense of humor. You are best when you can highlight the positive.

- **Relator:** You enjoy close relationships with others. You find satisfaction in working together to achieve a goal.
- **Responsibility:** You take psychological ownership for anything you commit to and feel emotionally bound to follow it through to completion. Your reputation is that you are utterly dependable.
- **Restorative:** You love to solve problems and enjoy the challenge of analyzing the symptoms, identifying what is wrong, and finding the solution. You love to save things and give them new life.
- **Self-assurance:** You are confident in your ability to manage your life. You know that you make the right decisions and set ambitious goals.
- **Significance:** You want to be recognized and stand out. Your performance needs to be visible, and you need to be appreciated for your unique strengths.
- **Strategic:** You can sort through the clutter and find the best route. You have distinct way of thinking and seeing patterns where others see complexity. You are talented in creating alternative ways to proceed.
- **Woo:** This stands for *winning others over.* You enjoy the challenge of meeting new people and getting them to like you. You enjoy meeting strangers and can easily carry on conversations.

I include this list to whet your whistle, but I encourage you to delve deeper into assessing your strengths. You may want to purchase the book *StrengthsFinder 2.0* by Tom Rath (Gallup Press) and use the code in the back of the book to take an online assessment. The StrengthsFinder website at `www.strengthsfinder.com` will give you more information. Another alternative to StrengthsFinder is through the `www.authentichappiness.sas.upenn.edu` website, which offers a free version of the strengths assessment.

REMEMBER

The strengths movement is gaining momentum in the workplace, and companies are starting to realize that people work better when highlighting their strengths. For a long time, businesses focused on trying to help employees improve their weaknesses, and that practice still exists. However, improving weaknesses shouldn't be your focus, and companies are starting to get that message.

Remembering your weaknesses

Weaknesses define you almost as much as your strengths do. I like to look at weaknesses as guideposts for what you shouldn't spend your day doing. Weaknesses are often the opposite of your strengths, but they can also be your strengths on steroids.

A *weakness* is a pattern of disinterest, avoidance, or just plain failure at performing a task that hinders your success. For example, you may really enjoy doing something but have a serious lack of talent at it, which you may consider a weakness. (Anyone who watches the auditions for *American Idol* knows what I'm talking about.)

Other weaknesses don't involve talent (or the lack of it). To observe your weaknesses, you might first look to your top five strengths and ask, "What is the opposite of this strength?" or "What would happen if this characteristic went overboard?" To consider an example, think about the strength Connectedness, which is used by someone who feels that everyone is all connected and part of something larger. A weakness version of that strength may be someone who can't mind his own business.

Give it a try: Take one of your strengths and consider what would happen if that strength were overused. This is a good first step to understanding your weaknesses.

Analyzing your strengths and weaknesses (SWOT)

It is common practice in a business setting to look at strengths and weaknesses through the lens of a SWOT analysis. This analysis examines your **S**trengths, **W**eaknesses, **O**pportunities, and **T**hreats. Here are the questions you're asked to answer:

- **Strengths:** What do you do well? What do others see as your strengths? What unique resources do you have to use?
- **Weaknesses:** What can you improve? What holds you back? What do others see as your weaknesses?
- **Opportunities:** What opportunities are available to you? What trends can you take advantage of? Can you turn your strengths into an opportunity?
- **Threats:** What is your competition doing? What can get in your way? What threats do your weaknesses expose you to?

Spotting your freak factor: What makes you unique

Your *freak factor* is a quality that you've probably worked hard in your life to hide in hopes that no one will find out about it. It's a unique quality that makes you different and unusual, at least to the people you knew early in your life. This unusual characteristic feels so individual to you that it may have actually been a source of pain when you were growing up.

Lady Gaga spoke about her freak factor in high school during her interview with Barbara Walters. She felt alienated and odd in high school and has now added this to her mission as an artist. She said, "I want to liberate them (her fans) from their fears and help them create their own space in the world."

It's a thrilling moment when you meet another freak and realize that the unique quality that previously caused you stress is shared with someone else. At that moment, you've found your tribe; you're accepted for your uniqueness. You may still look like a freak to the general population but not to the right group. Being a freak doesn't mean that you have a characteristic that is obvious to the outside world; instead, you have a characteristic that makes you feel different on the inside. Perhaps you are an exceptionally bright and beautiful blonde woman living in an environment where beauty (especially the blonde kind) is assumed to mean lack of brains. If you're actually smarter than everyone else in that environment, you're going to feel out of place.

Finding the right group to share your uniqueness with is important. To the wrong group, you may seem strange. But the right group will accept you for the brilliance of the gift that you bring (fulfilling your need for belonging/love that I discuss in the section "Knowing your needs," earlier in the chapter). Everyone fits somewhere, and you need to ask yourself whether you're willing to risk exposing your unique self in order to embrace who you really are. Revealing your unique self takes a lot of courage, especially if you feel your qualities may alienate people you care about.

Beautiful blonde freak

Consider the beautiful, brilliant blonde. Even though she took honors classes in high school, she still didn't feel like she fit in. Say that she follows her true path and enters a graduate program in her chosen area of study. By doing so, she may finally find a place where she feels like she fits in and doesn't feel like a freak. She can finally flaunt her intelligence and fit in because of it.

In his book *The Freak Factor* (CreateSpace), David J. Rendall describes how people have taken their weaknesses and created a unique life for themselves by embracing their differences. He talks about the reasons you should be proud to be different. A key reason to flaunt your differences is this: When you're different, you stand out. You are unique, original, remarkable, and influential to others. Being "normal" means that you may be ordinary, forgettable, predictable, and invisible. Dave encourages people to welcome their differences and be proud of them.

It's tough to get over that feeling of being in junior high school, where you would rather die than stand out as different. Many people never get over the shame of feeling different. But personal branding is about owning your freak factor, loving your uniqueness, and knowing that who you are is the most powerful differentiator of all as you build your brand.

Figuring Out What Else You Bring to the Table

Your strengths and freak factor (if you have one) aren't the only things you bring to bear when trying to set yourself apart from the crowd. In this section, I focus on examining your personality, education, work experience, and other components that come into play when building your brand.

Letting your personality shine

What do people think of when they think of you? Are you funny, serious, approachable? Your *personality* is the face that you show to the world. The descriptions that others give of you are most likely your personality traits.

The following list offers some descriptors of your personality characteristics. Think about (and perhaps circle or write down) which traits apply to you.

accessible	accurate	active
adaptable	adventurous	aggressive
aloof	ambitious	argumentative
assertive	authentic	beautiful
big personality	bold	bright
calm	carefree	caring
charming	cheerful	collaborative
colorful	committed	community-oriented
competitive	confident	connected
conservative	convincing	cool
cooperative	creative	dependable
devoted	diplomatic	direct
dramatic	driven	dynamic
easygoing	efficient	empathetic
energetic	enthusiastic	ethical
experienced	extroverted	flexible
friendly	fun	generous
genuine	healthy	helpful
honest	humorous	imaginative
impatient	independent	inspiring
innovative	intelligent	international
introverted	intuitive	kind
leader	likeable	loving

loyal	materialistic	methodical
moody	motivated	objective
open-minded	optimistic	orderly
organized	original	passionate
persuasive	philanthropic	precise
procrastinating	productive	professional
quick learner	quirky	refined
resilient	resourceful	responsible
restless	results-oriented	risk-taking
sensitive	shy	sincere
sophisticated	spiritual	stubborn
successful	supportive	talkative
temperamental	tolerant	team-oriented
thorough	trend-setting	trusting
visionary	wise	witty
youthful		

Why does personality matter so much in the workplace? William Arruda, President of Reach Personal Branding, says: "People want to work with people who are interesting. They likely won't choose you if you don't meet the minimum requirements, but when deciding among many people who meet the basic requirements, they are going to choose someone who they find engaging."

You can break down personality attributes into two broad categories:

- **Rational:** They describe a solid quality that people trust in you. Perhaps you are organized or accurate. When someone depends on you (whether at work or at home), you need to bring these rational attributes to the table.
- **Emotional:** These attributes are the reasons people want to be around you — for example, you're humorous or empathetic.

Arruda describes the difference between rational and emotional brand attributes this way: Rational brand attributes are the table stakes that get you into the game. Without them, you won't even be considered. The challenge is that usually many people meet these minimum requirements. It's a competitive world, and whether you're seeking to get a job, a promotion, or a new client, relying on your rational brand attributes would be a failed strategy. Emotional brand attributes, Arruda says, are those traits that get people excited about you. They are your personality characteristics and life experiences. You layer them on top of the rational brand attributes and use them to make emotional connections with those who are making decisions about you. Together, your emotional and rational brand attributes speak to your unique promise of value.

Highlighting your educational accomplishments

Does your education enhance or hinder your brand? As you look to develop your brand, you need to consider how your level of education and place of education impact your personal and professional reputation. Does your education history say that you complete what you start or that you lack focus? Does the college you attended have a strong academic reputation, or is it known as a party school?

As you gather the pieces to build your brand, your education is something that you can highlight or minimize. Do you look current with your professional development? Or have you not set foot in a college classroom for 20 years?

If you are positioning yourself as a person of credibility, you need to look current. On-the-job experience is the best way to demonstrate how you are using — and building on — your expertise, but taking courses, gaining certifications, or adding a credential to your portfolio can enhance your brand and help you establish yourself as an expert.

REMEMBER

In personal branding, you want to stand out from the crowd. Adding formal or informal educational programs can help you do that. Many high-profile universities offer certificate programs that are shorter than academic degrees and let you still claim a degree from a prestigious university. For many professions, certain certificates or credentials are the door openers to new opportunities. For example, an accountant gains a certain credibility when she obtains her Certified Public Accountant (CPA) status, and she distinguishes herself even further if she goes on to become a Certified Fraud Examiner or a Certified Management Accountant (or any other type of accounting specialist).

As you begin to formulate your brand, it is helpful to see what kind of educational and training background people you admire have. I always do a little sleuthing to see what I can learn through a Google search or by studying the profiles of people in LinkedIn. Ask yourself this: "What training or education do they have that I don't?" Also ask, "What education do I have that they don't?" and "What do I have that I haven't been using?"

What can you highlight from your education to build your brand? Here are some ideas:

- **Academic education**
  - Did you receive a degree?
  - What were your core classes? Special interest classes?
  - Did you do a senior project or highlighted project?
  - Will any of your professors act as a reference for you?

- **Credentials and certifications**
  - Have you earned any certifications?
  - Did you receive a credential in a specialty area?
  - Are your certifications or credentials state or nationally recognized?
  - Do you have initials you can use to highlight your accomplishment?
- **Professional development**
  - What specialty courses did you take?
  - Is the venue where you took the course an important asset?
  - Did you learn new skills that you can add to your area of expertise?
  - Are you current in your professional development?
  - Did you take a class that is not directly related to your profession but shows that you are an interesting person?

Your education not only gives you the substance to show that you know what you are doing, but also it can provide a foundation of people who support your brand. If you went to the No. 1 party school and feel as if your academic achievements are not viewed as valuable, take from that experience what you can and emphasize the positive. On the plus side, if your school was a big party school, you probably made a lot of friends and are a well-trained socializer-networker. Look for the most positive attributes and use them to build your brand.

Placing a value on your work experience

Nothing takes the place of actual work experience: getting in and doing the work to learn about an industry or functional role that you play. Personal branding actually started in the workplace because people realized that although they often did a good job, they were not always visible in their accomplishments.

For the purposes of your personal brand, here are some key factors that you can use to highlight your brand from the workplace or your community work:

- Where did you work? Is the company that you worked for one that offers prestige or reputation that supports your credibility?
- What titles did you hold? Are they impressive, inconsequential, or a good description of what you know how to do?
- Did you work with interesting clients or companies that have a strong reputation?

- What were your key work projects? (In the next section, I show you how to turn them into accomplishment statements.)
- Have you volunteered with the community in a leadership capacity that highlights skills you haven't yet used in the workplace?

Using your work experience is one more component to solidify your credibility. If you are not encountering the kind of experience that you feel you need in the workplace to build the brand you are looking to build, consider volunteering with a community nonprofit. Nonprofits are often much more willing to let you try something new to help you become who you want to be.

Realizing what makes you proud

When you were a kid, you were probably taught not to brag. So thinking about, writing down, and (gasp!) saying out loud what you're proud of can be very hard. But realizing what makes you proud is an important step in the branding process because it gives you the stories you use when promoting your personal brand. (I devote Chapter 8 to learning how to write your own story.)

One of the hardest things I have found for people to do is to remember and write their accomplishments. The best way to do so is by developing *accomplishment statements* — powerful tools that show what you know, how you problem-solve, and that you can produce results. These statements are written as specific examples of action you took and the results that you produced, as well as how someone benefited because of your actions. These statements form the foundation for your stories.

I like to use the PAR/CAR (**P**roblem-**A**ction-**R**esult and **C**hallenge-**A**ction-**R**esult) formula for writing accomplishment statements:

1. **Begin with a problem that you had to solve or a challenge that you overcame.**

   For example, "*Sales were declining, and the company was losing market share. As the Sales Director I needed to solve this.*"

2. **Use action words — verbs written in past tense — that describe as vividly as possible the action you took.**

   "I contacted all current clients and did a market analysis of the products. I reevaluated the competition and repositioned the product with a new marketing strategy."

3. **If you can, add a quantitative or qualitative result based on your activities, even if it is only estimated.**

   "Sales increased by 14 percent, and the company gained a 5 percent market share. Customers were excited to work with the company again. The sales team all received increased sales bonuses."

TIP

To enhance your accomplishment statement, include facts, figures, money volumes, percentages of increase or decrease, numbers of people involved, or geographical scope to make the result clear and shows the positive impact of your action.

As you try your hand at writing your own accomplishment statements, also consider these questions:

- What were some personal qualities that best described you in solving these problems?
- What are some of your favorite words or key phrases that appear in the statements?

ANECDOTE

I met a woman on a walk through my neighborhood. She was an older woman trying to get some exercise after a hip replacement surgery. She was walking with crutches and moving slowly. I commented on how we had to walk on the street now that they were paving the regional trail that I usually walk on, and she said, "I am the one who pioneered that project and made the trail happen 40 years ago." We talked some more, and I realized that although I will not remember her name, her signature accomplishment has become a lifelong personal brand for her: To me, she is the Trail Lady.

Do you have a signature accomplishment that defines your brand? If you are known for something specific, the personal branding process can capitalize on it. (Conversely, if you are known for something negative, you can use the branding process to try to minimize it.)

Gaining a 360° View of Yourself

Any time you seriously want to do some branding work, you need to know the opinions of others. Most people would prefer *not* to know what others really think about them, but in order to build a real brand, you need to collect data from a broader base than just your own personal opinion about yourself. After all, sometimes others perceive you differently than you perceive yourself.

Businesses often use what is called a *360° assessment.* The idea is that you gather information from all facets of your workplace, such as your boss, coworkers, subordinates, and administrative staff. These 360° assessments are used to gather information about your performance and behavior at work.

- Personality descriptors or personal attributes
- Your skills and abilities
- Your strengths and weaknesses
- General comments

In this section, I show you how to use online tools — in particular, the 360Reach — to accomplish a 360° assessment.

The 360Reach assessment

Most of the 360° assessments that I've seen obtain feedback about your performance at work or look at your leadership capabilities. While those things are important at work, for the purposes of personal branding, you need to ask different questions. An assessment that I like to use in the personal branding process is the 360Reach that was designed by Reach Personal Branding. It is the leading personal branding assessment that helps you understand your brand from the outside in. The 360Reach provides insights that you might otherwise not be able to gain about yourself.

One of the reasons that I like the 360Reach is because it answers the question "Who are you?" It looks at your character and pulls out information that is at the heart of your brand. It gives you an opportunity to understand how you are perceived by those around you. It helps you understand your reputation and take action that will help you reach your goals.

360Reach is being used as a development tool in 20 percent of the Fortune 100 companies and has been used by nearly 1 million people. There is a free version that you can take to gather your raw data, but the full version provides a great, very user-frendly report. You can find out more at `www.reachcc.com/360v5register`. You can buy a full report for about $50.

In addition to gathering data about personal attributes, skills, strengths, and weaknesses, the 360Reach contains two *projective exercises:* questions that seem unrelated but actually gather great insight. There are four questions, from which you choose two to answer:

- What kind of car would *(your name)* be?
- What kind of household appliance would *(your name)* be?
- What kind of dog would *(your name)* be?
- What kind of cereal would *(your name)* be?

I find it amazing how creative people can be when answering these questions. This is often the place where the best data comes from. For example, if *blender* comes up in the feedback over and over again with various comments about being able to mix it up, this person might consider building her brand on her ability to network and bring people together.

Conducting a self-analysis

To get a complete picture in a 360° assessment, whether you're using 360Reach or another online tool, your opinion of yourself needs to be one of the points of input. You would think this step might be the easy part, but I have often found that people are especially hard on themselves. The goal here is for you to look at yourself objectively and give a good evaluation of your strengths, weaknesses, and attributes, as well as figuring out just what kind of household appliance you would be! (If you find that all you can come up with is a floor mop, you know that you need to first work on your self-esteem before you go any farther.)

Try to have fun with your self-analysis; enter into this process with an open attitude and a clear idea of who you think you are.

Asking for insights from friends and family

Whenever you ask for other people's opinions, they will want to know that their comments are anonymous. Any 360° assessment tool that you use should have this feature. The 360Reach, for example, is completely anonymous.

TIP

The way an online assessment tool works is that you supply names and e-mail addresses, and the company running the assessment reaches out to those people on your behalf. To gain the best results, it is important that you choose people who know you well enough to answer questions about your top strengths or attributes. Ideally, you need to get 15 to 30 responses, so you need to request feedback from around twice that number of people. (Response rates normally run at between 40 and 50 percent on these types of assessments.)

You will get better results if you also send your own e-mail alerting your contacts that this assessment will be coming, that their responses will be anonymous, that it is something that you really would like them to do, and that you appreciate their honest feedback for your professional development.

You will get responses in both the free and paid version. The paid version neatly organizes the comments and allows you to make more sense of the data. For those of you not interested in doing a 360° assessment, you can always just poll your contacts with questions that you would like to know the answers to about yourself and what they think of you. It is not anonymous, but you may still get good feedback.

Getting feedback on the job

When you received grades at school, the experience may have been positive or negative. Grades can be an objective evaluation of your work, or they can feel subjective and personal.

The workforce offers its own version of being graded through your annual review. This review can be a scary process because if you get bad grades here, you may lose your job and your income.

My point is that being evaluated is likely an experience you don't really look forward to. Take a 360° assessment can bring up those feelings of being judged. I suggest that you enter into this process with the spirit of professional development and know that this process is one that you control. The feedback you request is the same as for any other group in that you submit workplace colleagues' e-mail addresses to the online assessment. The feedback is for your use only and allows you to choose how you will apply it.

Reacting when people see you differently than you see yourself

I think one of the biggest surprises in receiving the results of a 360-degree assessment occurs when what you think of yourself looks different than what others think of you. The 360Reach has a comparison column stating the top attributes that you see for yourself next to the top attributes that others see in you. If you see yourself differently than they see you, you can ask one of two questions:

- Do I want to be seen more as I see myself?
- Do I want to be seen as they see me?

When a gap exists between your own and others' view of you, chances are that you think less of yourself than others think of you. To close the gap, you must devise a plan so you can start thinking more highly of yourself. Setting some goals is a logical step, which I cover in the next section.

Bridging Who You Are and What You Want

Moving to the goal-setting stage means taking the ideas in your head and the values in your heart (an inner process) to the action stage (an outer process). Setting goals sets forth a plan to make personal branding real and outlines the changes you need to make to put your plan into action. In this section, I show you how to set goals and how (and why) to invest in yourself.

Setting goals to enhance your brand

Certified Personal Brand Strategist and Career Coach Randi Bussin outlines a goal-setting strategy and how you can best use it in developing your personal brand. Following are Randi's own words to describe this process:

In Randi's opinion, goal setting is a crucial exercise for career reinvention, job search, and personal branding coaching for the following reasons:

- Goal setting helps you get clear on what you want.
- Goal setting helps you identify what distractions may be blocking your success.
- Goal setting, including writing your goals, helps program your subconscious mind and activate mental powers that will enable you to accomplish these goals.
- Goal setting helps motivate you, especially when you get overwhelmed in the fast-paced society in which we live.
- Goal setting leads to success, increased income, and greater career/life happiness.

Brian Tracy, in his book *Goals! How to Get Everything You Want — Faster Than You Ever Thought Possible* (Berrett-Koehler Publishers), states that "only 3 percent of adults have goals, and everyone else works for them." You've probably read about the Harvard study that Randy discusses next, but it's worth reviewing again as you dedicate some significant time and energy to your decision to get serious about designing the life you want to lead.

Mark H. McCormack, in his book *What They Don't Teach You at Harvard Business School* (Bantam), tells of a Harvard study conducted between 1979 and 1989. In 1979, graduates of the MBA program were asked to set clear, written goals for their future and their plans to accomplish them. It turned out only 3 percent of the graduates had written goals, 13 percent had goals but they were not in writing, and 84 percent had no specific goals at all.

Ten years later, in 1989, the researchers again interviewed the members of that same graduating class. They found that the 13 percent who had goals that were not in writing were earning, on average, twice as much as the 84 percent of students who had no goals at all. Most surprisingly, they found that the 3 percent of graduates who had clear, written goals were earning, on average, 10 times more than 97 percent of their graduating class. The only difference between the groups was the clarity of goals they had set (and spelled out) for themselves when they graduated.

Randi has identified ten steps to help you get through the goal-setting process:

1. **Create a big picture of what you want to accomplish in your life.**

   Take a piece of paper and write down everything you want to accomplish in the next ten years. Or, use whatever format works for you — Microsoft Word or Excel, for example. The format doesn't matter; just get your ideas written. Be sure to include goals for all major areas of your life:

   - Career
   - Education/professional development
   - Volunteer/community service
   - Family
   - Health and physical condition
   - Financial
   - Hobbies and pleasure

   As you make a list of your goals, be sure they are what you want to achieve, and not something desired by others, such as your parents, your significant other, or your employer.

2. **Prioritize the goals by time frame.**

   Go back to the list you just created and break the long list of goals into three smaller time frames. When you prioritize your goals by time frame, it prevents you from feeling overwhelmed by having too many goals. It also helps you focus on the ones that are the most important and those you must hit in order to reach your longer-term, lifetime goals. Three categories of goals Randi suggests that clients aim for are

   - Next 12 months (short term)
   - Two to five years (medium term)
   - Six to ten years (longer term)

   The remainder of this section focuses on your goals for the next 12 months. Longer term goals will be revised each year moving forward and are less crucial to the discussion at hand.

3. **Rewrite your short-term goals in SMART goal format and also be sure the goal is written as a positive statement.**

   SMART goals are

   - **Specific:** This means stating what you are trying to accomplish and why. You are typically trying to answer the "who, what, when, where, and why" questions. The "why" question is very important. You need to understand **why** you want this goal and how the goal aligns with your values.

Example: A general goal would be "Get in shape." A specific goal would be "Join a health club and work out three days a week so I feel more energized during the day."

- **Measurable:** This establishes how you are going to measure progress toward the attainment of the goal you have set. To determine whether your goal is measurable, ask yourself these questions:
  - How much?
  - How many?
  - How will I know if I have achieved this goal?
- **Attainable:** When you list goals that are important to you, you begin to find ways to make them come true. You develop the attitudes, skills, and abilities to reach them. Make sure that the goals you set are attainable. If it is too far of a reach, you probably won't commit to doing it and will get frustrated. You want the goal to stretch you a bit so you will feel motivated to attain it. For example, a goal to lose 30 pounds in 1 week isn't achievable. But if you set a goal to lose 1 or 2 pounds a week, that is more realistic. The success of reaching your goal helps you remain motivated and set a higher goal next time.
- **Relevant or Realistic:** A *realistic goal* is an objective that you are both motivated to achieve and realistically able to do so. Remember to set your goal high enough to stretch yourself. If you find you have achieved your goals too easily, set the bar higher next time. If the goal took a dispiriting time to accomplish, make the next round of goals a little bit easier.
- **Timely or Time Bound:** A goal should have a time frame associated with it; by anchoring your goal with a time frame, you set your subconscious mind into motion to begin working on it. With no time frame, there is no sense of urgency to reaching the goal.

4. **Type your goals, put them in several places where you can see them, review them daily, and revise them as needed.**

   This action of putting your goals in a visible place sets the intention to the greater universe and becomes a daily reminder of what it is you are trying to accomplish. Spend a minute every day in front of your list of goals and read them to yourself. Review your goals regularly and revise them if you reach them too easily, or if they are too difficult. Also, if you notice a deficit in your skills despite achieving a goal, then think about what you would like to do to fix this.

5. **Identify the obstacles that you will have to overcome to achieve your goals.**

   What is going to get in the way of you achieving your goals? Brian Tracy states that there is usually one limiting factor that gets in the way of reaching your goals, and that this one factor is usually internally focused. What is that limiting factor for you? What within yourself is holding you back?

6. **Identify the knowledge, skills, and competencies you need to achieve your goals.**

   Which skills do you need to be at the top of your game? What one skill, if you developed it, would have the greatest impact on your life or career? What one skill, if you developed it and did it consistently, would help you achieve your most important goal? Identify it and begin to work on it every single day.

7. **Identify the support team you need in place to achieve your goals.**

   To achieve big goals, you will need the help and support of many people. Who is your support team or board of advisers? Identify the list of family members, work colleagues, and mentors you need in your life. Your list also may include your coach, an industry consultant, and individuals who belong to a professional association. As you think about your support team, think about ways in which you can be a giver and not necessarily a taker.

8. **Celebrate successes.**

   When you achieve a goal, take time to enjoy the satisfaction of having reached the milestone. Treat yourself to something to mark the accomplishment. You do not have to spend a lot of money; it can be a simple gift such as a book, a dinner out, or something more extravagant such as a massage. Just take the time to relish in your success, which will help boost your confidence.

9. **Organize your 12-month goals into smaller more manageable steps, from the beginning to the completion of the goal.**

   Planning is very important to reaching your goals. The 80/20 rule states that 80 percent of your results will come from 20 percent of your efforts. So how will you spend your time? The more detailed you can be in outlining your activities, the more you will accomplish in less time. Plan the next 12 months, month by month. For each month, list two or three activities that you must accomplish that would have the most profound impact on the bigger picture. Ask yourself the following question: If I could only do one thing in the month of January, what one activity would add the most value to my goals?

10. **Take action every day.**

    Randi always tells his clients that lots of baby steps add up to big goals. If you're having a very busy week at work, don't beat yourself up. Just do one thing, one little thing each day that will keep the momentum going and keep you moving forward.

Investing in yourself

So what are you going to do with all of the self-awareness you are gaining? For now, you are going to collect each insight you've gained in this chapter. You will record them in your personal brand profile, which I explain in Chapter 7, to build the information you need to write your personal brand statement.

Your brand is built upon *all* your factors — even the ones that you feel everyone else shares. The gift is in the layering. Imagine yourself as a wheel, and each quality (your needs, values, interests, strengths, personality, freak factor, education, work experience, and so on) is a spoke. You look for the point where they all meet, and you build your brand on that unique point of intersection.

Through this process of self-assessment, you may be realizing that some areas require your attention. Maybe you now understand that you need further training, which requires you to go back to school. Or maybe you are discovering a strength that you haven't yet tapped in your work life. Now is the time to invest in yourself.

Beginning the personal branding process makes you take a hard look at yourself so that you can realistically and aspirationally build your brand. In order to do that, you need to be a lifelong learner and continue to invest in yourself. Don't skimp on the investment; give yourself the time and tools you need to get where you want to go. Doing so will undoubtedly pay dividends in the long run.

Chapter 5

Spotting Your Target Audience

In This Chapter

- Identifying who qualifies as your target market
- Finding out as much as possible about your targets
- Lining yourself up with your target audience
- Writing a positioning statement

Your target audience is the people you want to know about you, such as potential employers, community groups, or your current boss. You market your personal brand to these people so that your brand has a specific direction. After all, not everyone is interested in you!

In this chapter, I show you how to aim for your target audience. That process begins with figuring out who, exactly, they are.

Recognizing Who You're Trying to Reach

Before you can communicate your brand to the right people, you must identify who needs to know about you and what you have to offer. They are the people and companies that are just waiting to experience and appreciate your brand.

One of the biggest mistakes that budding personal branders make is trying to appeal to everyone. Think about the game of darts: You have to aim in order to hit the board. (If you let your darts go without aiming them, you probably won't be very popular.) If you hit the board, you score. And if your aim is very good and you hit the bull's eye, even better!

In Chapter 4, I help you define yourself with the aim of getting closer to defining your product, which is your brand. With that budding definition in mind (which you'll refine when you work through Chapter 7), I want you now to ask yourself these key questions:

- Who will buy this product?
- Where do I want to sell this product?

My clients often shy away when I ask these questions, but the truth is that someone will be buying, and you are selling your personal brand.

REMEMBER

Creating a personal brand is a self-driven process. If you don't like your product or don't know what you have to offer, you need to do more work before you can get dig deeper into knowing who you are trying to reach.

Imagining your ideal client or workplace

If you could wave a magic wand, what would be your ideal scenario? Can you imagine the kind of client you'd like to have or the type of workplace you'd like to go to each day? For example, you may want to develop your brand as a philanthropist, so you'll want to look at what causes or nonprofit agencies align with who you are.

You can follow many practical steps to spot your target audience, but open your imagination and try to visualize yourself working with your ideal client, company, service, or scenario. For example, I thought about the characteristics of my ideal client, and here's what I came up with:

- Appreciates the work that I do
- Pays me well and pays in advance
- Loves the service that I provide
- Trusts my expertise and lets me use my best judgment
- Refers other dream clients to me
- Promotes my work to everyone he talks to

Wouldn't this client be great? Dreaming about the perfect situation is a good beginning because it gets you thinking about who would actually be the right target audience for you to put your time, energy, and effort into pursuing. Your target market begins and ends with the customer in mind, whether that customer is an employer, a job, new friendships, teams, or companies. What do these customers need that they're not getting? What do you have that they may want?

Your target audience will vary depending on how you plan to use your personal brand. If you're using your personal brand for a job search, you'll be identifying potential employers. If you're an entrepreneur interested in using your personal brand to develop more business, you'll target your future customers. If you are happily employed and want to build a stronger brand within your company, you'll be looking at the people you work with as your target audience.

Personal branding is about expressing your authentic self and making you an active partner in creating the direction of your life. To find the right target, you need to review your needs, values, strengths, interests, mission, vision, and unique personality traits. If you haven't already done so, I encourage you to spend time with Chapter 4 before moving forward.

Focusing on potential employers

Identifying potential employers is a key step in the process of a job search. What would be your ideal place to work? If you're unemployed, it's easy to get caught in the desperation of "I just need a job!" But a job that's the wrong fit for you likely won't last long. The best-case scenario in finding your next employer is that on the first day of a new job, you walk in feeling happy to be there, and they are happy to have hired you. You have the skills and personality that they are looking for, and this new employer welcomes you with open arms.

Okay, so I'm an idealist! But I do believe that if you have a clear idea about what you want, you are much more likely to get it.

In this section, I show you how to look at this process as one of elimination. I identify the filters you need to apply to the mass of potential employers out there so you can get specific about your target.

When you feel you don't belong

Think about times when you have felt like you didn't belong. Consider the following scenarios:

- Think of a job where you felt like you could never relax and be yourself. How did you feel at the end of the day?
- Think about a time when you attended a party and couldn't figure out why you were invited because there was no one there you could relate to. Did you feel like grabbing the serving tray and pretending you were the caterer?
- Have you ever been on a team loaded with players who were a lot better than you? How did that make you feel?
- Did you ever go on a date and wonder why on earth a dating site (or a mutual friend) thought you were compatible with this person? Did you end the date early?
- What happens if you tell a joke and no one laughs? Do you want to crawl under the table?

These situations capture moments when you're not with the group you belong to; you aren't working within your target audience. They illustrate the stress and discomfort that can occur when you're aiming for the wrong target.

Geography

The first filter you apply is an obvious one: geography. Unless you're willing to move, you may need to focus solely on the employers in your area.

TIP

I say *may* because geography is becoming less of an issue for some people and some industries. If you do a type of work that could allow you to telecommute from your current home, the geography filter simply may not apply; your potential employer could be located a thousand miles away.

Your product

What you have to offer the potential employer is crucial. Obviously, what you are selling needs to be something that a company wants to buy, so you must identify employers that need the work you can do. If you have a skill like accounting, which most employers need, this filter may not weed out too many potential targets. But if your skill is quite specific — say, for example, that you design amusement park rides — you'll have much fewer employment options. (However, your skill may be so highly valued that you'll be sought after by those few targets.)

How do you find out which employers might need what you have to offer? I offer tips in the upcoming section "Researching Your Targets."

TIP

When you begin to develop a network of people who work at companies of interest to you, ask them not only about those companies but about competing companies as well.

Personality and values

The next potential employer filters are personality and values: Both of them must be a good fit. You are looking for an employer whose environment matches your personality and values. This filter may be a bit tough to apply because you don't always know what goes on within an organization until you're there. However, reading as much as you can about the potential employer and (if possible) talking to people who already work there can teach you a great deal about whether it's a good fit for you.

REMEMBER

Corporate culture is the atmosphere created through the shared values, traditions, customers, philosophy, and policies of an organization. Corporate culture is the personality of an organization and impacts the way a company does business and how it conducts itself. If corporate culture is the personality of the organization, you need to make certain that your personal brand fits in. Do the two personalities blend well, or are they like oil and water? If you are a free spirit, for example, working in a financial audit firm may not serve you (or the company) well.

Finding a match with the corporate culture begins with looking at the top values that you identify through your work in Chapter 4. Do they match the values of the company? Line them up side by side and see how the two sets of values compare.

For example, if you had a strong value for environmental issues but applied for a job at a company that had pollution violations, it would be a bad cultural fit. Think about your own values and look for the alignment with a potential employer.

Listed in Table 5-1 are some companies and what they stand for to the public. If you worked for one of these companies, would you agree with what they stand for?

Table 5-1 Companies That Stand for Something

Brand Name	***What the Company Stands For***
BMW	The ultimate driving machine
Apple	Innovation, cool
Facebook	Social, connected
Disney	Happiest place on earth, family fun
Maytag	Dependable, never needs repairs
Polo	Class and sophistication
Volkswagen	Fun, trendy, nostalgia
Starbucks	High-quality, individualized coffee drinks, with locations consistently everywhere

REMEMBER

After you're employed by a company, you can only be as individual in your personal brand as the company culture allows you to be. During your job search is the best time to consider personality and values — both your own and the company's.

Using the ACE Method

EXPERT OPINION

Susan Guarneri, the Assessment Goddess of the great north woods of Wisconsin, uses a specific methodology to guide her clients in finding their target audiences. She begins by asking them to do the type of self-assessment I help you do in Chapter 4. She then builds on that information using what she calls the *ACE Method.* The ACE method is a great tool for job searches and identifying potential employers. Here are the steps it entails:

- **Assess** all your career and personal assets:
  - Personal brand
  - Motivated skills (the skills you are good at *and* enjoy using)
  - Talents and aptitudes
  - Passions and interests
  - Personality type
  - Work and life values
  - Career and personal goals
  - Education and training
  - Licenses and certifications
  - Work/business experience
  - Industry knowledge
  - Career and business network (relationships)
- **Clarify** what's important:
  - Your top three motivated skills/leadership competencies
  - Your top three passions and interests
  - Your top three personal brand attributes
  - Your unique promise of value (see Chapter 7)
- **Evaluate** the best fit for what's important to you:
  - Your preferred career target (job function) or business target — your dream job or dream client
  - Your preferred work environment: which sectors, industries, companies? (The five sectors are corporate [for-profit], nonprofit, education, government, and self-employment.)
  - Your preferred projects or solutions to problems (results)

Guarneri notes that golden opportunities will come more easily if you are clear about what you want and able to articulate your value, if you determine what you want to offer and recognize which target audience is attracted to what you have to offer, and if you proactively pursue your target audience.

Targeting future customers

In the section "Imagining your ideal client or workplace," earlier in this chapter, I list the qualities that I would like in my ideal client, and I encourage you to do the same. To find your target audience, you then need to add some specific criteria so that you can begin your search for where you'd find these people. If your target audience is potential customers, you need to define them using characteristics such as lifestyle, occupation, geographic location, income, gender, life stage, beliefs, or ethnicity.

After you list the characteristics you're looking for, you need to research where you might find people who fit them. You gather as much data as you can to outline your ideal customer profile. (The upcoming section "Researching Your Targets" can help.)

For example, consider the case of an attorney who specializes in construction-defect cases. She needs to conduct research to find out the following information:

- Who has construction defects? The attorney needs to consider whether she wants to represent the people causing the defect, insuring the defects, or impacted by the defects.
- Are there enough potential clients in the area to keep her in business? If not, she may need to extend her geographic reach.
- Who can pay the bills? In other words, who can afford to hire a lawyer to address their needs?
- Where can she meet these people? She could trace who is involved with construction defects and strategize where she might meet these people by checking out construction business networking groups or meeting insurance claims representatives or attorneys at bar association meetings.

After asking these questions, the attorney may determine that she wants to work with insurance companies that represent construction defects in the state of Nevada for builders that build casinos. That's a pretty specific description of her ideal future customers!

REMEMBER

By carefully defining your target audience based on thorough research, you solidify your brand and differentiate yourself from others. In other words, you begin to figure out your niche — a topic I discuss in detail in Chapter 6.

Keeping your eyes on the company you work for

If you're not looking to change jobs, your target audience is already in front of you. Your job in this case is to get to know your current employer in as much detail as possible.

Each company has a brand reputation and personality. Sometimes that brand persona is strongly driven from inside the company with a mission statement that the employees believe in and carry forward into their work with clients.

That strong internal brand is reflected to the outside world. If you worked for this company, you would know what the company stands for and your role within it. A company like this is often most open to an employee expressing his personal brand because the company's message is well-defined.

Unfortunately, this ideal isn't always reality. More common is a disconnect between what a company says on its website and how company management acts behind closed doors. For example, a company may state that it's a family company, but the employees consider it a dysfunctional family. A company without a clear sense of its own brand message may not be too interested in employees who are developing their personal brands.

Be observant. Use political savvy and read your company's mission statement. Watch the key players and identify opportunities for you to become known for something that is part of the brand you'd like to convey.

What kind of employee does your company value? Ask yourself these observational questions about the company you work for:

- What have you been praised for during your performance reviews or during informal feedback from your boss?
- Who has valued your work most frequently?
- What tasks do you excel at doing?
- What conditions or work environments allow you to be your best?
- When have you been most effective or most efficient?

The answers give you clues as to where you will find the best conditions in which to build your brand at your company.

Researching Your Targets

When you've identified your target audience (see preceding section), you want to find out as much as possible about it. Information is power, and a well-researched target list will give you the confidence to move forward in reaching out to the people who need to know about you.

If you've identified your target audience, you should have an idea of the kinds of companies you're interested in and perhaps people you would like to meet. Where I see people get stuck is in how will they find these targets. Accomplishing that step is much easier with the Internet. However, because you have access to so much information, it can be overwhelming so it's best to start with a plan. I outline some basics here, but if you want more details on researching companies, you should consult a good career search book, such as *Get The Job You Want Even When No One's Hiring* by Ford R. Myers (John Wiley & Sons, Inc.).

Searching for information online

Your goal with an online search is to gather information that you can use not only to build a profile of your target audience wish list but also to help you learn how you will connect with them. You're not looking for job openings here; you're looking at criteria that match your target audience profile.

Start with a simple Google search where you put in the keywords that you've identified as important to you about your target audience. In addition, try these online searches:

- Conduct a `www.LinkedIn.com` search of people, companies, or answers in the query box of LinkedIn.
- A site with loads of resources is `www.job-hunt.org`.
- Fortune Magazine's list of 100 Great Places to Work in America is at `www.greatplacestowork.com`.
- Find your city's business journal site at `www.bizjournals.com`.
- Go to specific company websites to search for their annual reports, which can be chock full of great information.
- Subscription business databases like Hoover's and Dun & Bradstreet are often available at your local library or at a business college.
- A good business resource site is `www.vault.com`.

TIP: Building your target audience list is a research project; get organized about how you want to approach it. Make a list, develop a spreadsheet, set up files, and use whatever organizational system that you need to make the best use of the information you find. Some people find this step to be boring, but it's crucial to help you build a solid brand, not one just conceived in your head.

Going straight to the source (if possible)

One of the scariest suggestions I might make to you is to call someone and ask about a specific company. I am the first to admit that doing so could bring up all your fears of rejection and any insecurities you might have about talking to new people.

Always the best way to go straight to the source is through a personal introduction. Starting with your target wish list in hand, first ask friends, neighbors, and colleagues if they know anyone at XYZ company or — more specifically — your key contact at that company. You can do your asking online via LinkedIn, Facebook, Google+, or Twitter, as well as in personal conversations. (You can find out how to use your personal brand on social media in Chapter 11.)

If you find someone who has the information you need, ask whether she could introduce you to that contact. If that person is willing to do so, you greatly strengthen your odds of having a conversation with your target contact.

You may have luck locating your target audience through your local Book of Lists — an annual publication by `www.bizjournals.com` noting the top businesses in your geographic area. You can also attend professional meetings, community events, award banquets, and company open houses. The more visible you are at these type of events, the more you will look like you belong with this target audience.

Attending conferences and trade shows

One of my favorite ways to learn about a target audience is to attend a professional conference or trade show. Here you get to see how people within a profession act around each other. Vendors are always eager to talk to anyone who stops by their booth. Some of the best informal networking takes place at a conference because people aren't at work, are generally open to socializing, and have name badges to help with introductions.

Conferences and trade shows have the most cutting-edge information being presented by speakers and at the break-out sessions, as well as at exhibitor booths. Often, the best information you learn will be during a conversation around the breakfast table or while waiting in line. If you have the opportunity to attend one of these events as part of your research into target markets, grab a pocket full of business cards and take advantage of every opportunity to learn and meet members of your target audience.

Aligning Yourself with Your Target Market

After you define and research your target market, you want to make sure that your actions are in sync with your audience's needs. In other words, you want to stay authentic to the brand that brought you to this specific target in the first place. In this section, I offer suggestions for doing just that.

Catering to the psychographics and demographics of your market

As you research your target audience, you find information that fits into two broad categories:

- **Demographics** are the statistical characteristics of a population including gender, race, age, disabilities, mobility, home ownership, employment status, and even location.
- **Psychographics** look at consumer lifestyles to create a profile of likes, dislikes, activities, interests, and opinions.

Your target is a good fit when both demographics and psychographics match with your goals, and you never want to lose track of them.

Suppose that you're a dentist and want to open an office next to a retirement community. You find out that most of the people are over 70 years old and that 64 percent were women, 40 percent of whom did not drive. The largest social group is the knitting club. You wouldn't want to market to this group through the Internet, and you wouldn't want to defer to male pronouns in any marketing materials. Perhaps, instead, you could have introductory offers printed on postcards attached to balls of yarn that you hand out in person at knitting club events. You could even have a van to provide free transportation to your office.

Bottom line: Don't forget your audience! Knowing your audience allows you to best meet their needs and highlight your personal brand to the people who want to know about you.

Appealing both rationally and emotionally

Your target market will be attracted to you for different reasons. In Chapter 4, I note that rational attributes are solid qualities that people trust and depend on in you, whereas emotional attributes are often the reasons people want to be around you. These attributes (which I mention in Chapter 4 in the context of defining who you are) appeal to your target audience.

The people interested in working with you first want to know if you have what it takes to do the job. These rational attributes are tangible qualities that they need from you. For example, they may want to know that you are professional, international (you speak other languages), and a leader. Rational attributes are qualities that you need to get you through their gate. You must be able to show your target audience that you have the right education, experience, certifications, and solid skills to do what they need you to do.

The emotional attributes, such as sense of humor, empathy, friendliness, and loyalty, are the qualities that appeal to your target audience and attract them to want to work with you or do business with you.

In your target market research, you find the people who want the attributes you've got. And when you're pursuing your target audience (such as an employer or customer), you need to be sure to highlight the attributes that you know are important. As an example, after I am clear on who my ideal client is, I ask a potential client more specific questions to determine if we're a good fit. I highlight my strengths and am clear about what I don't do. The right clients are as thrilled to find me as I am to find them.

Highlighting your benefits to your market

Anticipating the reaction you'll receive from your target market is tough. Building your personal brand and beginning to use it can be a little scary because you don't know the reaction that you might receive. Highlighting your rational attributes is the easiest place to start because you can back them up with tangible evidence of degrees, certifications, or a work experience track record.

Then, be sure to ask yourself this question on a regular basis: What's in it for your audience? You always need to consider the ways in which you benefit your target audience. This group wants to know why they should spend energy and money on you. Always keep their needs at the top of your mind while you're both defining a target audience and setting the wheels of your personal brand in motion.

As William Arruda of Reach Personal Branding says, "Personal branding is not about being famous; it's about being selectively famous. It means knowing who needs to know you and being ever-visible to them. To this group, you are a leader, an inspiration, a resource. To the rest of the world, you are completely unknown."

Creating an emotional bond: Investing in relationships

Personal branding is all about communicating your message to the right people. You're remembered by others through your actions, accomplishments, and the emotional connections you make. Personal branding requires consistent behaviors so that people know what to expect from you.

You can't build a solid brand without relationships, but building relationships doesn't come easily to everyone. The most important thing you can do is to be consistent in your message the first time you make contact with a potential employer, future customer, or other target audience member. Then, be sure to read Chapter 15 about building and nurturing your network to work on your ability to create and nurture relationships.

Developing a Target Market Positioning Statement

A *positioning statement* is a tool used in business to identify how a brand will be positioned in the market. It puts into words what makes a brand important and differentiated so that it is noticed by those who need to know about it.

Before you focus on finding your niche and differentiating from your competitors (see Chapter 6), I want you to try a hand at writing your own positioning statement. Your statement gathers information from the research you have done on your target market and asks you to think about how you want to position yourself. It guides you in developing a position that will best serve your brand identity and communicating your personal brand to the right people. Positioning yourself will keep you in the minds of your target market and attract the right people to seek out your expertise.

Here's how to develop your own positioning statement:

1. **Define your target audience (who do you want to serve?).**

   Who are you interested in directing your brand toward? Your target audience is who you want to know about you. Your first target audience must always be yourself because you need to believe in your brand before anyone else will.

2. **Figure out your frame of reference (what is your point of view?).**

   The frame of reference sets the tone for the space you want to occupy. What category do you want to participate in? Who wants to have the same role or achieve the same goals? What is your unique point of view in this category?

3. **Identify points of difference (how will you uniquely do this?).**

   The point of difference is what makes you different from others in the space you play in. What distinctive benefits do you bring to your target audience? How do you stand out from all the rest?

4. **Offer support (I am credible because . . .).**

   Support is the evidence that your positioning statement is true. You need credible proof that you are what you say you are. You are giving the *because* statement for the points of difference. This is the reason that your target audience will want to work with you or seek out your expertise.

5. **State your promise or core benefit (who, where, uniquely how, because).**

   Here, you pull the four previous pieces together to let your target audience know what the net benefit is to them. What's in it for them?

Chapter 6

Knowing Your Niche — and Your Competitors

In This Chapter

- Securing your sweet spot
- Taking ownership of your niche
- Diving in to differentiation
- Getting to know your competitors

Competition is a word that brings out ambition for some and makes others recoil. We live in a competitive society but are praised for being collaborative; is it any wonder we're sometimes confused about how to get ahead?

In personal branding, I want you to look at competition as a way of understanding where you fit, who else does the same type of work you do, and how you can better identify your uniqueness. If you understand these factors, living your personal brand will allow you to find a place where what you offer stands out from others and creates a less competitive space in which you can thrive.

Owning the Business — of You

Having a personal brand is a little like having your own business. As such, you need to look at all aspects of who you are, including who else does work like you do and how you compare. This step applies whether you're an independent professional or an employee in a workplace.

A 4-year-old boy I know, tired of being told what to do and what not do, finally replied to his mother, "I am the boss of my shoes." Well, you are the boss of your own shoes! Your personal brand is something you can manage and direct, even if you can't completely control how others perceive it.

Identifying the sweet spot in which you want to compete

There is an intersection where what you have to offer, whom you want to work with, the markets that you serve, and the ideas that you have to share all come together. That point is called your market niche or your *sweet spot,* and it is uniquely yours. When you have found your sweet spot, you have found the niche that you want to use in developing your personal brand.

I have a friend who is a corporate trainer. He found his sweet spot in working with emerging leaders in an internationally diverse company. He claims his sweet spot is training these leaders in leadership development and helping them grow to be better managers. He likes to work with mid-level professionals who are eager to improve in their careers in a global environment.

Finding your sweet spot allows you to stay true to yourself, and it should give you direction to form a strategy for developing your niche. This concept applies whether you're an entrepreneur or working in a company. (Your sweet spot in the workplace becomes something that you are uniquely known for.)

Assessment guru Susan Guarneri, whose ACE Method appears in Chapter 5, has outlined a process for finding your sweet spot (your niche). Many of the questions in this process also appear in Chapter 4 or Chapter 5, so if you've worked through those chapters, you've got some of this territory covered. I encourage you to take a few minutes and work through this process, writing down any additional answers in your personal branding journal.

- **Who** is your target audience?
  - Who do you most enjoy working with? Why?
  - With which people have you had the most success?
  - Which people share your values and passions?
  - Do they have a common problem for which you have a solution?
  - Describe them using one or more of these: demographics (for example, age, gender, location, education level, career field); psychographics (for example, interests, hobbies, desires, needs, emotional intelligence); key problems or obstacles; and values and goals.
- **What** do you offer to your target market?
  - What solutions to problems? What proven results?
  - What products or services, or combination of both?
- **Where** is your target market?
  - Online or offline or both?
  - If offline, what is your geographic locale?

- **Why** will your target market choose you?
  - Out of all your brand attributes, which ones would your target market value?
  - Do you offer credibility and shared values?
- **How** can you capture the interest of your target market?
  - How is your personal brand and unique promise of value (which I define further in Chapter 7) different from your competitors?
  - How can you add even more value?

Owning your niche

Owning your niche means you are creating a mini-kingdom where you are the king or queen of a particular target market. When people think of that niche, they think of you. The niche and your personal brand become synonymous.

You can begin to create your own niche by picking a specific area that you want to be great at and claiming it. If you're stuck, ask yourself which problems you're especially good at solving or who seems to be drawn to you. Years ago, I kept getting lawyers as clients. I wasn't really sure that was who I wanted to have as my target audience. But when I thought about it, I realized that I had been raised by an attorney, was married to an attorney, and had a neighbor and many friends who were attorneys. It became an easy and obvious choice for me to specialize in that niche.

REMEMBER

You need to let go of the idea of serving everyone when choosing a niche. The world is filled with experts, and you simply can't know that much about everything. Many of my clients are afraid to eliminate people from their niche because "What if I narrow so much that I don't have any clients or work to do?" Because they are afraid to let go of those who no longer fit into their target audience, people often stay too broad in who they serve. Don't make that mistake: You don't want to end up with no defined niche and not being known for anything.

If you have no idea how to choose the type of people for your niche, think about your favorite people to work with and choose to name them as your niche. Perhaps you're a tattoo artist and you find that you prefer to work with women and your favorite tattoos to do are roses. It doesn't mean that you don't work with other clients, but you make it known to everyone that you especially love to work with women who want rose tattoos. Narrow your niche to one or two choices and then start learning everything you can about your target audience. (See Chapter 5 for hints to get started.) Devote two to three hours a week gaining knowledge about your niche. Investigate questions like: What are trends in this industry? What kinds of meetings do these people attend? Who in my company belongs to a professional association or has an area of expertise that I can learn from?

EXPERT OPINION

What's the difference between a niche and a personal brand?

I asked my colleague Susan Guarneri how she helps her clients determine the difference between a niche and a personal brand. She offers this quiz to help answer that question.

What are the search results when someone Googles your name or company name? Are those results about your personal brand or your niche, or both? Often the terms "personal brand" and "niche" are used interchangeably. But, are they really the same?

Here is a quick quiz to help you better understand both of these essential terms.

1. A niche is the same as a personal brand. T____ F____
2. You can own more than one niche simultaneously. T____ F____
3. You can own more than one personal brand simultaneously. T____ F____
4. The best way to determine your personal brand is to choose it. T____ F____
5. Your niche and your personal brand are essential to your career / business identity. T____ F____

ANSWERS:

1. False. Tom Peters originally wrote an article about "The Brand Called You" in August 1997 and coined the phrase "CEO of Me, Inc." Subsequently, William Arruda of Reach Personal Branding defined personal branding as "a unique promise of value." His definition encompasses "identifying and communicating what makes you unique, relevant, and compelling so that you can advance your career or business."

   Niche, however, is "a place, employment status, or activity for which a person or thing is best fitted; a specialized market" as defined by the Merriam-Webster dictionary. Thus, your personal brand is the intersection of *who* you are (the authentic you), the *value* you deliver to your target market (niche), and the *differentiation* between you and your competitors who may be serving the same niche.

2. True. According to Wikipedia, targeting your "niche market" is "the process of finding and serving profitable market segments. . . . " You may decide to start with one niche market, perhaps an outgrowth of one of your passions or subject-matter-expert knowledge. But you can certainly expand that niche to serve other market segments. As you move through new life experiences, other niches may arise.
3. False. Your personal brand is grounded in the authentic you. Your top brand attributes and strengths are apparent to others through your communications, behavior, and activities. The more transparent and authentic those interpersonal interactions, the stronger your personal brand. Trying to project a different persona than what you really are is extremely difficult to consistently and convincingly attain.
4. False . . . and True. Your brand is experienced and defined by others. Perception is

reality. However, your personal brand can be aspirational as well. You can strengthen select attributes and characteristics to reinforce your preferred brand theme. Simply increase the conscious transparency and visibility of your attributes of choice.

5. True. You may want to increase your visibility online and/or offline for your job search or business or social cause or event. Identifying your niche will allow you to educate, inform, persuade/influence, entertain, and/or build relationships with the right target market. Clarifying your personal brand will allow you to express the *value* you can bring to that market (niche) based on *who* you are and *how* you are different from your competitors.

Cultivate yourself as an expert in that niche. Become the go-to person for a particular group of people or become a subject matter expert. In my former work at a consulting firm, if there was work to do with attorneys, they were always sent to me. I think everyone else was afraid of them, but they were the people I enjoyed serving!

Become an expert. Write articles, blog, speak, and do whatever it takes to be known in that niche. (I show you how to craft a communications plan in Chapter 10.)

Claim your niche: Own and be known!

Differentiating Your Brand

You can't ignore your competitors when you need to understand who their target markets are, what their strengths are, and where they are weak. At this stage in the branding process, you want to do a thorough analysis of your competitors to see what they do well and what you can learn from their best practices. You want to look for opportunities that your competition may be missing and determine what needs are going unmet that you can serve.

This process is a continuation of discovery from Chapters 4 and 5 that will help you know where to target your brand. You may be a hip hairstylist and have developed a look to show that you're modern, trendy, and cool. You will want to see who your competitors are in your target of chic salons in an urban area. Knowing your competition helps you know where you fit.

Finding your potential competitors

You need to define who your competitors are, where they are located, and what they do, so you need to ask yourself a few questions. Whether you're an independent business person or you work inside a company, ask yourself

- What businesses or people are like your business in terms of what they do and how they do it?
- What businesses or people are competing in your target market in terms of who they sell to? These can be people doing something different, but you have the same target market.
- Are your competitors located locally, nationally, or internationally? Or are your competitors borderless and compete in the online space?

Finding this information can be easier than you think now that you have access to research at your fingertips. Depending on the markets you are targeting, you can find your answers in some of these places:

- **Yellow Pages:** Yes, they still exist! Look up your profession or line of work to see who else is listed.
- **LinkedIn:** Do an advanced search on LinkedIn and list your professional title, keywords, and geography for the work that you do. Remember to think of all the titles someone could be called for the work that you do.
- **Professional meetings:** Attend professional association meetings and see who is there. Are these the people whom you compete against?
- **Google:** Search for keywords and geographies, putting quotes around searchable items to narrow your results.
- **Yelp:** For local businesses, Yelp has become a resource to see what people say about you and your competition.

If you're trying to compete against people within your own workplace, identify the people who are the prized employees. What do they offer your employer that you don't? How can you find your niche within the workplace?

Gather as much information as you can about anyone who might fall into the category of competitor. What is your impression about their brand? Note what they seem to do well and notice what is missing. What can you learn from the information that you've assembled?

Determining how you and your competitors differ

Think about your competitors or peers, both actual and potential. What do you all have in common? You must have certain qualifications to play in your target audience's arena, so being similar is a good thing to begin with. For example, if you're an attorney, you had to pass law school, and if you want to practice law, you need to have passed the bar exam in your state. All attorneys practicing law in your state need those things. That makes you similar. But as you build on what you know, your similarities become fewer, and your differentiation will become more apparent.

When you do the same thing as your competitors and there is no real differentiation, you become a commodity. *Commodities* are items based on price, not differentiation, and give you no leverage other than asking if you are the least expensive. Your job in personal branding is to distinguish yourself as a sought-after brand because when you are differentiated, people will pay a premium to work with you.

Think of it this way: If you were a coffee, you would want to be Starbucks because people would be willing to pay more for you and would be loyal to your brand. To become your own version of Starbucks, highlight your differences as you build your brand.

The same/different exercise

William Arruda of Reach Personal Branding likes to use the *same/different exercise* to illustrate differences that you can use in the personal branding process. This exercise is used with his permission. The same/different exercise illustrates where you are the same as, and where are you different from, those who do what you do. Here is an example of differentiating two recent college graduates:

Same	**Different**
Bachelor's degree in business	Double major in business & Spanish
Semester abroad	Semester at sea visiting 14 countries
Fraternity membership	Fraternity leader for two years
Summer internship	Chosen from 500 internship applicants
Computer savvy	Programmed three Facebook business sites
Senior project	Award-winning senior project
Dean's list	Dean's list for six semesters

Take a piece of paper and draw a line down the middle. On the left side write the word Same, and on the right side write Different. Now make your own list of how you are the same as your competitors and what qualities make you different. Record these in your personal branding journal.

Follow the link `http://bit.ly/same different` to a video by William Arruda explaining the differences between you and your competitors.

Being able to highlight what makes you different is a key to a dazzling personal brand. After all, personal branding is all about your unique promise of value. No one will remember you if everything you stand for is no different than everyone else. We hunger for our own uniqueness and want to be seen for the individuals that we are. Therapists know that often their best work is to listen to someone tell his story so that the client feels special enough to be heard. Your differences allow you to be heard.

What makes your brand different than your competitors? What makes you stand out? Do their weaknesses provide an opportunity for you to highlight your value to that market and more fully live your brand?

TIP

I want you to list the qualities that make you special or that you uniquely possess. Think of this list as a statement of fact and not a bragging exercise. Look to Chapter 4 to spark ideas and list as many things as you can think of. This list may include certifications that you hold that others don't or a language that you speak. A quality may even be something like, "I get more done in a shorter period of time than my peers."

If you find that you don't have many differences from your competition (which you may not have early in your career), think about how you might tell your story in a different way. I recently did business with two people who did just about the same thing. Both were excellent in how they did their work, but one was more engaging and worked to develop a warmer bond between us. I chose to continue to do work with that person because in addition to doing excellent work, he made me feel good. Mr. Feel Good can use his friendliness as a brand differentiator.

REMEMBER

When you're lining up all the tangible, rational attributes that you have to offer, don't forget the emotional attributes. These can be your key differentiators that you have to offer and that your competition is missing.

I find that some people can't see that many of their qualities are anything special. Don't judge what is or isn't special; just make a list of what you have to offer while looking at it with a critical eye and asking "Is this the same as or different than my competitors?" If you need more help, see the sidebar "The same/different exercise."

Understanding Contenders for Your Target Market

When you know your *contenders* (worthy competitors), you have options of what to do with that information. You may choose to define a very narrow niche so that you don't have any competitors, or you may find that you want to band together with your competitors, creating a strong alliance providing more business for all of you.

In your workplace, your contenders are the people doing well inside your company and those from the outside who may be hired to do work that you're not demonstrating that you can do. Continue to observe and gather information so that you can direct your brand.

Comparing, not competing, for the same dollars

How do you compare to the competition? Ask yourself these questions:

- What are your competitors missing? Is there a gap in the services they provide that could be an opportunity for you?
- Are you targeting the same market? What tactics do they use, and do the tactics seem to be effective?
- If you were that company's customer, what would the experience of doing business with them be like?
- How do they find their opportunities?
- What can you learn from them that would help you develop your business or move into a position you would like to have in your company?
- Are you trying to occupy the same space as someone else who has done it longer and better? (If so, you will need to think of a new angle.)
- How will I price what I do?
- Does the market dictate what I can charge for the work I do? (If yes, you will need to price yourself in relationship to others doing similar work and focus on other aspects of your business to stand out.)
- Is there room for the price to go up or down depending on what I offer? (You may be able to answer this question after you've been doing business a little longer and can find added value in your service before raising your prices.)
- How did you arrive at what you are going to charge? Did you do a comparison of the competition? Was your value determined geographically? (What you could charge in New York may be very different than what you could charge in Tampa, for example.)
- Does what you charge support your personal brand? (If you're branding yourself as a luxury person but are undercharging, you're not being true to your brand.)

Overcoming your fears in the face of competition

Personal branding involves taking your authentic self out into the world. It is easy at this point to be overcome with the fear of *what if no one wants this brand? What if I can't compete?* It's a very real fear, although you won't often hear people say it out loud. Putting yourself out there is scary, and if you don't have the self-esteem to back up your brand, you won't get very far.

The best way to overcome your fear of competing is to stay true to your personal brand with strategies that spell success:

- **Stay authentic.** You know who you are. Don't be afraid to be that.
- **Play fairly.** Don't fling mud because it will take you down and dirty your reputation.
- **Have a good attitude.** Be known for your good nature and for being pleasant to work with. People like doing business with nice people.
- **Don't say yes just to agree.** Great brands stand for something, and when you are called to do that, stand up for what you believe in.
- **Start early and overdeliver.** People like to know that they can count on you to be there and that you will do what you say you'll do.
- **Communicate better than anyone else.** Build your brand loyalty by being a great communicator.
- **Find support from people who believe in you.** Nothing helps overcome your fears like having a fan club.

Defending your brand

The more successful you are, the more enemies you will have. Some people won't like you just because you are doing well. The old expression "keep your friends close and your enemies closer" comes into play here.

As you gain success, you may encounter a competitor who does whatever he can to sabotage your success. A saboteur draws attention to you through negative attention. Sabotage is an attack on your reputation, and how you handle the incident can give you further credibility. The extra attention is your opportunity to turn your audience around with what you have to offer, your positive attributes, and a forum to take the high ground.

Keeping professional boundaries

Professional boundaries are simply knowing where you end and where another person begins within your profession. Professional boundaries are important because the boundaries define acceptable behavior and identify the limits for the relationships that you share in the workplace. Having clear boundaries causes less stress in the workplace. Professional boundaries are like good manners in that they make everyone feel comfortable.

REMEMBER

Having a resilient personal brand built on solid values, using your key attributes, and having supporters who believe in you are the best defenses against a saboteur. Developing clear personal boundaries sets you and your brand apart from the ugliness. In other words, don't get involved in dreadful gossip at work or people who pry too deeply into your personal life. Always keep clear professional boundaries, and your foes will have less ammunition if they decide to target you. Boundaries are the best protection for preserving your emotional energy and defending your brand.

Asking for advice from colleagues

Now, this advice may seem contrary to the idea of competition, but I think one of the most valuable resources you can have is your colleagues (*a.k.a.* your competition). However, you need to apply some strategy here: You need to find competitors who aren't really direct competitors.

Perhaps you can locate people doing the same work with the same target audience as you, only they are in Illinois and you are in California. Or you may look for someone inside your company who works in a different division. People share much more freely when they don't feel threatened. As a matter of fact, it often makes them feel good to know that they are helping someone and can act as a mentor.

TIP

One of the best ways I have found to learn about an industry is to find alliances that you can partner with. In business, that may mean working with a group that needs someone who does what you do. The alliance is an offshoot of the core business; they take a cut of the fee but refer business to you. These alliances will share information with you because they know if you are good, they too will make more money. Your good personal brand enhances their brand.

Some other sources to learn more from colleagues are found through professional groups in person and online:

- **Yahoo! groups:** There is a Yahoo! group for everything. When you join a Yahoo group, you can receive the e-mails that the members of the group send to each other. This is a connected way for you to ask a question and have it answered by someone who shares your interest.
- **LinkedIn groups and LinkedIn questions:** LinkedIn has a plethora of business groups that you can belong to, begin discussions with, and gain credibility with to learn more from professionals in your field. With LinkedIn questions, you can pose questions and hope that someone answers them.
- **Industry-specific websites:** These can give you information about the work that you do and the markets that you serve. Industry experts are often featured here.
- **Professional associations:** You can meet people in person to expand your network, listen to speakers, and learn who the players in your industry are.
- **Industry newsletters:** The articles may provide valuable insight into the work that you do and the people you serve.
- **Twitter:** It's fast and immediate and gives you more information than you will know what to do with. Experts abound here, so check it out.
- **Facebook:** In particular, the business pages connect you to colleagues with your interests and provide relevant information to learn.

REMEMBER

Study your competition, but don't be afraid of it. If your market has competition, you know that you have found a niche that others find attractive as well. Personal branding positions you to compete with an authentic approach to your target audience.

Chapter 7

Crafting Your Personal Brand Profile

In This Chapter

- Arranging your defining building blocks
- Promising uniqueness in your value to others
- Expressing the essence of your personal brand
- Preparing to take your brand public

Personal branding is about finding your own voice, taking ownership of your own career path, and feeling empowered in what you contribute to the world. It's also about managing how others perceive you. In this chapter, you synthesize all your qualities into a statement that is the foundation on which you will communicate and live your brand. This statement is the heart and soul of who you are and what motivates you.

In Chapters 4, 5, and 6, I introduce you to the defining pieces composing your brand. In this chapter, you gather the building blocks from those chapters to craft a personal brand profile that highlights your authentic self. In doing so, you bring to light your unique promise of value, which allows you to then write your personal brand statement and develop a strategy for using your brand.

The pieces of your puzzle come together in this chapter, allowing you to see the whole picture of who you really are. Working on the personal brand profile can be really exciting, and you'll walk away having a clear sense of what makes you tick.

Compiling Your Personal Brand Profile

If you work through Chapters 4, 5, and 6, you can gather a lot of information about yourself that you can use to craft your personal brand profile. If you haven't yet read those chapters, you're absolutely welcome to keep reading here, but I encourage you to refer to them at some point so that you're able to fully utilize the tools in this chapter. In this section, for example, I show you how to place all those tidbits into a personal brand table so that you can see at a glance who you are and where you want to go.

Gathering your stepping stones to success

Each of your characteristics is like a piece of a quilt; it's important, but it's only a part of a greater whole. Only after you assemble the larger product is its true beauty revealed.

Your quilt pieces — the building blocks of your brand — are these characteristics, which I discuss in depth in Chapters 4 and 5:

- **Needs:** The necessities you must have. Needs direct your feelings and influence your values.
- **Values:** The emotional currency of your life. Values are the core principles that give meaning to your life and are defined as a set of standards that determine your attitudes, choices, and actions.
- **Interests/passions:** Things that intrigue you and motivate you to devote energy to them. They determine how you want to spend your time.
- **Mission:** Statements that clarify what you are all about and what you want to do in life.
- **Vision:** Your ideal version of how you will use your mission. Expressing your vision involves describing what you see as possible in the world.
- **Strengths:** Patterns of interests and abilities that consistently produce a positive outcome in a specific task.
- **Freak factor:** A unique quality that makes you different and unusual.
- **Personality attributes:** Words describing the face that you show to the world.
- **Education and work experience:** Solid brand attributes that you can use to describe yourself.
- **360º feedback:** Information about your character, which is provided by people who know you best (such as friends and coworkers).
- **Goals:** What you want to achieve.
- **Target market positioning statement:** A tool used to identify how your brand will be positioned in the market. The statement puts into words what makes your brand important and differentiated so that your brand is noticed by those who need to know about it (see Chapter 5).

Creating a personal brand profile table

I have found that the best way to capture your information is to build your personal brand with a profile table. By having your information in one place, you can see your patterns emerge. Taking this step allows you to see the words that best describe you and synthesize them into an authentic personal brand statement.

You won't use everything that you gather in your table. However, when you have all the pieces together, you can easily extract the pieces that best convey your essence.

Figure 7-1 is an example of a personal brand profile table that has been filled to show you how you would fill out your own table.

Developing Your Unique Promise of Value and Personal Brand Statement

Your unique promise of value and your personal brand statement are closely linked; the statement is an expression of the promise. Both of them focus on what your target audience expects from you; they create an expectation of what you can deliver.

These pieces of your personal brand profile are probably the most important (no pressure!), so you want to take your time and get them right before you start to communicate with your target audience. In this section, I walk you through how to develop each of them.

Identifying your unique promise of value

Your unique promise of value is a promise that you make to your target market (see Chapter 5) that your brand will fulfill. It is the personal aspect of your brand that is aligned with your mission and values. Your promise of value is the essence of what you have to offer and guides you in how you will live your personal brand. It clarifies and communicates what makes you special — what makes you different from other people. Crafting this promise requires understanding your values, interests, strengths, and personal qualities and using them to distinguish yourself.

Personal Brand Profile	
Mission	To empower others to use their talents in the world.
Vision	I am a change agent and leader for programs and organizations to bring about the value of each individual and live in a world where each person can contribute to society using their unique talents authentically.
Needs	Income to pay for necessities of life and support my business — for example, a certain dollar amount per year. An environment that is safe and flexible, where I can express my creativity. Connections to friends, family, and my community. Challenging work where I am continually learning. The ability to use my talents to serve others.
Values	Integrity, creativity, choice, community, congruency, learning, courage, enthusiasm, financial independence, intuition.
Interests & Passions	Coaching, counseling, facilitating, managing people and projects, envisioning the big picture, helping others grow, teaching, leading, inspiring.
Strengths	*Individualization:* I'm intrigued by the unique qualities of each person. I focus on the differences between individuals. I find the right person to play the best part. *Strategic:* I can sort through the clutter and find the best route. I have a distinct way of thinking and seeing patterns where others see complexity. I am talented in creating alternative ways to proceed. *Learner:* I'm energized by the journey from ignorance to competence. I thrill at the growing confidence of a skill mastered. Activator: I make things happen by turning thoughts into action. Arranger: I enjoy managing all the variables, realigning them until I have found the most productive configuration possible. I am a great example of effective flexibility.
Personal Descriptors (Freak Factor, Education, Work Experience)	National Certified Counselor, Professional Certified Coach, college professor, Spiritual seeker, avid reader, Vespa rider, world traveler.
Personality Attributes (360° Feedback)	Inspirational, energetic, dynamic, extroverted, enthusiastic, supportive, creative, solid, community builder, pragmatic intuition, intelligent, fun, adventurous, challenger of the status quo.
Goals	Serve professionals as both private individual clients and corporate clients. Run weekend workshops that are affordable to the general public. Conduct corporate trainings.
Unique Promise of Value	I am known for my creativity, enthusiasm, and intelligence by serving each client with respect, giving them individual attention, and treating them with unconditional positive regard. I am an expert in my field and use my knowledge to help my clients and students excel. My clients appreciate my solid, grounded approach during times of transition and trust my guidance through the process.
Personal Brand Statement	I bring creativity and enthusiasm back into the lives of professionals using my expertise in career development with an intelligent, customized approach.
Target Audience Professional services and law firms. I understand this market and its unique position of maintaining a professional identity and trying to build clients within a firm setting.	**Differentiation** Professional Certified Coach Certified Change Management facilitator Four years of experience running corporate training change management programs Highly rated evaluations from former clients.

Figure 7-1: A personal brand profile table lets you see patterns.

Lida Citroën, in her book *Reputation 360* (Palisades Publishing), offers this advice when crafting your brand promise:

> *Your brand promise should look something like this: "In order to be known for (your desired brand qualities), I will hold myself out to others in this way: (your behavior, actions, attitude); and I will demonstrate authenticity in this way: (how you will let people see you as real, genuine). I will know my brand promise is working when I see this: (benefits, goals you hope to achieve)."*

You must be able to live up to your promise of value. You're always better off underpromising and overdelivering to those you serve. Your brand promise is what you want to be known for. It can be the promise of value of who you are today, or it can be written as who you aspire to become.

Here is how I've written about my own unique promise of value:

> *I am known for my creativity, enthusiasm, and intelligence by serving each client with respect, giving them individual attention, and treating them with unconditional positive regard. I am an expert in my field and use my knowledge to help my clients and students excel. My clients appreciate my solid, grounded approach during times of transition and trust my guidance through the process.*

Moving from your promise to your personal brand statement

After you're satisfied with what you've developed as your unique promise of value, you can turn your attention to writing the all-important personal brand statement.

One method I like to use when I am developing a personal brand statement is to look at someone's profile and get a feel for the whole person. That's why I consider it so useful to compile a personal brand profile table. (For an example, refer to Figure 7-1, earlier in this chapter.)

When you work on your own statement, keep in mind the central themes that emerge from your profile table and think about your attributes. Then, envision your best self! I often put keywords on separate sticky notes and stick them to a blank wall. Doing so gives you time to think about what the core of your brand is and what message you stand for. It may take a few days and several rounds of rearranging the words, but eventually a statement will emerge.

To begin your thought process on what your brand might include, answer the following questions:

- What three or four key words describe your essential qualities quickly and clearly?
- What is your *essence factor,* the core of who you are? "I know I am in my element when __________."
- What is your *authority factor,* the knowledge that you hold and skills that you possess? "People recognize my expertise in _________."
- What is your *superstar factor,* the qualities that set you apart? (This factor is how you get things done or what you are known for.) "People comment on my ability to ___________."

Adapted from Be Sharp (CreateSpace Publishing) by Paula Asinof and Mina Brown.

Peppering your statement with "wow" words

TIP

When writing your personal brand statement, you want to use words that best describe what you offer. The words you use should highlight your emotional attributes and motivate you so that you can deliver that brand to your target audience.

Chapter 4 is filled with multiple word lists. If you haven't done so, I encourage you to review the values, interests, strengths, and personality characteristics lists for the words that best describe you. Add those words to your profile table.

Then, to communicate the action in your message, add key verbs like the ones I list here. For a more complete list of "wow" words, see *Best KeyWords for Resumes, Cover Letters, and Interviews: Powerful Communication Tools for Success* by Wendy Enelow (Impact Publications).

Accomplish	Analyze	Articulate	Budget
Calculate	Capitalize	Classify	Close
Collaborate	Communicate	Conceptualize	Conclude
Decrease	Demonstrate	Distribute	Educate
Empower	Engineer	Enhance	Examine
Exceed	Generate	Identify	Influence
Integrate	Listen	Manufacture	Mastermind
Maximize	Navigate	Network	Organize
Pilot	Pioneer	Prospect	Rebuild
Redesign	Reengineer	Rehabilitate	Simplify
Slash	Sold	Strategize	Supervise
Systematize	Teach	Transition	Upgrade

Drafting your statement

To give you a sense of what a personal brand may look like, I offer some sample brand statements courtesy of William Arruda of Reach Personal Branding:

> *I use my quirky nature, confidence, and passion for fun to motivate creative teams in ad agencies and marketing departments to work together more effectively to drive greater value for their organizations.*
>
> *Through my natural enthusiasm and my empathy for others, I inspire research and development professionals to develop innovative products in biotechnology.*
>
> *I deliver Zen-like teleseminars and online learning programs to stressed-out, overworked police officers, firemen, and other emergency workers to help them identify, manage, and reduce stress.*
>
> *In working collaboratively with designers, I write witty, pithy, timely, and compelling copy for marketing materials for B-to-B companies.*
>
> *Sitting at the intersection of technology and business, I use my passion for communication to help IT professionals in Fortune 100 companies express themselves in ways that are understood by business people.*
>
> *I use my 25 years of experience in — and passion for — marketing to help senior marketing executives in large organizations succeed by making marketing valued inside the organization.*
>
> *Through my intuition and genuine concern for — and interest in — others, I build long-lasting, fruitful relationships with my team, my business partners, and clients to drive consistent, recurring revenue for my company.*
>
> *I encourage seniors living in North America to connect with their passions, kick over the rocking chair, and live rich, fulfilling, active lives.*

My own statement reads this way:

> *I bring creativity and enthusiasm into the lives of professionals using my expertise in career development with an intelligent, customized approach.*

To help you get started writing your statement, I offer this fill-in-the-blanks template, in which you can place your keywords from your personal brand profile. Don't be constrained by the language I suggest here! Simply use it as a starting point for writing your statement, and then let it simmer until you know how you want to express yourself.

Summing up your personal brand in a tagline

A *tagline* or slogan is a phrase that follows your brand name and sums up your unique promise of value. A tagline is shorter and catchier than your personal brand statement, but it serves a similar purpose: It distinguishes you in the minds of your target market, expresses your personality, and/or gives a sense of what you do. A tagline is a short one-liner that you can add to a business card or to the signature of your e-mail.

In Chapter 2, I discuss the power of branding by illustrating how corporations use an element such as a tagline (a slogan) to create a lasting impression on target audience members. For example, you're likely to recognize the phrase "Just do it!" as Nike's tagline. And even though it has tried to transition to "So good!" in recent years (to emphasize an increased focus on healthy foods), Kentucky Fried Chicken's "Finger lickin' good!" was such a constant in its ads for half a century that people still associate KFC with that earlier tagline.

TIP

Taglines are best when they're simple and easy to remember. With 11 or fewer words to convey your message, you have to work hard to craft a worthwhile tagline. If you struggle with this step, keep in mind that a tagline isn't absolutely essential; it's just a helpful tool for getting (and keeping) your audience's attention.

Some people use famous quotes as their taglines. (Maybe you have a friend whose e-mail signature line always includes such a quote.) Some people display a great sense of humor in their taglines, which speaks volumes to their personality. If you're going to use a tagline, just remember that it must align with your unique promise of value and your personal brand statement. Otherwise, you'll just confuse your target market.

REMEMBER

A well-done tagline is so clear that anyone who reads it can determine what business you're in, even if she's never heard of you. See Chapter 2 for a list of real-life examples of corporate taglines and consider these effective solopreneur taglines:

- **Barbara Smith Accounting:** Making accounting personal
- **Abigail Marks Marketing:** Make your mark with Abigail Marks Marketing
- **Thomas Fuller, Personal Trainer:** It's Not Just Fitness . . . It's Personal
- **Susan Guarneri:** The Career Assessment Goddess

TIP

Here are some guidelines to develop your tagline:

- Write it in the present tense.
- Keep it short and make sure that it's consistent with your brand.
- Use your unique characteristics to make it catchy.
- Make sure that it's easy to say. (Practice saying it out loud.)
- If you're using your personal brand tagline internationally, know how your words translate into other languages.
- Google your phrase and see who else uses that tagline.

Test-driving your personal brand

If you've navigated all the steps I outline earlier in this chapter, you're ready to launch your personal brand and take it for a test drive. Taking your brand out to the public for the first time can feel very strange. You'll be saying words about yourself that up until now have been only on paper or only in your head.

Your very first step is to talk about your brand to yourself, maybe in front of the mirror or while driving to work. After all, no one will believe your brand unless you do! Make sure that you can speak the words with confidence before you say them to anyone else.

Then, the easiest way to introduce your brand is by trying it out on people who genuinely care about you and understand your message. Solicit their feedback about your personal brand before moving on to your target audience at large.

The key is to begin using your key personal branding words. I had a client who was attending a conference of her professional colleagues. I gave her this assignment: "Say your branding statement in some form in ten separate conversations during the conference." She was to start with a word or two, and as she got comfortable saying her brand out loud, she was to add another word. By the end of the conference, her goal was to be able to articulate her brand message and not feel embarrassed to do so.

When you first test out your brand, do so in person — not via written materials. Here's why:

- You can see how comfortable you are with your new brand and what it sounds like out loud.
- How you phrase your brand when speaking may sound different than how you phrase it when writing.

The idea is not to quote your written brand but to weave the essence of the brand into a conversation. Saying it out loud will allow you to observe the reaction from others. At this stage in the game, you need to play with the idea that you have a brand and that it is ever evolving. So give it a try!

In Part III, I show you how to develop a communications strategy using a variety of communications tools to help you take your brand to the public. You definitely want to take your brand for a test-drive before jumping in to a full-blown communications strategy.

Gearing Up for Your Personal Brand Strategy

All the steps I discuss in this chapter (which build on work I outline in the preceding Part II chapters) are the hardest part of the personal branding process. These steps helps you discover more fully who you are; who you want to work with; your needs, values, mission, and unique promise of value; and maybe more than you wanted to know about yourself — the good, bad, and the ugly.

The work I discuss in Part II involves mostly self-reflection and examination. Developing a strategic plan for your brand and implementing it puts your brand into action. For most people, this step requires hard work and the devotion to live a more authentic life.

What will your personal branding strategy be? Will you market yourself as the first to do something, as a leader in your field, or as an expert or by using your race or gender or by aligning yourself with a cause?

Before you begin devising a strategy, look at your brand from your target audience's point of view. If you were to stand in their shoes, what would it want from you? You must identify the key reasons that your target audience would want to work with you or do business with you.

In addition, you must take a series of crucial steps to bring your personal brand to market. These steps, which I discuss in upcoming chapters, include

- Writing your brand story (see Chapter 8)
- Determining how you can best communicate with your audience (see Part III)
- Fashioning your image (see Chapter 12)
- Creating your visual marketing materials (see Chapter 13)

In other words, much of the rest of this book is dedicated to helping you devise your strategy for moving from the self-reflection stage to the "Look out world, here I come!" stage. But before I talk about that work, I want you to think about two crucial topics: money and time.

Figuring out the finances to take your brand to market

Personal branding requires money, though not necessarily a lot of money. Obviously, the amount depends on what you're doing to build your brand.

Starting a business requires a bigger plan and a bigger budget than simply trying to stand out and create a certain image (for whom creativity may matter more than money).

As you look to the future to build your personal brand, ask yourself what you need to support your brand:

- Do you need additional training or education?
- Will you need career-related materials, such as a resume, bio, business cards, or letterhead?
- Does your wardrobe need updating?
- Will you need money for a website or online marketing?
- Does your transportation fit your personal brand?

Thinking about your financial needs early in the personal branding process will prevent angst during the implementation phase. Take the time to look at your finances now so that you aren't surprised by your money needs later.

Scheduling your successes

TIP

I encourage you to set a timetable to make your personal brand happen. In Chapter 4, I explain that the most successful people in this world are often those who set goals for themselves up front rather than just waiting for success to happen. I want you to succeed, so I want you to set specific goals for yourself — now!

When it comes to moving your personal brand into the public eye, map out the initial steps on your calendar. Pick a date for completing each step and stick to it. Then, as you get close to completing that list, add more deadlines to your calendar to keep you moving toward the goals that I outline in Parts III and IV. Don't let your brand stagnate! Set firm deadlines for yourself and make every effort to stick to them.

Spending focused time on this activity helps it go more quickly. I suggest devoting at least an hour a week to work on furthering your brand. Here are suggestions for beginning steps you may want to mark on your calendar:

1. **Make a list of what you want to achieve and what you're willing to commit to make it happen.**
2. **Review your goals (see Chapter 4) and determine your personal objectives for taking your personal brand to market.**

   Your objectives can include becoming a more visible leader, strengthening the relationships with your customers, or being known as a thought leader in your industry.

3. **Write your elevator pitch (see Chapter 8).**
4. **Implement your personal brand in some small, initial way.**

   See the earlier section "Test-driving your personal brand" for ideas.

Where you go from this section is largely determined by what you're trying to accomplish. Part III helps you get a handle on the next steps that make the most sense for you.

Chapter 8

Writing Your Story

In This Chapter

- Appreciating the power of stories
- Storytelling your brand
- Pitching your story in 30 seconds
- Rehearsing your personal commercial

Personal branding is about authoring your own life. It's how you create your story, live your story, and then tell that story to the right audience. Stories are personal, and nothing will build your brand like a good story. A good story makes you human and connects you emotionally with your audience. Personal branding uses your story in crafting a stellar biography and an engaging introduction or elevator speech.

In this chapter, you discover how stories unite you with others and how you can tell your story in a compelling way.

Why People Like Stories

The first time I remember telling a story to a group was when I was speaking at my high school graduation. I wanted people to remember me and remember my story. I decided to tell a story of why I had stayed in high school for my senior year even though I had enough credits to graduate early. My message was to show why high school had given me a strong foundation on which to build my future.

As I started to write my speech, I couldn't find the words I wanted to say to make my point. I was completely blank, even though those who know me would say I always had something to say. My mother came home one day with a story that seemed to illustrate my message. You may have heard it, but here is the story that I told:

This fable originated during the cathedral building period during the Renaissance in a city somewhere in Europe. Workmen were laying the first blocks of the foundation, and an overseer was inspecting their work. Coming upon three workman who were busily engaged in their tasks, the overseer asked the first workman, "What are you doing?"

Without looking up, the workman answered, "I am laying bricks."

The overseer then asked the same question of the second workman. Like the first, he answered without looking up. "I am making sure that the blocks are level and plumb."

Turning to the third man who had a trowel in his hand and was obviously spreading mortar, the overseer asked, "And what are you doing?"

The workman stood up, removed his cap, cast his eyes upward as though visualizing the beautiful walls and spires that would someday occupy the now empty space, and answered, "I, sir, am building a cathedral."

Had I just given a speech about why I thought education was important, how I had gotten a lot out of the activities, and how I had grown as a person, no one would have cared other than my parents. Instead, the story engaged the audience and connected them with the universal theme of hope for the future and a vision of what might be.

Crossing all cultures

Fairy tales, myths, legends, and stories are told in every culture as entertainment, education, and cultural preservation. These stories are filled with characters that teach lessons and make people think about their own values as they make decisions in everyday life.

There is a universal desire to want to belong. All cultures use story to connect people to each other and teach them cultural values. Revolutionaries are often master storytellers and are able to lead a movement through story. They're able to connect with their listeners on every level, inspiring people to follow them.

Folk and fairy tales speak to people in the symbolic language of archetypes. *Archetypes* are representative patterns of behavior that cross cultures. *Hero* and *mother* mean basically the same thing across every culture, and stories have a way of connecting people with the human elements that make them the same through these symbolic patterns. These patterns are understandable by almost everyone in every culture.

Years ago, I went to the caves of Lascaux in southwestern France. The drawings told the stories of Paleolithic life in 15,000 BC. I had thought the drawings were just animals until I saw the stories in the art. I realized that to tell a story is to be human, and I was witnessing a deep human desire to communicate and be heard.

When you tell a story, you're aligning yourself with your listeners. Connecting with the other person and sharing what you have in common are what make stories so powerful.

Realizing how brains create and use stories

Think about when you've listened to a vivid story or watched a scary movie. Were you on the edge of your seat with your heart racing and adrenaline pumping, breaking out in a sweat? To the brain, an imagined experience is processed the same way as a real experience. People crave experiences and love stories, whether they're listened to, read in a book, watched on a screen, or interacted with in a video game.

Stories are the brain's way of organizing information. You're bombarded with information daily, so your brain tries to make sense out of the information and create order. Your brain creates a story to put all the pieces together.

Stories connect your logical left brain with the feeling right brain to create a holistic experience. Storytelling is effective because it engages the whole brain, not just the dry facts that appeal to the left brain or the artistic, visceral experience in the right brain. (Not sure what left and right brain functions are? Take a look at Table 8-1.)

Table 8-1 Brain Functions

Your Left Brain . . .	*Your Right Brain . . .*
Is logical and analytical	Uses feeling
Likes details	Looks for the big picture
Focuses on facts	Enables your imagination
Excels at words and language	Understands symbols and images
Comprehends the present and past	Comprehends philosophy and religion
Helps you study math and science	Finds meaning
Comprehends	Believes
Perceives order and patterns	Feels appreciation
Is based in reality	Has strong spatial abilities
Forms strategies	Is based on fantasy
Is practical	Focuses on the present and future
Is concerned with safety	Sees possibilities
Likes a plan	Is spontaneous
Calculates risk	Takes risks

The brain doesn't like gaps and will fill in missing information. The brain takes disconnected pieces of information and adds a story line to connect them. I used to tell my teenagers that it was better to tell me what really happened than let my imagination come up with a much more vivid story!

Stories connect the facts of who, what, why, where, and how and create a multidimensional experience for the listener. A listener may not know whether a story is true, and it may not matter, because the meaning is in the moral or essence of the story.

Using Storytelling to Illustrate Your Life

Storytelling illustrates events through words, images, and sounds. A story has a basic structure: a beginning, middle, and end. The best stories pull you in from the beginning, keep your interest in the middle, and leave you with a satisfying ending, wishing for more. Each story takes on a life of its own, thanks to the unique voice, gesture, and sense of humor of the storyteller. Stories tap in to your deep sense of imagination and trigger the heart of what makes you human.

People tell stories every day. The simple question "How are you?" asks you to tell the person your story. If the answer goes beyond "Fine," then a story begins. The most common story told in an interview begins with the question, "Tell me about yourself."

The telling of a story is always personal. Whatever walk of life that you come from, your stories define you. Your story becomes your personal brand, and you need to think about which stories you tell to others to illustrate who you are. Reflect on those people in your life who tell stories of complaint, hardship, and angst. What messages do those stories send to you when you hear them? Certainly not one of competence and command. Your story is an expression of your life, so put some thought into what you tell (and don't tell) others. See the upcoming section "Keeping gossip out of your brand" for some thoughts about what types of stories *not* to tell.

Even stories shown in advertising and the media are personal. Envision your favorite commercial. Why do you like it? Most likely, it has a message that connects with you both emotionally and visually. You feel the product will solve your problem or fulfill your desires. You find commonality with others, and through the message, you're able to make a decision. Take beer commercials, for example, which have been featuring pretty girls for years to sell their products. The message at an emotional level is "If you drink this beer, you, too, will have pretty girls surround you." Not likely, but the suggestion often works!

In this section, I help you think about the type of story you want to tell about yourself — one that helps you accomplish your goals and live your brand.

Finding the plot in your story

The good news is that, unlike a novelist or short story writer, you don't need to determine who the characters in your story will be. The central character is predetermined, and it's you! To begin, then, your focus should be on plot. That's what this section is about.

EXPERT OPINION

To tell a good story, you need to have a good story. Here are 20 questions from Bernadette Martin, author of *Storytelling About Your Brand Online & Offline* (Happy About), to get your story started. If you're a natural storyteller, these questions will give you more material to work with. Most people need suggestions, and the following questions are a good start:

- What is the funniest experience you've ever had?
- Have you developed, created, designed, or invented something?
- What was your bravest or most courageous moment?
- Have you ever received an award or special recognition?
- What's the most impulsive thing you've ever done?
- What's a story you never tired of hearing from your mom or dad?
- Were you ever unexpectedly left "carrying the ball," and you jumped to the plate?
- How have you increased sales (if that's ever been part of your job)?
- When have you identified problems others did not see?
- Have you ever developed or implemented a new system or procedure?
- When have you effectively handled a crisis situation (professional or personal)?
- Who's the most influential person you've met?
- Have you ever had an experience where you accomplished the seemingly impossible?
- When have you done something where you really had to laugh at yourself?
- Have you ever had an experience in a foreign country that was a revelation of cultural differences?
- What was the one moment or highlight in school you'll never forget?

- In which competitions have you excelled?
- When have you juggled many projects simultaneously under deadline pressure?
- What was the one event in your childhood that had the greatest effect on your life?
- What is the one lesson you've learned that you still live by today?

Creating trust through stories

Telling a story is a way to build trust. Every brand wants you to trust what it stands for. When you tell a story to your target audience, whether it be a business colleague, a child, your partner, or a friend, you're creating a bond with that person. A story lets your listeners decide for themselves whether they'll trust you and the brand you're presenting.

To create trust, you need to know how to tell a variety of stories about yourself:

- **Who are you?** This story doesn't need to be personal, but it does need to represent your values. This story shows your humanity and your ability to recognize your flaws.
- **Why are you telling this story?** This type of story reassures the audience that you have good intentions. It connects you with your audience and shares your reason for telling your story to these particular people at this particular time.
- **How does your vision relate to your audience's vision?** With this story, you share your own ideas about what's possible and connect them with what your audience wants to believe is possible.
- **What do you value?** This story helps your audience know what your values are and how they guide you in daily life.

When your storytelling skills are strong enough, you can also work on telling a story that anticipates what your audience is thinking. The goal is to make your listeners wonder if you've got psychic abilities! But really, what you're doing is simply paying close attention to your target audience and mirroring their hopes and concerns in your words. By doing so, you build empathy and create the foundation for strong relationships.

REMEMBER

Stories are designed to influence your listeners and are generally more effective than a recitation of facts. If you want to have the greatest influence possible, tell a story first and save the facts for afterward. When your audience is feeling connected with you, they'll be much more willing to hear the rest of your presentation.

Using stories in the workplace

Businesses have taken an interest in storytelling in recent years. They're finding that both employees and customers are more interested in listening to stories than to factual presentations.

Daphne A. Jameson, a business communications expert, researched the way language is used in business meetings. She found that when managers used storytelling to resolve conflicts and address difficult issues, they were more successful in communicating those conflicts. This insight especially applied to situations where a direct conversation wasn't possible. For example, say that one member of a team is behaving badly, but you can't call that person out in the team meeting. Instead, you can tell a story about a past difficult situation and what the group learned from the difficulty. You insert different players and hope the team understands the moral of the story. You are teaching a management lesson without naming names or pointing fingers.

Storytelling plays an important role in decision-making practices. Jameson's research shows that in meetings, managers prefer stories instead of theoretical arguments or statistical calculations. When the situations are complex, stories allow them to include more information and help the participants put the discussion in context. I often tell stories of past situations to illustrate a point that can help my clients navigate their problem situations. I guide them through story rather than tell them what to do. Through story, I illustrate complex relationships and create scenarios that help them better strategize their own plans.

Keeping gossip out of your brand

Gossip is a form of storytelling about what other people are doing. Gossip uses the same key elements of stories and usually includes a plot, characters, and a point of view. Americans loves gossip and have built an industry around the spreading of celebrity gossip in magazines, television shows, blogs, and other forms of communication.

However, being known as a gossip is bad for your brand. Gossip can hurt the reputations of all involved: the person spreading the rumors, as well as the person being talked about. A gossip gains a reputation as someone who can't mind his own business and, worse, can't be trusted. When people know you are a gossip, they always wonder what you're saying about them.

Think of it this way: Gossiping is like the dark side of networking. If you find yourself being a bit of a gossip, turn that ability to connect with others into being a dynamic networker. Say positive things about other people instead of negative things. Keep clear of gossip and foster your network instead.

Making your story memorable

Personal branding showcases your authenticity, and the strength of your brand is based on how others relate to your experiences and character. Today's economy is an experience economy where people crave experiences and want to connect to others in a personal and memorable way. If you don't create an experience, you won't stand out.

When you live your life authentically, your story and your connections with others create something special. That experience not only makes you memorable but also, with the right expression of who you are, leaves impressions that create a transformative experience for those who interact with you.

Crafting Your Personal Commercial

A number of terms can describe your professional introduction to another person — for example, the *elevator pitch,* the *30-second commercial,* or the *personal commercial.* Regardless of what you call this introduction, you need to be able to describe (quickly!) who you are, what you do, and the elements of your personal brand. Depending on your situation, this spiel may last from 15 seconds to usually no more than 2 minutes.

TIP

At its best, your personal commercial sparks the interest of the listener. You say something interesting to get that person's attention and ask for more information. The personal commercial is one of the most critical pieces of your communication toolbox because you use it to develop other tools, which I describe in Chapter 9.

I find that the personal commercial is one of the hardest pieces of the branding process for people to feel comfortable with. It seems to contradict all the messages you hear about not bragging or tooting your own horn. Discovering how to introduce yourself the right way, though, can boost your self-esteem.

Avoiding common mistakes

When you begin to build your personal commercial, you aren't really answering the full version of "Tell me about yourself." Not everyone in every situation cares to know all about you. Before you respond, you need to put your statement in context and adapt what you're going to say to your audience.

For example, if you were at your high school reunion, you might speak about yourself one way. You'd want a different message for a professional association or work-related meeting, however.

Common mistakes people make when introducing themselves include the following:

- **Being too personal in a business setting.** Telling a potential employer *"I love to eat bonbons and watch soap opera reruns on the weekends"* is bad form; no one cares except your closest friends. Also, be wary of sharing too much information about a difficult family situation — a divorce or illness, for example. Share only the basics of your personal life when first meeting a business colleague. (*"I'm married and have two grown children"* is perfectly appropriate.)
- **Giving your complete life chronology.** Almost always, such a retelling of your life story will be too much information. *"I was born in Minnesota, and we lived there until the third grade. Then we moved to Chicago where I went to two high schools."* Maybe — just maybe! — you'd share this kind of info on a first date with someone who seems really interested in you, but even then I'd caution you to err on the side of leaving some gaps.
- **Reciting your resume.** I'm talking about statements such as *"I was a department manager and then promoted to buyer. I stayed there three years and then was promoted to District Manager for two years."* If you're interviewing for a job or trying to win an interview, you want to home in on the highlights of your experience and skills. If you've already secured an interview, you can assume that the potential employer has spent time reading your resume and doesn't need to be reminded about every last detail.
- **Sharing inappropriate information about yourself and others.** Believe it or not, some people think it's okay to share info such as *"I was just at a medical appointment and had this mole removed."* Yikes! When you're introducing yourself to someone — whether for business or other purposes — steer clear of any subjects that could make your listener squirm.
- **Sharing inappropriate information about others.** I discuss the dangers of gossip in the section "Keeping gossip out of your brand," earlier in the chapter. Especially in a business context, saying something like *"My ex-boss was a bit of an alcoholic — I was always having to cover up for her"* is not going to win the trust of your audience. Show that you have some restraint and stay far away from gossip of any kind.

Another mistake some people make is relying completely on their rehearsed personal commercial when introducing themselves. I was running a networking group several years ago, and a man called to inquire about the group. I asked why he was interested, and he launched into his canned, well-rehearsed commercial that had nothing to do with me or the group I was running. I let him know in a very nice way that I wanted just to know a little about him and to put his commercial away. He fell silent and really didn't know how to talk to me. Don't be that guy. Understand who you're talking to and adjust your commercial to that audience.

Building your personal commercial

After you have a sense of what *not* to do, you're ready for some tips on how to introduce yourself effectively. I used to struggle to help my clients sound professional, unique, and personable. I was happy to discover a book called *Be Sharp* (BookSurge Publishing) by Paula Asinof and Mina Brown that brilliantly laid out a personal commercial in three key steps:

1. **Make your first impression.**

   Your *essence factor* describes the essential qualities you exhibit as a professional. Write three or four words that describe your essential qualities as a professional. Add an adjective that describes a dynamic quality about you. Describing your professional self this way sets the stage for a great first impression. For example, *"I'm Mary Brown. I am a strategic financial planner for Squirreled Away funds."*

2. **Be in the know.**

   Your *guru factor* identifies your knowledge and expertise. To find your guru factor, list your special areas of knowledge. Choose one or two areas of expertise that are relevant to your goals. If you struggle with this step, try finishing the statement "People recognize my expertise in . . . ."

   The guru factor is about what you know, not just what you do. For example, *"After spending 12 years with a major accounting firm, I took my expertise in financial management with key stakeholders and opened up my own firm."*

3. **Identify your best stuff.**

   Your *star factor* is what makes you special in how you get things done. It can describe your personal qualities, professional characteristics, or your style in how you apply those qualities to your work life. To find your star factor, list the qualities and attributes that set you apart from your peers. Choose a few that are important to your success and describe why they matter.

   The star factor includes words that describe you, such as "I'm known for . . . ," "I'm recognized for . . ., or "Others describe me as . . . ." Tell how your star factor is important to what you do. For example, *"Clients trust my advice and feel secure in how I manage their money."*

When you've taken all three steps, put them together to create your personal commercial:

> *I'm Mary Brown. I am a strategic financial planner for Squirreled Away funds. After spending 12 years with a major accounting firm, I took my expertise in financial management with key stakeholders and opened up my own firm. Clients trust my advice and feel secure in how I manage their money.*

Many cultures teach that it's impolite to talk about personal accomplishments. When you're creating your personal commercial, though, you shouldn't feel shy about what you've accomplished. Gather all this information as a factual account of what you know.

TIP

Not sure how to begin identifying your own accomplishments? In Chapter 4, I walk you through how to write accomplishment statements: powerful tools that show what you know, how you problem-solve, and that you can produce results. They also explain how someone benefited because of your actions. These statements form the foundation for your stories.

Aligning your message with your brand promise

I devote a good portion of Chapter 7 to explaining what your brand promise is. Delivering on your brand promise means putting into action what you want to be known for. When you understand your brand, you can more effectively tell your story. Doing so makes you able to live your brand in all aspects of your life.

After you draft your personal commercial, I encourage you to revisit your brand promise and make sure that it's represented in the message you plan to convey. If it isn't, you need to revise your personal commercial until the message and the brand promise are in synch.

REMEMBER

You want to be able to live up to your unique promise of value. Crafting a remarkable personal commercial — as well as other stories about yourself and your brand — is an impressive way to highlight to your audience what you're capable of doing.

Honing your personal pitch

Before you take your personal commercial on the road, here are a few tips to help you build your strategy:

- Know who you are talking to.
- Put yourself in the other person's shoes.
- Understand your personal brand and the unique promise of value that you bring to your audience (see Chapter 7).
- Be authentic in your enthusiasm for who you are and for what you do.
- Show confidence — even if you lack it. Don't let anyone see you sweat.
- Be genuinely personable.

- Convey a sense of presence.
- Avoid acronyms and technical jargon unless you're among people who understand what you're talking about.
- Keep it short and simple.
- Rehearse your statement over and over until it sounds natural (see the next section for tips).
- Rehearse some more (read the next section again!).

TIP

One clever strategy is to let the other person go first with introductions. That way, you have a better chance of knowing your audience before you begin speaking.

Practicing Your Pitch

After you craft your personal commercial, you need to practice it. When you do, try to be as objective as you can. As personal as this personal commercial feels, it's not personal. It's factual, and you need to talk about yourself with neutrality.

TIP

One technique I use with my clients is to have them pretend that they're describing someone else. I have them write their commercial in the third person and then go back and insert "I" for their name.

EXPERT OPINION

Bernadette Martin, author of *Storytelling About Your Brand Online & Offline* (Happy About), gives her basic formula to help put your pitch together. Follow these steps, filling in the blanks as you go:

1. **Hello, my name is . . . .**

   Include your title and company name.

2. **I work with . . .**

   Describe your target audience.

3. **who experience . . . ,**

   Add the challenge or problem.

4. **which means that . . . .**

   Give the outcome of the problem.

5. **What I do/offer is . . . .**

   Describe your product or service.

6. **This means that . . . .**

   List the outcome or the solution.

Bernadette gives an example of her 60-second commercial using this format.

> *My name is Bernadette, and I am Founder of Visibility Branding where I help individuals — who could be executives, entrepreneurs, professionals, MBA participants, or consultants — message the story about their personal brand and what makes them unique. My clients can be in career transition or just want to increase their professional visibility online and offline. Their challenge is often how to integrate social media into their communication strategy and how to write an effective bio. I help them in these areas, as well as with developing a networking strategy with a karma-based attitude. Working virtually or onsite in one-on-one or group sessions, my clients learn how to clearly communicate or tell the story about their personal brand in a compelling way to their target. As a start, I offer a complimentary personal brand assessment. Could we exchange contact information?*

TIP

When you actually deliver your personal commercial to a live person, pay attention to your handshake, make eye contact, and have good posture. (For more about image, see Chapter 12.)

Part III

Communicating Your Brand with the World

The 5th Wave By Rich Tennant

In this part . . .

In this part, I show you how to present a central message to the world. I help you write your own story — a story that, when pared down to its essence, becomes your very own commercial. I also demonstrate how to tailor all the traditional tools of business communication (including resumes, cover letters, and bios) to highlight your story and promote your brand.

Because so much communication occurs in the virtual world, I devote an entire chapter to taking your personal brand online and making it stand out in a sea of bloggers and social media users.

Finally, I demonstrate how to craft a savvy communications plan so that you can reach out to the appropriate people; become known as a trusted expert; present a clear, consistent, and constant message; and stay ever-present in the minds of your target audience.

Chapter 9

Branding Your Traditional Communication Tools

In This Chapter

- Producing a great resume, bio, and cover letter
- Crafting effective presentations and articles
- Appealing to the public in speeches and on television

You may assume that you communicate pretty well because, after all, *you* understand what you're talking about! The truth is that most people don't communicate well. In face-to-face situations, they don't really listen to what others are saying, don't pick up nonverbal cues, and don't speak clearly and effectively to communicate their own message. And in writing — when voice and appearance are removed from the communication equation — they may struggle even more.

This chapter is full of information about how to master the traditional communication tools that you can use to promote your personal brand. I show you how to maintain consistency and get your point across whether you're writing a resume or a cover letter, shaping a presentation or an article, or giving a presentation or a TV interview. (When you're ready to dive in to the details of communicating your brand online, be sure to check out Chapter 10.)

Setting Yourself Up for Success: Branded Job Search Documents

In this section, I cover how to create communication tools that are most often associated with a job search. I'd like you to think about these documents through a personal branding lens. Personal branding highlights your uniqueness and makes each document more than a set of facts. Your goal is to tell your brand's story — to engage and impress your audience with your personality as well as your skills — whether via your resume, bio, or cover letter.

Before you work on these tools, I share some tips and the introduction to a case study so that you can better understand how personal branding comes into play when creating them.

Showcasing your talents in writing

Kelly Welch, a Career Branding Strategist at YES Career Services, is a featured contributor to this chapter. Kelly wrote a case study called "The Story of Daniel Perlino" (which you can read in the next section) so that you have concrete examples of each type of job search tool discussed in this section. The case study is based on a real person, whose name has been changed.

Welch offers the following tips about creating branded documents:

- Present the same philosophies, sayings, taglines, and attributes throughout your documents to gain consistency.
- Use a thesaurus to look for similar words that convey consistency in branding without being overly repetitive. (Just don't go overboard and try to include every possible synonym for your keywords!)
- Identify your target audience carefully and understand what compels them (see Chapter 5). Then, reflect that information in your unique promise of value (see Chapter 7) that speaks to your audience in a compelling and relevant way.
- Seek to understand the problems that your target market faces and then offer solutions that highlight your brand.
- Communicate your message clearly, consistently, and constantly in order to attract the most relevant opportunities. (See Chapter 11 for my discussion of these three Cs.)
- Tune out the noise! Leave off details that don't support or promote your brand. This step is important to gain a clear and memorable message.
- Use brand attributes that are visible in everything you do. All your written materials (as well as your spoken communication) should tie back to your personal brand attributes (see Chapter 4). For example, you'll soon find out that Daniel Perlino (described in the next section) is creative, energetic, and collaborative; these attributes should be highlighted in every part of his communication.
- Practice writing and talking about your brand attributes and strengths when recounting your career stories or when strategizing a new plan. By doing so, you stay true to your core message and gain comfort and confidence when communicating about it.

Meeting a case study: The story of Daniel Perlino by Kelly Welch

Daniel came to me by referral of another client, who used to be his colleague. Daniel carefully admitted that even though he was a corporate product brand manager and master salesman, he did not understand how to brand himself. He could not ascertain his standout factors or articulate what attributes drove his behaviors. He was clueless as to how to tell stories about his achievements and extremely shy about self-promotion. Moreover, he was unsure how to thread a consistent message across all his career marketing materials. I knew he had come to the right place.

Daniel worked through a process that took about two and a half months. In that time, I coached him on his inner workings and strengths, and I gave him assessments that reflected how he and those around him view him as a "brand." We had deep discussions about the meanings behind his answers to critical homework exercises I assigned him. He took his work very seriously, was genuine and interested, and was always prepared. He even created a beautiful, color-coded mind map of his progress that included all the aspects of his life that the assignment related to. I was impressed with his approach to our work, as well as with how much he did consider impressive about himself.

Daniel came away with a fresh idea of who his target audience *really* was and what his unique value proposition was to attract them. He discovered his focus was on small to medium pharmaceutical companies looking for an energetic leader who was creative, inclusive, and tenacious in pursuing "good to great" campaigns and a motivating atmosphere. We built his communication toolkit to include a branded resume, branded biography, branded LinkedIn profile, and branded, targeted cover letter.

In the end, Daniel gained offers in consulting and for permanent positions of employment. After much careful comparison to his vision, mission, and overall brand, he accepted a generous offer to return to the earliest firm on his resume — a firm that had promoted him rapidly and purposefully rotated him through developmental assignments. He is now happily working within an agile, newly acquired group inside that firm, playing to his strengths and feeling true to his genuine brand.

Daniel's branded message boils down to this:

> Creative ⇨ Energetic ⇨ Collaborative

He sends this message regardless of the type of document he is crafting.

Creating a branded resume

The primary function of any resume is to create a picture of how you want to be seen now and in the future. When you create a *branded resume,* you use your personal brand to infuse your resume with your unique qualities. The result is a job search tool you're proud of that highlights your brand promise (see Chapter 7).

In other words, you want your branded resume to illuminate who you are and what you stand for. You can position this information in a summary section at the top of the resume, in a quote (from a professional colleague or a performance review) that is highlighted on the resume, and/or in an experience section that features your key accomplishments listed in bullet points.

A branded resume has some key elements that set it apart from a standard chronological laundry list of what you have done. To get your resume read, you need to show your *unique promise of value,* the personal aspect of your brand that is the essence of what you have to offer. Your unique promise of value clarifies and communicates what makes you different from other people. As I explain throughout Part II of this book, arriving at your own unique promise of value requires understanding your strengths and using them to distinguish yourself for a specific opportunity.

To create a branded resume:

- Use your brand promise in the summary section and revisit it in other parts of the resume. Show that you are energized and passionate about your work.
- Write accomplishment statements that highlight the valuable contributions that differentiate you from others.
- Don't waste space on lame, clichéd words. Use powerful descriptors that give substance to your brand.
- Break away from boring and let your enthusiasm shine through in your statements.
- Deliver the message that you want to send to your target market. Emphasize the experience that promotes your brand and minimize your off-brand work history.
- Remember to reflect who you are now and who you aspire to be. Let your resume have a future focus.
- Make the design of your resume align with your brand identity. (Chapter 13 addresses your visual identity.)

Most resumes will be two pages long. However, someone new to the workplace or returning to the workplace after a long absence faces special challenges when crafting a resume. Often without the work experience to fall back on, creating a branded resume seems much harder. After all, you just don't have as many accomplishments on which to draw. In cases where professional experience is lacking, creating a one-page resume featuring community service or internship experience is perfectly acceptable. *Resumes For Dummies* by Joyce Lain Kennedy (John Wiley & Sons, Inc.) offers lots of information and examples that may help.

Figure 9-1 present Daniel Perlino's branded resume. Note some of the branded highlights in Daniel's resume:

- In the summary paragraph at the top, he uses phrases like "Participative management style" that speak to elements of his personal brand.
- In the experience section (labeled "Career Narrative" on Daniel's resume), the phrase "Reinvigorated relationships" again reinforces his brand.
- Two quoted sections (one on each page of the resume) provide powerful testimony indicating that other people have recognized Daniel's brand attributes.

Penning your branded biography

A *branded biography* is a narrative of your brand story. It tells the story of your unique promise value to your target audience. Your bio needs to emotionally connect with your readers and be written in a way that engages them. It positions you for how you want to be known going forward while giving relevant confirmation of your experience and qualifications. It expresses who you are, what you offer, and what is important to you.

Bios are most frequently written for people in the workforce who wish to emphasize their professional accomplishments. However, you can write a bio during *any* stage in your life. A bio tells your story to an identified audience that is important to you. If you're looking for work after an absence from the workplace, for example, that story could focus on your achievements in raising a family, performing community service, serving in the military, or completing your new college degree.

555.555.5555
Annapolis, MD

DANIEL PERLINO, MBA

danperlino@gmail.com
linkedin.com/danperlino

MARKETING EXECUTIVE | BIOPHARMACEUTICALS

Known for a winning record of accomplishments by consistently applying a "good to great" mantra across the board. Confident, win-win problem solver who walks the talk. Participative management style drives ideas from *me* to *we* with resounding success. Brand champion with marketing and sales lenses. Recent accomplishments in both new product launch / lifecycle planning.

Product Launches ▪ Brand Strategy ▪ Sales Management ▪ Managed Care Marketing
Cardiovascular ▪ CNS ▪ Dermatology ▪ Endocrinology ▪ GI ▪ HIV ▪ Infectious Disease ▪ Oncology ▪ Respiratory
Matrix Empowerment ▪ Situational Leadership ▪ KOL Diplomacy

CAREER NARRATIVE

SENIOR DIRECTOR, STRATEGIC BRAND MANAGEMENT
Pharmascope, Inc. ▪ 2009 to Present
Recruited to immediately organize, develop, and launch two brands within a 12-month period. Promptly developed the positioning and messaging platform for back-to-back launches of two GI brands, SENALTA and AKRINEN. Leveraged launch planning capabilities to develop awareness campaign for a new drug development facility in France. Successfully integrated a new agency of record. Four direct reports.

- Accelerated the launch planning process for two back-to-back IBD brands.
- Captured launch goals for SENALTA by capturing 9% share of the once-daily market segment within 6 months.
- Exceeded expectations of early adoption with 15% of GI's prescribing SENALTA within 90 days.
- Designed and implemented the first web-based interactive patient compliance program for Pharmascope.
- Reinvigorated relationships with the Sales Force, gained trust and partnership to propel global launches and presence.

> *"I know I speak for our entire team when I say how impressed I am...This has been the most seamless and energizing launch in terms of available resources plus clarity of value proposition coming out of the gates that I have ever seen in 19 years of pharma experience."* Executive VP's comments, day after SENALTA launch.

EXECUTIVE DIRECTOR, ALLIANCE MANAGEMENT
ClinVar Group, a division of Biovast ▪ 2004 to 2009
Recruited to govern a portfolio of commercial alliances that represented a market value of approximately $150M. Provided commercial direction for NDA submissions, assisted with commercial due diligence, and partnered with each alliance CEO to maximize the launch of their respective brands.

- Governed team charters for the launch of two brands: TROVOX — CCJ Labs / QUIMOL — Geneu Labs.
- Collaborated with R&D and project management for Phase III clinical trial for the alliance with TANDOL.
- Improved alliance ROI 23% by developing and implementing an Alliance Management Training Guide.
- Co-authored white paper on the value of alliance management and due diligence as an emerging capability.

SENIOR DIRECTOR, PHARMACEUTICAL ALLIANCES & MANAGED CARE MARKETING
SciMatrix, Inc ▪ 2002 to 2004
Manufacturer of the HXG IDPROFILE Infectious Disease risk diagnostic.
Recruited to direct the commercial strategy for contracting, and account management with Managed Care Organizations (MCO). In addition, directed late-phase clinical research alliances with Clinsos, FKL, and Tanio, Inc.

- Accelerated a contract strategy that increased revenue by $5.4M, or 19% of total income within 6 months.
- Developed a new tactical plan targeting MCO Medical Directors that increased sales by 21% in 6 months.
- Employed, 'hire tough, manager easy' motto to hire, train, and coach four *star performing* Account Managers.

Kelly Welch.

Pharmastarion • 1988 to 2002
Promoted or rotated for development six times through roles in both marketing and sales management. *Highlights:*

Directed the end-to-end strategic and tactical marketing campaigns:

Drug:	**RINATOL**	**ZINCIL**	**Dermatology Franchise**
Annual Sales:	**$1.28B**	**$734M**	**$573M**

- Developed lifecycle campaign that rapidly increased sales by $87M for ZINCIL within 6 months.
- Devised an innovative targeting strategy that grew RINATOL market share by 9% within in 90 days.
- Gained wide approval from both VPs of Sales and Marketing for instituting a fresh and highly effective means for coordinating and implementing new tactical marketing programs.
- Directed regional launches for SURVASE, RINATOL 100MG TABS, PALNON, INTROVAN, ANOSTAT, and XALTIN.
- Created and distributed a new marketing capabilities tool to streamline launch planning for newly appointed brand directors and brand managers.

Titles held:
- DIRECTOR, US COMMERCIALIZATION & LAUNCH PLANNING
- SENIOR PRODUCT MANAGER
- SENIOR REGIONAL MARKET DEVELOPMENT MANAGER
- SENIOR MANAGER, SALES & MARKETING OPERATIONS
- DISTRICT MANAGER
- SENIOR SALES REPRESENTATIVE

"Daniel has played several key roles in his tenure, and never fails to innovate campaigns and empower his teams and partners to heights beyond expectations. He 'walks the talk', and he delivers." — Excerpt from senior management team on 360° performance review.

EDUCATION

- MBA, Marketing — Stephen M. Ross School of Business, Michigan State University, Ann Arbor, MI
- BS, Business Administration and French — Columbia University, New York, NY
- Medical Marketing Certification — New York University, New York, NY

Figure 9-1: Daniel Perlino's branded resume.

Kelly Welch.

Here are some other specific situations when a bio can be very useful:

- If you write a work proposal, a bio offers insight into who will be working on the assignment.
- On your website, you likely want to include a bio in the "About Us" section.
- If you plan to give a speech, you want to give your host a bio so that you can be properly introduced.
- When you're looking for a job, a bio offers potential employers and network contacts an overview of who you are that is more personal than a resume.
- If you have the opportunity to serve as a committee chair, your bio can be shared with constituents of the committee so that they understand your qualifications.
- Eagle Scouts write bios to present themselves at an Eagle Court of Honor.
- Authors write short bios that appear in their books.

Biographies are especially powerful when your resume looks disjointed or when your experience doesn't follow a traditional path. A bio can weave the threads of your work experience and your personal brand message into a meaningful story that makes sense to the reader.

Your bio should feature information from the personal brand profile table in Chapter 7. You want to include your interests, strengths, personal descriptors, unique promise of value, and personal brand statement. The bio should effectively complete these statements:

- People recognize my expertise in . . .
- I know I am in my element when . . .

In other words, what are you really good at? And what things do you do related to this target audience that you have enthusiasm for?

If you read Chapter 8 and worked on writing your stories, they definitely come in handy when creating a branded bio. Tell one or two shortened versions of those same stories in your bio to show your accomplishments through an interesting narrative. To find out more about crafting an excellent professional biography, I suggest that you read *Be Sharp* (CreateSpace Publishing) by Paula Asinof and Mina Brown. If you need additional help with the writing process, you can always hire a professional resume writer to write your biography for you.

Figure 9-2 shows Daniel Perlino's branded biography. (For more on Daniel, see the section "Meeting a case study: The Story of Daniel Perlino," earlier in this chapter.) Note how the biography catches your attention with the first sentence. Not only does his bio tell you what he does — *a creative strategic marketing leader* — but also it tells you how he does it — *with a love of life and a passion for excellence.* Both what he does and how he does it are important elements of his brand. Read his bio to discover how the language used paints a picture of his skill set and his personality. His bio ends with some keywords that remind the reader of his key knowledge and show his personal brand's leadership style.

DANIEL PERLINO, MBA

PROFESSIONAL BIOGRAPHY

Cardiovascular ▪ CNS ▪ Dermatology ▪ Endocrinology ▪ GI ▪ HIV ▪ Infectious Disease ▪ Oncology

Daniel Perlino is a creative strategic marketing leader with a love of life and a passion for excellence. He has extensive brand expertise in the therapeutic areas of oncology, HIV, respiratory, cardiovascular, migraine, and antibiotics. He derives energy by adapting to rapidly changing business conditions and is always "looking for a better way to do things." Truly playing to his strengths as a confident visionary and motivator, Daniel has created and led blockbuster marketing campaigns with annual sales exceeding $1.25B. He has provided the tactical vision for commercial alliances, strategic client services, and commercialization and launch planning.

Daniel consistently applies his "good to great" mantra and counts himself fortunate to have had multiple wins in the specialty pharmaceuticals arena. Most recently, as Senior Director, Strategic Brand Management for Pharmascope, Inc., Daniel's collaborative, rallying approach led the strategic vision and positioning for a new gastroenterology franchise. He represented two brands with projected revenue of $200M; under his leadership the sales exploded at record speed. His ability to manage through obstacles became very apparent as he simultaneously managed the lifecycle transition of another brand to generic.

Before this, Daniel accepted a proposal to join the ClinVar Group as Executive Director, Alliance Management. In this role, he managed an investment portfolio of three commercial alliances with a market value of $150M by cultivating relationships with the partner CEOs and building efficiencies within the processes.

Previously, Daniel was recruited to join SciMatrix as the Senior Director of Pharmaceutical alliances and Managed Care Marketing. In his tenure, he increased Managed Care sales by 21 percent in just six months. He also revamped the contract strategy, increasing revenue by $5.4M (19 percent) within his first six months.

Daniel launched his career in business development at Pharmastarion, Inc., immediately winning recognition as a best-in-class salesperson. He progressed aggressively through sales and product management positions of increasing responsibility. Rising up the ladder, Daniel has always threaded his success with his resolve to finding win-win solutions.

Behind him, Daniel leaves a legacy of accomplishment by innovation and perspiration in his wake. He holds true to his personal commitment to leverage the energy of his organization and to exceed company objectives. He uses his grounded persona and sense of humor to lead by example and involve and motivate his teams.

Daniel holds an MBA in Marketing from the Stephen M. Ross School of Business at Michigan State University, and a BA in Business Administration and French from Columbia University. He resides in Annapolis, Maryland, with his wife and three children.

Product Launches ▪ Brand Strategy ▪ Sales Management ▪ Managed Care Marketing

▪▪▪

Matrixed Empowerment ▪ Situational Leadership ▪ KOL Diplomacy

Figure 9-2: An example of a branded biography.

Kelly Welch.

Writing letters of introduction

Your cover letter or letter of introduction offers you the opportunity to connect with your reader in a more personal way than afforded in a resume. This letter differs from a branded bio because it's more concise and formal, and it's tailored to the specific work opportunity available. In the letter, you can express your personal brand and point the reader to sections of your resume that you would like to draw attention to.

The cover letter is written in the first person and should be tailored to each reader personally; you don't want it to sound like a template. This is your opportunity to discuss your understanding of the targeted company's issues and use past accomplishments to show your ability to solve similar problems. You want to be sure to promote your authentic self in the letter (not overstating your achievements or minimizing your skills) and show your strong value proposition (your unique promise of value).

Your cover letter may mirror much of what you have written in either the bio or the summary section of your resume. People often worry that they are repeating themselves. As long as your materials are written well and send a clear message, repetition is fine! Your job in the cover letter is to paint the picture for your reader of what you have to offer and to look interesting enough to compel the reader to spend time with your resume or bio.

Here are some fundamentals to keep in mind while writing the letter of introduction:

- Let your personal brand shine through. (In doing so, you'll let your personality shine through as well.)
- Make sure that everything is spelled correctly and that you use proper punctuation.
- Address the letter to a person whenever possible. Even if the job description asks you to send your materials to a blind box or to "Human Resources," do some research and try to find out the name of the person you would report to if you got the job. Address the letter to that person, but be sure to follow directions and send the letter to the blind box or HR department or wherever the description states.
- Remember that your goal is to convey what you can do for the employer and how you will help solve their problems.
- Summarize your experience, highlighting your best stuff.
- Keep your letter to just one page.

- Send references only when you're asked and never write the phrase "references available upon request." That fact is assumed, and the phrase is tired and outdated.
- Proofread your letter before you send it! Read it aloud to yourself and listen to how it sounds. Ask someone else to proofread it as well.

Figure 9-3 shows a cover letter written by Daniel Perlino. (For more on Daniel, see the earlier section "Meeting a case study: The story of Daniel Perlino.) Note that his letter begins by emphasizing his brand attributes ("my creative, energetic, and collaborative approach") that appear in all of his documents. He then highlights his strengths in the center of the letter, where he gives specific examples of what he can do. After providing an overview of his career, he ends with a statement of action ("I will call you on Tuesday, January 25th to follow up"). If you are sending a letter to a blind box or an HR department, meaning that you don't know exactly who to follow up with, you might substitute a sentence like "I look forward to meeting or speaking with you soon."

Compiling a printed portfolio

A *portfolio* is a collection of documents that validate your accomplishments and professional achievements when you go on a job interview (or when you meet with a new client). This tool helps you remember all that you have done in your past to build your personal brand. Portfolios provide evidence of your credibility. Having possession of your documents not only provides proof of your work to use as a marketing tool but gives you the confidence to speak to your brand.

Your portfolio may be compiled in a section of your file cabinet, scanned into an electronic file on your computer, or put into a file box. These days, portfolios are often saved to online repositories, such as `www.manifestyourpotential.com` and `www.efolioworld.com`, that provide electronic access to all these documents.

But even as society moves away from paper and toward the computing cloud, I encourage you to create a portfolio binder that contains paper copies of documents that demonstrate who you are. Sharing such a binder with a prospective employer or new client is an impressive way to highlight and prove that you have done what you have said you could do on your resume. This printed portfolio is especially helpful for people who need to show writing samples or visual representation of their work.

Victoria Chalmers, President
Baylon Research
444 Medicine Way
Any Town, NJ 12345

January 19, 2011

Re: Pharmaceutical Marketing Brand Director

Dear Ms. Chalmers,

I am thrilled to lead complex pharmaceutical brand launch initiatives that bring promise or hope for those consumers who so desperately look for it. I seek out specifically challenging campaigns so that I can truly leverage my creative, energetic, and collaborative approach and propel those brands to success. I understand that Baylon Research is poised for a breakthrough launch. Considering me for the Brand Director position will ensure your firm has the best positioning for increased market share.

To illustrate some points of support:
Matrix Empowerment and Leadership: I have the unique capability to rapidly gain the confidence and respect of R&D teams through Sales and Key Opinion Leaders, which has led to many notable wins.

Alliance Management: I strategize to set the foundation for long-term success with alliance team charters. Garnering near-immediate trust paves the way for establishing long-term partnerships.

Champion of Change: I have a tenacious commitment to gain clarity, refine objectives, and seek a better way to do things. I energize the matrix players around evolution for the good of the brand.

My career has been marked by progressive promotions with challenging assignments. This is a key reason why I am interested in Baylon Research. I have admired your company as a strong competitor of my most recent employer, and I firmly believe that my marketing, sales, and alliance management background are just what Baylon needs to set it on a trajectory toward a blockbuster future!

I look forward to presenting my qualifications in greater detail. Thank you for consideration. I will call you on Tuesday, January 25 to follow up.

Sincerely,

Daniel Perlino

Enclosure (resume)

Figure 9-3: A sample cover letter.

Kelly Welch.

Taking writing and computer classes

I communicate for my profession, yet I often feel I will fall behind at any minute. There is so much to learn just to keep up, let alone keep ahead of the curve! Consider taking classes to boost your communication skills, whether college courses, online courses, webinars, or self-study courses.

If you feel unsure about your basic writing skills, take a basic composition class at your local community college or sign up for an online course. If getting credit is not important, audit the class so that you feel you can learn without having to perform for a grade. If you've got a handle on the basics but want to improve as a writer, look for business technical writing classes (or even creative writing classes, depending on what you do for a living and the type of audience you're trying to attract).

In addition, the hottest adult education classes (including at libraries and community centers) focus on how to use technology to communicate your message. If you feel uncertain about your computer skills, consider taking a class in social media strategies, using LinkedIn or Facebook, publishing your own newsletter, or designing your website. And you can always improve your skills through the use of web-based training or YouTube how-to videos. (You can find out how to do just about anything through a YouTube video! Pick a topic, such as "how to write a better business e-mail," and you may be surprised what you'll find.)

Here are some things to include in your portfolio:

- Your branded resume
- Your branded biography
- Letters of recommendation, at least one or two of which are current
- Sample projects
- Articles that you have written
- Past business cards
- Academic degrees
- Certifications and licenses
- Employee reviews
- A list of key successes from your work
- A list of awards you have received
- Volunteer service documents
- A list of professional contributions, such as committees you have chaired or evidence of how you have contributed to your profession

- Thank-you notes you have received
- Social networking site profiles
- Print copies of multimedia presentations you have created

Taking Your Message Public

When you embody your personal brand, you also find your voice. This process can take you to a new level of confidence where you want to express what you think and what you know. By taking your message to the public, you can become known as a thought leader in your particular area of expertise.

In this section, I offer tips for mastering traditional types of public communication: printed articles, speeches/presentations, and television interviews. Of course, more and more often, people are establishing their expertise and reaching out to their audiences online, so be sure to check out Chapter 10 as well.

Reaching a wider audience with articles

Articles express your expertise and help develop your presence as a thought leader in a particular area. Writing articles is much easier than writing a book and can expose you to a large number of people in your target market. If you write with frequency, you can become known as an expert in a relatively short period of time.

Not sure where you would try to get an article published? Most professional groups have a newsletter and are often looking for people to write articles for them. You may not be paid, but the point is to get yourself in front of new readers; you reap rewards by building your reputation. Also, search for reputable websites that relate to your field of interest and expertise; fresh, well-written content should find an online home fairly easily. In Chapter 5, I show you how to identify your target audience. Begin with that information and develop a list of print and electronic media to contact regarding article submissions.

As far as what you should write about, ask yourself these questions:

- When I'm talking about my work, what do I enjoy discussing?
- Who would like to read what I'm qualified to write about?
- What topics demonstrate my expertise?

If you're writing with a specific newsletter, website, or other medium in mind, be sure to inquire about the preferred length of an article and whether you need to follow any specific conventions when writing. The more closely you align your material with the medium's needs, the greater your chances of having an article accepted.

If you're comfortable with writing, ideally you want to generate articles on a regular basis so that your name stays fresh in the minds of your audience members.

Mastering public speaking and presentations

In survey after survey, people rank public speaking as one of the scariest things in the world. Speaking in public ranks right up there with death! That's because people are afraid of not knowing what to say, forgetting their words, looking dumb, or being rejected.

One of the quickest ways to ruin a speech or presentation is to deliver a message that feels false. As I note often in this book, a personal brand stems from living your authentic self from the inside out. To be a truly great presenter, you need to learn to speak from your genuine center. Audiences know when you're not coming from your true self and can feel when a presenter is disingenuous. For example, I once attended a presentation given by a well-known and highly regarded speaker (who charged high fees!). She had interesting things to say, but everyone in the audience could feel that she didn't really care about the people she was speaking to. Her content was spoken with authority, but she had no connection with her audience. Most people walked away disappointed and felt ripped off by her presentation.

With so many ways to go astray, should you just avoid speeches and presentations altogether? Of course not! You want to put yourself in front of your target audience whenever you have the right opportunity. Just be sure you're ready to deliver the genuine goods.

Toastmasters International suggests tips, which I've adapted to help you overcome your fears and deliver a winning speech, whether you're giving a presentation in front of five colleagues or standing in front of a packed, 2,000-seat auditorium:

- **Be knowledgeable about your subject and choose something you are interested in.** Know more about the subject than you include in your speech. Use humor, personal stories, and conversational language to enhance your speech.

- **Rehearse, make adjustments, and rehearse some more!** Rehearse out loud with all equipment you plan on using. Time yourself and make sure that your speech flows easily. Revise as necessary.
- **Understand who you are speaking to.** Say hello to the audience members as they arrive.
- **Familiarize yourself with the room.** Arrive early and get comfortable with the speaking area. Practice using the microphone and visual aids.
- **Take a deep breath, and smile.** Begin by addressing the audience. Pause, smile, and count to three before you say anything. Transform nervous energy into enthusiasm.
- **Visualize giving a successful speech.** Imagine yourself speaking with a loud, clear, and confident voice.
- **Recognize that people want you to do well.** They are happy that you're the one giving the speech and not them. Audiences want you to be authentic, interesting, informative, and entertaining.
- **Don't remind your audience about mistakes or apologize for your nervousness** — the audience probably didn't notice it.
- **Focus on the message.** Draw your attention away from your own nervousness so that you can concentrate on your message and your audience.
- **Your speech should represent your personal brand** — as an authority and as a person. Experience builds confidence, which is the key to successful speaking.

Consider joining Toastmasters (`www.toastmasters.org`) to improve your public speaking skills. Toastmasters International is a global leader that helps people learn to communicate more effectively. Toastmasters trains its members to become more confident speakers through weekly participation in speaking groups. Toastmasters is great skill-building training, and many people enjoy the community building aspects of the speaking groups as an added benefit.

Developing your personal brand on television

This section was written by Tara Kachaturoff, the creator, producer, and host of Michigan Entrepreneur TV.

Television is the ultimate branding experience where all the components of your personal brand blend together in a three-dimensional expression of who you are. From your first contact with the producer or media representative, to the final handshake as you leave the studio after taping, each and every interface provides an opportunity to express your very best.

Whether you're scheduled to appear on network television or a local cable station, everything you do, from your first interface with producers, to doing the actual interview, is revealing your personal brand. Regardless of the media venue, professionalism trumps all. You never know what connections you may make or what opportunity may lead to your next big break. Always be mindful that your reputation will precede you!

Keep your television debut in perspective. While your heart may beat uncontrollably when you land your very first TV interview, the reality is that your reputation or personal brand is only as good as the last interface anyone had with you. How people experience your personal brand is an ever-evolving experience, not a one-time event. And chances are this first-time experience will not be the last time you're in the media's eye!

Unless you're an A-list celebrity, any inklings of being a "high-maintenance" guest can potentially jeopardize your opportunity. Everyone is busy; and TV shows have deadlines, policies, and procedures. Do your homework up front, or have your PR person do it for you. Do whatever you can to meet the host's requirements, or else you risk the chance that the whole experience may unravel — and very quickly.

Preparing for your TV debut

If you want to make the best impression during your TV debut, you've got homework to do! Here are some ideas for how to get ready:

- **Use a folder to keep all your notes about your upcoming appearance in one place.** This helpful reference reduces stress and serves as a useful resource for future media events.
- **Listen to and follow all the instructions you receive from your producer or other contact.** Ask this person what to wear, what to bring, and any other necessary details.
- **Make a list of the names, titles, and contact information of everyone you interface with.** Take notes after each conversation and note any follow-up items.
- **Watch several episodes of the show.** Note the general format, how the host interacts with guests, conversation patterns, segment lengths, appropriate dress, and so on.
- **Draft notes around your interview topic.** Include key talking points. Keep in mind that your interview may be heavily edited and may turn out differently than expected. Don't rehearse or memorize anything.
- **Pack everything you need a day or two prior so that you don't forget anything.** If you're an author, pack several autographed copies of your book to present to the host. Make sure that you have directions to the studio and its phone number.

Your appearance

Following are tips for ensuring that your hair, clothing, and makeup are appropriate for the interview:

- **If time permits, have your hair professionally styled prior to taping.** This is definitely not the time to experiment with a new hair color or cut. It's amazing what you can do with a little trim and a lot of hairspray!
- **Clothing does make the man or woman, especially when it comes to your personal brand.** Select garments that sum you up at a glance — those that are on brand for you. Accessories like glasses and jewelry are fine but should be muted so as not to distract viewers. Avoid noisy jewelry like bracelets because the microphones magnify sounds. Don't wear patterned clothing and avoid wearing solid black, white, or red because they don't come across well on camera. Also, avoid wearing clothes that blend in with the background. You may want to bring an extra outfit just in case you decide to do a last-minute wardrobe change.
- **Wear makeup.** Not just for women, makeup application is an essential ingredient to freshen your look, even out skin tones, and make you look your best under the bright lights and camera close-ups. The crew will probably add extra liner under your eyes to make them more visible, and depending on the venue, they may actually do your full makeup.

On the day of the interview

Here's what to do when the big day arrives:

- **Warm up your voice on the way to the studio.** Sing along with the radio or talk through your key points as you're driving. It's a great way to get energized and psyched-up at the same time!
- **Arrive early so that you have time to acclimate to the studio environment.** Doing so also helps you calm any jittery nerves. Introduce yourself and shake hands with staff as these simple gestures decrease stress immediately.
- **Be prepared for things to change.** Much can happen between the time you're invited as a guest and when you "go live." The key is to go with the flow and be flexible and accommodating.

After the show

When your interview is over, you still have a few things to do:

- **Send the host a handwritten note of thanks for the invitation.** Few people send thank-you notes, so you're certain to stand out.
- **Immediately write everything you remember about your experience.** Describe the people you met, how you felt, what you enjoyed, the highlights of your interview, and anything that memorializes the experience.

You'll be glad you captured the moment because this material may be usable for a future book, blog posts, or other projects. Also, write down how you can leverage this opportunity to convey and further extend your brand message to your target audience.

- **Find out how you can obtain a copy of the interview for your own use.** Be mindful of copyright issues and how you're allowed to use the material. Check with the producer for more information and secure any necessary permission.
- **Celebrate.** While it's easy to do a self-critique of your interview — what you didn't do and what you could have done better — instead choose to celebrate your success and the fact you've had the opportunity to share and offer value to others.

Above all, keep moving forward. Remember, this is one step on a much longer personal branding journey!

Chapter 10

Communicating Your Brand Online

In This Chapter

- Staying on message
- Creating a website or blog
- Using LinkedIn, Facebook, Twitter, and other social media
- Adding online video or podcasts to further your brand
- Managing your reputation online

What was the last message you posted online for the world to read? How about the last picture you posted? If a complete stranger were to read that message and view that picture, what impression would she get of who you are and what you stand for? Would she think you're thoughtful and organized? Silly and playful? Rude and disrespectful?

Maybe you don't intend for your personal brand to be viewed online by people who are in the position to hire or evaluate you. But guess what? It will be. So you absolutely *must* pay attention to what your online presence says about you. If you ignore your online presence, or if you assume that you don't even have one because you've never joined any professional sites or done any online networking, you run the risk of letting other people create your image for you. Don't! Get proactive about how you present yourself online. In this chapter, I show you how to communicate a positive message about your brand online.

Determining Your Online Message

Your future employers, competitors, and fellow employees could be searching your name online right at this moment. Does that fact make you excited or uncomfortable? Are you certain you know what these people will find when they look for you?

In a 2011 study by Jobvite on social recruiting, 89 percent of respondents said that they will recruit for positions in their companies through social media this year. Before you interview with a potential employer, attend a business meeting where you'll meet new colleagues, or give a presentation, the people you're going to meet will almost certainly do some homework to find out about you. A savvy business person checks out anyone he's going to meet to get a sense of who this person is: what her qualifications are, where she went to school, and whether she looks like she'll be good to do business with. Therefore, your online presence often creates the first impression of who you are.

The earlier chapters in this book walk you through the process of understanding why your personal brand matters and constructing a brand message that represents you effectively. Your message online needs to be based on the same principles that I explain in those chapters. Your message online highlights your unique promise of value, the promise that you make to your target market that your brand will fulfill. (I discuss target markets in Chapter 5 and your unique promise of value in Chapter 7.) Your promise of value is the essence of what you have to offer and guides you in how you will communicate your personal brand online. It clarifies and communicates what makes you special — what makes you different from other people.

Your online message should describe the essential qualities you exhibit as a professional. You want to identify your knowledge and expertise, as well as what makes you special in how you get things done. Your message should exhibit your personal qualities, your professional characteristics, and your style in how you apply those qualities to your work life.

Social media impressions can be even more personal than your written communication tools (see Chapters 8 and 9) because your online presence almost certainly includes visual elements, including pictures of you. Your visual message needs to send the same consistent message as what you write or say.

Attracting Your Audience to a Profile Hub

A *profile hub* is any central source online — such as a website, blog site, or personal web page — that guides people who are interested in your services to the multiple paths in which you communicate. Using a profile hub allows you to influence the impression that people have about you when they search for your name. You can set the look and feel of your brand, and the hub acts as a portal for the information seeker to find out about you.

Your profile hub can serve as a central point for all your sites, including your blog, LinkedIn profile page, Twitter and Facebook accounts, YouTube channel, Flckr photo gallery, and other online platforms. By coming to your central hub, people get a good idea of who you are and what you do.

Content for your profile can include

- A brief bio about who you are
- Links to your social media sites (such as LinkedIn, Twitter, Facebook, YouTube, and Fan pages)
- The name, products, and/or services of your business
- Your key clients (if appropriate)
- Your education
- Special features that enhance your personal brand, such as a favorite quote or testimonial
- Your photo
- Links to — or PDF versions of — articles you've written or slides you've produced

LinkedIn, which I discuss later in the "Showcasing Your Personal Brand on LinkedIn" section, has become the most popular profile hub. It's free, easy to use, and widely used by millions of people. Other social networking sites that can act as a profile hub include About.me, Google+, or a Facebook Fan page, among others.

Whether you're fresh out of college or facing a career transition past middle age, you can (and should) master popular social media, such as LinkedIn, Facebook, Google+, and Twitter, so that you can boost your online reputation. (I discuss this subject in detail in the section "Measuring Your Online Reputation," later in the chapter.)

While any of the social networking options may be fine, your profile hub of choice may likely be your own website and/or blog site.

Setting Up a Website

Websites are no longer scary to create and certainly aren't the sole property of businesses with lots of money. Anyone with a basic understanding of computer tools and a little creativity can create a website in a few hours. A website or a blog site is the primary tool to highlight your brand online. If you're in business for yourself, you won't be taken seriously if you do not have a website. (And your website can easily have a blog component.)

Decisions, decision: Create your own site or hire a pro?

When you consider what you want a website to accomplish, you may wonder whether you need to hire a pro to create the site for you or whether to try creating it yourself. Do-it-yourself websites make sense when

- You're a small business or solopreneur and do not have much money to invest in your initial website.
- You're willing to learn the skills to be able to add content to your site as you build your business.
- You're comfortable enough with the computer that you aren't afraid to play with creating a site.
- You want a simple site without extra functionality.
- You enjoy the designing process.

Consider hiring someone to build your site if

- You're too busy to set up your own website.
- You're looking to build a site that has increased functionality and needs a professional to add plug-ins and widgets.
- You have no design sense and can't figure out how your brand might look when put into your website.
- You're not comfortable with computers, and web design would be very stressful for you.

TIP

The difference between a blog and a website

A blog and a website aren't really that different because many web designers use blogging software to manage and publish websites. The basic difference between a blog and a website is that the pages of a website remain more static in their information. True blog sites are changing regularly with new blog posts and interactions with readers.

Websites often follow a more formal or professional style of presenting information to the site visitors. Blogs are usually more informal in their approach as they try to engage their visitors in a blogging conversation. Chapter 13 explores the visual elements that are important to include in your website or blog site.

Regardless of how you create the website, keep in mind that you want the site to highlight keywords that correspond to your brand message, and you want the visual impact of the site to mesh with your visual brand image. As always, consistency is key! To remind yourself how you want to phrase your brand message, refer to Chapter 7. For help with your brand's visual identity, be sure to read Chapter 13.

When you decide to do it on your own . . .

If you decide that you feel up to the job of creating your own website, you won't truly have to go it alone. You can find several major sites to help you create your own website:

- **Wordpress.com:** The basic version of this website/blog site is free. You can choose from more than 100 templates.
- **GoDaddy.com:** You can register your domain name at this site as well as create a professional website.
- **Vistaprint.com:** Offers printing services and helps you create a basic website.
- **TypePad:** This free blog site also allows you to customize your site by using one of its templates.
- **Miniblog Tumblr:** It allows for free e-mail publishing from your desktop or phone to create instant blog posts.

Many other online resources can help you create your own website. Some easy and popular ones are Google, Intuit, and Yahoo!.

Becoming a Blogger

This section on blogging was contributed by Rachel Gogos, president of theBrandID.com ("Making the web more personal").

To blog or not to blog: That is the question. Yes, we live in different times than Shakespeare did, but undoubtedly, if he were living today, he would have a blog.

However, blogging isn't for everyone. It's time-consuming, tedious, and not very glamorous. On the other hand, a blog boasts content that is 100 percent in your control; it's your little piece of real estate on the web; it can be a powerful web-marketing and personal branding tool; and it's a great outlet.

This section walks you through the blogging process, from deciding whether to give it a go to posting content that keeps your readers coming back for more.

Considering the merits of blogging

How do you decide whether a blog is for you? Here's a list of questions to ask yourself before building a blog:

- What are your goals on the web?
- Can blogging help you achieve your goals?
- Is it important for you to be perceived as very knowledgeable in your industry, niche, or job? If the answer is yes and you work for someone else, is it okay with your employer that you have your own blog?
- Who is your target audience?
- Can you reach your target audience on the web? If the answer is yes, will your target audience read a blog?
- Do you like to write?
- Do you have time to post to your blog? If not, can you build a cadre of guest bloggers to help lessen your writing load?

Blogging is a great way to stand out on the web and build your personal brand. To date, more than 50 million WordPress sites exist on the web. (WordPress is the most popular blog content-management system on the web.) While not all these sites may have active blogs, clearly the blogging world is a big one, which means getting noticed online is tough.

If you're running a business, having fresh content on your site frequently can help your site stay up in the Google rankings. One of the few places it makes sense to update content frequently is in the blog section. Also, providing valuable, informative content on your site can help you build a loyal following on the web, which can translate into customers.

If you're part of a larger organization or company and want to start building your brand online, blogging can be a way for you to do so. You can write about your industry or your expertise. If you know you want to transition into a different industry or different type of job, you can blog about those topics as well.

A blog is one of the very few slices of real estate on the web that allows you to author your own content and, therefore, control it. It's a place for you to share your knowledge, resources, and value. It's a space where you can communicate your personality, strengths, skills, and passions.

TIP

If you can blog under your vanity name (such as *rachelgogos.com),* you achieve a higher-ranking Google result if someone searches your name. (Keep in mind that almost 90 percent of recruiting and employment executives Google people before meeting them.)

Creating an online ecosystem

If you're on the fence between building a website or a blog site for your new venture, don't fret. These days, the only difference between the two is whether or not you post fresh content to a section of your website known as the blog. If you think you may opt to blog in the near future, definitely build your website using an easy-to-update content-management system. You can simply keep the blog function and page hidden or unconstructed until you're ready to start blogging.

The beauty of a blog (or any self-managed website) is that it allows you to coordinate an otherwise unwieldy amount of online content; it lets you aggregate your online content so that you're not recreating, writing, and rewriting constantly. In other words, a blog lets you build an online ecosystem.

Your online ecosystem is your profile hub (see the section "Attracting Your Audience to a Profile Hub," earlier in this chapter), which pulls together everything you do online. A profile hub compiles all the various tools that you work with to promote your personal brand: LinkedIn, Facebook, Twitter, Google+, YouTube, and so on. All your online roads should lead back to your blog. You can also add some nifty tools to it that automate the process of a new post being sent directly to your Twitter, Facebook, and LinkedIn accounts.

Your blog is the epicenter of your ecosystem. If you were to draw it, it would look like Figure 10-1.

You push content out via your blog, but with your other online activity, you're also pointing people in toward your blog.

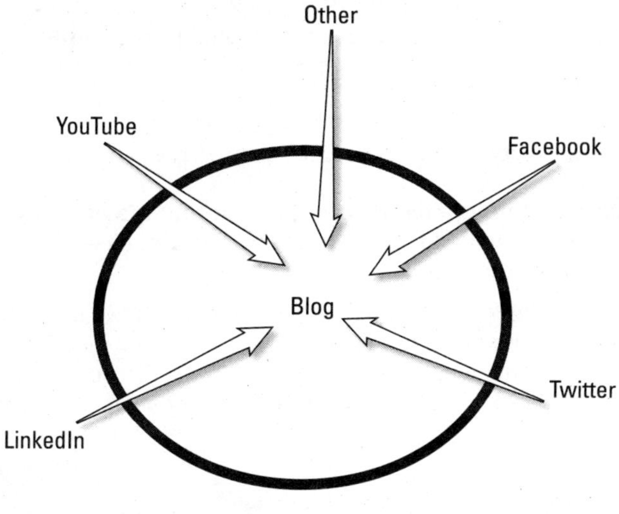

Figure 10-1: Your blog sits at the center of your online ecosystem.

Rachel Gogos.

Getting started

Blogging is fairly easy if you like to write. If you don't like to write but believe you must have a blog presence, be sure to check out my tips in the upcoming "Sharing your wisdom" section and actively search for outside contributors who generate content your audience can use.

To get started, here are some decisions you need to make:

- **Platform:** Select a content-management system that is right for you. Some are free, and others cost a small amount. You can host your own blog site, which costs a minimal monthly amount, or you can have a harder-to-find URL (such as `NAMEyouCHOOSE.blogspot.com`) that is hosted for you and is free to use and set up.
- **URL:** Select a username that is in line with your personal brand and what you want to communicate. Ideally, you can blog under your vanity URL (your name). If you have a common name, pick a URL that is a combination of your name and niche (such as *johnsmithcutlery)* or perhaps use your middle initial if you tend to do so anyway. If you're going to blog about a topic that ties in to your expertise, you can omit your name and let the URL reflect your area of expertise.
- **Topic:** Decide what you're going to write about! Leave yourself some latitude when deciding your topic(s). For example if you're going to write only about various kinds of poison ivy, you may run out of material. Instead, you can write about plants and vegetation that agitate the human body.
- **Design:** Design your blog site. Pick a color that communicates a little more about who you are and what you stand for. (For tips, see the video called "What Color Is Your Brand" at `www.youtube.com/watch?v=XDohoPavchc`.) Add a professional photograph of yourself. Pick a font that is your style and that matches what you use on your other branded materials.

Here are some other ways to make your blog site great:

- **Make your social media icons prevalent so that it's easy for a reader to follow you in other places on the web.** Also, make sure those icons match the look of the rest of your site.

  TIP: Use a social media icon on your blogsite *only* if you're active in that medium. Don't get caught up with trends. Use social media that help you meet your goals and reach your target audience. If your target audience isn't using Facebook, you don't need to use Facebook for marketing your business.

- **Have an RSS (Really Simple Syndication) feed icon.** This technology allows readers to subscribe to your site and follow your blog posts. RSS feeds help the reader stay informed by retrieving the latest content.
- **Create a place for your readers to comment.** Have a comment feed section on your site for readers to contribute their thoughts.
- **Have a spot on your blog that tells your readers a little more about you.** You can have a mini branded bio or a lengthier bio on a separate page of your site.
- **Include a photo of yourself on your blogsite.** Using a photo is really important because it builds a stronger connection between you and your reader.
- **Include video *posts (vlogs)* or simply one video of yourself talking to your readers.** Using video builds an even stronger connection than posting photos.
- Make your posts easy to share via readers' social media accounts by adding a plug-in for them to easily comment and forward your posts to their friends and contacts. You can use the Meebo bar (`www.meebo.com`) or a social media share bar plug-in from WordPress, among other online tools.

Sharing your wisdom

After you've set up your site, you're ready to write posts. Here are a few tips for writing blog posts:

- **Think seriously about your introductory post.** I like to make these posts *sticky,* meaning they will stay at the top no matter how many other posts you write. That way, if a new reader joins your growing community, he immediately knows what you're all about, what you're writing about, and what your intentions are right there at the top of your blog. The best way to describe the intro post is this: If your blog were a book, what would you write in the introduction?
- **Find your voice.** Be who you are and put your personality into your writing. (Just don't forget to spell check!) If you're funny when you're speaking with people, be funny in your writing as well.
- **Share relevant information.** Depending on the purpose of your blog, find the right combination of personal information laced with public information. In other words, watch out for TMI (too much information).
- **Keep it short.** Keep copy to a minimum, but get your point across. That doesn't mean you won't have an occasional longer post.

- **Keep it real.** Be honest with your readers.
- **Incorporate your passions.** Part of your personality has to do with what you are passionate about. If you're passionate about gardening but you are an HR professional, find ways to tie gardening into your HR content. You can do it.
- **Be creative.** The more creative you can be (while still remaining on topic), the more interesting your blog posts will be, and the more likely your audience is to read and recommend them.
- **Stay on topic.** Make sure that your content is consistently on topic for what you or your business claim to do. For example, if you're an executive coach, you don't want to write a blog about how to change oil in your car.
- **Connect to your reader.** Have a picture of yourself on your blog and write in the first person.
- **End with a question.** What better way is there to engage your readers than to end with a question? Encourage your followers to answer questions by using the comments section of your blog.
- **Respond to comments.** Make sure that you review and respond to comments frequently after posting fresh content. This step is key to building your community.
- **Set a pace for yourself and keep up with it.** Try to post on schedule and regularly. If you tell your readers you're going to post weekly on Fridays, then post weekly on Fridays. Ideally, you should post a few times a week.

Repurposing your blog content

When you start blogging, you can find endless ways to repurpose your content and use it in other ways to build your brand online and off, which adds to your ecosystem. Here are just some of the ways that you can repurpose your blog content:

- Online webinar
- Narrated PowerPoint
- E-book
- Book
- E-series
- DVD series
- Podcast

- In-person presentation
- Slide share
- Newsletter
- E-mail auto-responder series
- Print article (newspaper or magazine)
- Web news column (Huffington Post, local newspaper)
- Guest post on another blog
- Video on YouTube

Chapter 11 guides you in developing a communications strategy where you repurpose the same content in many different formats. Find a subject that you enjoy and use it over and over.

Showcasing Your Personal Brand on LinkedIn

This section was written by Robin S. Fox, a social media coach, trainer, and workshop leader.

If you're just beginning to think about using online tools to showcase your personal brand to your business and social networks, begin with LinkedIn. Success with social networking often comes at the intersection where you're sharing the right information to the right people at the right time and on the right social media platform. That equation doesn't always work as easily on Facebook as it does on LinkedIn.

It's a well-accepted fact that people do business with people they know, like, and trust. This was true well before the advent of the Internet. Think about it: Don't you prefer to work with people you like and trust?

While direct selling is frowned upon on LinkedIn, business conversations are not only accepted . . . they're expected. These are the same conversations that allow LinkedIn to do what LinkedIn does best: help build effective business relationships based on nurturing the "know, like, and trust" factor. With more than 120 million users, LinkedIn is the world's largest online professional network and is growing daily. The people you're trying to reach — those you know and those you don't — are very likely on LinkedIn.

Controlling first impressions

While there are many advanced tactics for sharing your personal brand on LinkedIn, you can accomplish a lot just by doing a few simple things well, starting with the information people see on the first screen shot of your profile and your summary statement.

The ultimate goal is to create your LinkedIn profile in such a way that it provides answers about you and your personal brand that visitors typically look for when visiting any website:

- Who are you?
- What do you do?
- What can you do for me?
- Do you have proof of what you say you can do?
- Who else can comment on your expertise?

You make a first impression online in much the same way as you do in person. The first step is to get your LinkedIn presence moving in the right direction. While over time you'll likely add more information and include and integrate some of LinkedIn's robust applications, there's no reason you can't work toward answering these five basic questions from the outset. Consider their answers as you fill in various LinkedIn sections.

Optimizing your snapshot: Headline and photo

Your *snapshot* is the information on your LinkedIn profile that shows in the search results when someone does a search within LinkedIn. It includes your name, headline, headshot/photo, geographic location, and industry. Figure 10-2 shows the format in which this information appears. Figure 10-3 shows a LinkedIn page.

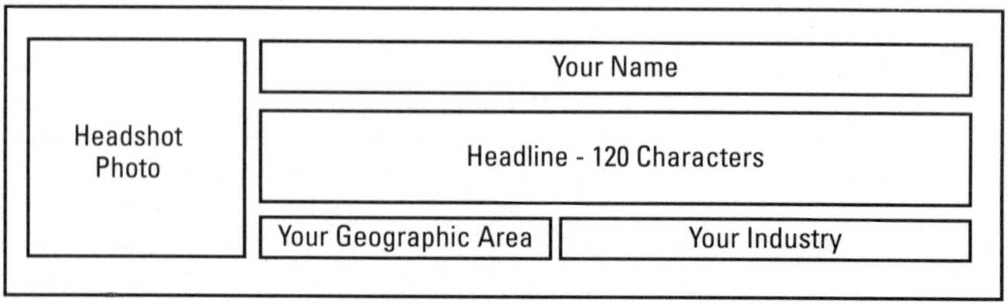

Figure 10-2: How your LinkedIn snapshot appears online.

Robin S. Fox.

Robin (Schoettler) Fox

Social Media Coach | Helping you raise brand awareness, build effective business networks and improve your online image

San Francisco Bay Area | Professional Training & Coaching

Current	**Instructor** at **LinkedIn Bootcamps**
	Social Networking Training & Online Community Management at **Lafayette Chamber of Commerce**
	Social Media Strategies Workshop Leader at **Public, Private & Corporate Venues**
	Social Media Coach at **Robin S. Fox Consulting** **(Sole Proprietorship)**
	Online Community Manager at **Friends Corner Book Shop**
	Content Creator & Blogger at **Robin S. Fox Consulting** **(Sole Proprietorship)**
Past	Traditional and New Media Communications Leadership (Outreach) at Organizations supporting Lafayette Library & Learning Center
	Freelance Journalist/Columnist. National/Regional clips at publications listed in description.
	Vice President and Corporate Client Manager (Corporate Finance & Lending) at Chemical Bank, a legacy bank to JP Morgan Chase
Education	Inbound Marketing University (Hubspot), Inbound Marketing Educator - Inbound Marketing Best Practices (Certificate)
	SMMU, Social Media Best Practices Certificate Program
	San Francisco State University -- Integrated Marketing Program (Certificate)
	Training in Client Management, Corporate Finance & Credit Analysis from Chemical Bank (now JP Morgan Chase)
	University of North Carolina at Chapel Hill
Recommendations	**30** people have recommended Robin
Connections	**500+** connections
Websites	Register - Linkedin Bootcamp
	Hire Social Networking Help
	Join Robin S. Fox on Facebook
Twitter	RobinSFox
Public Profile	http://www.linkedin.com/in/robinsfox

Figure 10-3: A LinkedIn profile.

Robin S. Fox.

Most of this information is obvious — and yes, it's critical to include a photo in which you look both professional and approachable. (For help with headshots, turn to Chapter 12.)

The number one mistake people make with their LinkedIn headline is to use the headline space to repeat their current position and employer — information that is viewable in Experience, the section that appears immediately below the Snapshot on your LinkedIn profile. Repeating that information in your headline is a missed opportunity.

The headline area is prime real estate on your LinkedIn profile. Make it work for you by using it to better clarify your personal brand promise. LinkedIn gives you as much as 120 characters to craft your headline. Start by thinking about your elevator pitch or personal commercial (see Chapter 8). How would you translate that pitch into a LinkedIn profile headline?

Alternately, focus on answering these questions in the headline: "Who are you?" and "What do you do?" But keep in mind that you're even better off taking the headline to the point where it answers the next question, "What can you do for me?" Here are a few good examples:

- Social Media Coach — Helping you raise brand awareness, build effective business networks, and improve your online image
- Advisory Partner, specializing in corporate investigations, forensic accounting, and fraud detection and prevention

Google considers LinkedIn a highly trusted site. As a result, when someone searches for you on Google.com, a link to your LinkedIn profile will likely come in very high in the search returns. When it does, Google pulls information from your snapshot and your most recent job listing to populate the link description. Test it and see — you may want to further adjust your headline to improve how those results look.

Filling in the other basic information on the profile

LinkedIn's resume-styled interface makes it easy to create an organized quick view that can help prove that you have sufficient experience, education, and/or expertise to successfully accomplish what you say you can do — in other words, to fulfill your personal brand promise. As a first cut, try to fill out this information completely, including any lists of examples of past projects completed that help substantiate your experience.

While it may look like a resume, LinkedIn is not one. It's a communication document. Consider your personal brand and include the experience, education, and expertise you have that support that brand promise. If functional titles would help your audience better understand that experience, then use them, too.

As you fill out these sections, try to use keywords that will resonate with your customers and prospects. In addition to making these sections much more compelling by doing so, you gain search rankings in Google if others search for your solution using the keywords you've chosen.

Links: Using custom anchor text

LinkedIn allows you to add up to three website links (not counting Twitter) on your profile. This is a great opportunity to send visitors to your website(s) to learn even more about you. Try to fill all three link spots — if not to your personal website(s), then perhaps to reach an article you wrote or were quoted in or something else you'd like to share that fits with your brand.

When you enter the URL for a link, LinkedIn asks you to choose a category (such as My Website or My Blog) that will serve as visible, clickable text in a hyperlink. Keep in mind that people are more likely to click a link if they understand where it will send them. In addition to the predetermined link categories, LinkedIn offers a way for you to customize the link category. To do so, choose Other from the drop-down menu of categories. When you do, a new comment field appears, and you can enter your own customized anchor text for the link you're adding.

When you create custom anchor text for your website links, include call-to-action verbs that help readers understand something they'll be able to do when they click that link. Examples of these verbs include *register, read, buy, download, view,* or *join.* For example, you may link your Facebook page URL using the anchor text "Join me on Facebook."

Gathering recommendations

One of the nice features about LinkedIn is the ability for others to offer recommendations for your work. To recommend someone, they have to be on LinkedIn, which some people find limiting. An upside is that the recommendation they write for you lives on their LinkedIn profile, too. This dual exposure increases the likelihood that more people will see that recommendation, including your recommender's network.

Pick your recommenders wisely because your network will pay attention to the author. You want to make sure that the source of your recommendation is someone reputable and whose own image meshes with your brand. You don't want a recommendation by someone who would reflect poorly on you or your character.

Crafting the summary section

One of the most important sections of your LinkedIn profile is the summary section. Here is your chance (in 2,000 characters) to really tell your personal brand story in such a way that it matters to the reader.

A successful summary helps a reader who is looking for a particular solution answer a basic but important question: Am I in the right place? When you write your summary section, consider it a one-on-one conversation with the person (or kind of person) you most hope will read it. What problems does that person have? What solutions do you offer that will help? Use keywords that will resonate with the reader and also help your profile get found when others search for the solutions you offer. If you mention your past experience, use it to prove that you are now ready to help the reader.

TIP

LinkedIn does not offer spell-checking. Draft your summary in Word or another editing program and then cut and paste it into LinkedIn.

To encourage business referrals from your LinkedIn network, use a portion of your summary section to explain what you do in terms that help others understand when someone else they know may need your help.

Stating your specialties

The LinkedIn specialties list is keyword-driven. Find the right keywords for your industry and add them here. These may be the words people would use to search for an expert. This section should mention skills or experiences that you consider your professional specialties.

Here are a few examples of LinkedIn specialties:

- Personal brand strategist, executive coaching, career coaching, career transition, strengths-based training, change management
- Research & Development, corporate strategy, engineering, management
- Nonprofits, real estate law, tax planning, code compliance, licensing
- Competitive analysis, financing, franchising, mergers and acquisition

Completing a LinkedIn profile worksheet

Figure 10-4 demonstrates a systematic approach to thinking about what you want to say on LinkedIn before you begin to add information to the site. In addition, it serves as a checklist to make sure you complete the most critical information people first see when they visit your LinkedIn profile. By following the worksheet, you'll be reminded about the sections of information you need to provide.

Your LinkedIn Profile Checklist: Quick Steps to a Better First Impression

1. Complete the basic items on your Profile, including your photo (see below)
2. Add a Summary Section and Specialties
3. Ask for Recommendations

☐	Update Headline	*Limit 120 characters • Focus on solutions you provide*	
☐	Add Headshot	*Professional looking • Cropped close to face • Be recognizable*	
☐	Fill in Work Experience	*Include relevant experience that supports your personal brand*	
☐	Complete Education Section	*Include college & graduate degrees, but also other relevant training*	
☐	Add Links with Custom Anchor Text	Link URL	Anchor Text
☐	Add Twitter Account		
☐	Claim Custom URL		
☐	Add Summary Section	Focus on Solutions You Offer • Avoid Jargon • Use Keywords	
	Keywords to Use: 1. 2. 3. 4. 5.		
☐	List Specialties		
☐	Add recommendations	*Who will you ask?*	

Figure 10-4: A LinkedIn profile worksheet.

Robin S. Fox.

Considering a case study: Daniel Perlino's LinkedIn profile

Chapter 9 introduces the case study of Daniel Perlino. Kelly Welch, a career branding strategist at YES Career Services, wrote this case study. In that chapter, you can see Daniel's resume, branded biography, and a sample cover letter. Here, the case study of Daniel's branded materials continues. Figure 10-5 shows Daniel's LinkedIn profile summary.

LinkedIn Summary, Daniel Perlino

- Builder of winning strategies; employs diplomatic mindset that builds trust with Senior Executives, R&D, and Sales Executives.
- Confident problem solver; leverages the power of team governances to provide and implement solutions.
- Visionary leader; seeks optimal solutions, focusing on: client satisfaction, alliance relationships, and maximizing ROI for all stakeholders.

Always 'looking for a better way to do things', I make it a point to truly play to my strengths as a visionary, motivator, and active contributor. I walk the talk and have led marketing campaigns for pharmaceutical and biotechnical brand names with annual sales exceeding $1.25B, as well as tactical vision for commercial alliances, strategic client services, and commercialization and launch planning. I am reputed for my organization, attention to detail, creativity, and participative management style. I am most energized when creating a strategic win-win plan and empowering a team to achieve it.

Personally, I am a firm proponent of educating and inspiring youth to aspire to great futures. I find my own inspiration fueled by history, the outdoors, and energetic, positive teams of people. I readily connect my role as Pharmaceutical Marketing Executive with my **joie de vivre** and passion for excellence. I bring lots of creativity and gain energy by successfully building strategies and collaborating with R&D and sales teams across the full product lifecycle to create blockbuster campaigns.

Some of my other icons are found in history, such as:

- JF Kennedy: Visionary and motivator of young people.
- Abraham Lincoln: Took charge of the challenges of the country by not trying to please the masses but focused on what is right.
- Martin Luther King Jr.: Gave our country a reason to believe that we all can do better... to protest without violence and see his grace as an inspiration to change.
- Teddy : A no-BS type of guy. He knew what he liked and he went after it with gusto. He was an outdoorsmen, and friend of the ecology, and loved being with nature.

Specialties

Antibiotics • Brand Management • Cardiovascular Commercial Alliance Management • Complex Commercial Initiatives • CNS • Dermatology NDA Submissions & Product Launches • Gastroenterology • HIV • KOL Diplomacy • Sales Management • Oncology • Respiratory • Strategic Vision • Team Empowerment

Figure 10-5: Daniel Perlino's branded LinkedIn Profile.

Kelly Welch.

Bonding with Facebook: Key Factors for Building Your Reputation

Social media coach, trainer, and workshop leader Robin S. Fox wrote this section as well.

It's hard to ignore Facebook's power as a personal branding tool — and not just because Facebook is the largest of the popular social networking platforms (although its extensive reach is a huge positive in extending your reach in the world).

What's more important is that Facebook is well designed to share the kinds of information — words, photos, video, website links, and more — that help tell your story in ways that simultaneously inform and entertain. This ability allows you to navigate the gentle balance of being social while also sharing enough of your personal brand to offer a satisfying taste of what others experience when they meet you in person.

Facebook needs a warning label, though: Sharing the wrong information to the wrong people in the wrong way can impact how people feel about your personal brand.

Even if you believe Facebook is strictly for personal use, don't skip over this section. Now more than ever, people do business with people they know, like, and trust. That means your target audience may very likely include the people who know you best, the same people you'll likely connect with on Facebook. If you want them to be your advocates, you need to clue them in, if only subtly.

Your reputation forms on Facebook in ways similar to how it forms in any community, online or otherwise. It's based on what others know about you — first-hand and inferred. Your reputation includes

- Ways you behave generally
- People you associate with
- Information you share
- Information others share

Looking at this list, you can see that you can't completely control your reputation on Facebook. Other people impact it as well, so remember the motherly words of wisdom: Be careful who you hang out with.

TIP

Whether you plan to use Facebook for business or not, it's a good idea to take some defensive measures to protect your personal brand. One of the best steps is to take advantage of what Facebook calls *notifications:* notices sent to your personal e-mail inbox based upon actions by others on Facebook. For example, you can ask for a notification when someone links a photo back to your Facebook profile, something referred to as *tagging.* The notification gives you a chance to be among the first to see that photo.

Considering your big-picture strategy

Your Facebook profile has lots of content areas to share optional personal information, a nod to Facebook's legacy as a college social networking site. Before deciding what to share, ask yourself basic networking questions:

- What do I need to share to showcase my personal brand?
- What other information am I willing to share?
- What should I keep private — or not share at all?

Your answers determine what really belongs in your profile and suggest a general framework for your Facebook behavior, including ongoing content sharing and privacy-setting strategies.

Optimizing what everyone can see

Everyone, including the online public, can see three things about your Facebook account:

- The name at the top of your Facebook profile
- Your Facebook account URL
- Your current profile picture

Making this information public is Facebook's way of making it easier for people to find you on Facebook. Consider customizing all three to your advantage:

- **Recognizable name:** Facebook makes you use your real name to set up your account but gives you flexibility when it come to the name that shows at the top of your profile. Use a nickname if it helps you be more recognizable and better matches your brand.

- **Unique username:** When you claim your custom username, Facebook uses it to create a professional-looking URL for your profile that's easily shared: `www.facebook.com/`*`Username`*. With so many people on Facebook, getting your first choice may be difficult. Be creative in thinking of alternatives but remember that you can add this URL to your business card and e-mail signature. The username has to make sense for your personal brand.
- **Public profile photo:** This photo falls outside of any privacy settings, meaning anyone can view it. Therefore, choose one that is both friendly and professional.

  TIP

  Optimize the profile photo space by using a larger profile picture (up to 180 x 540 pixels) that includes additional content — words or images — to help showcase your personal brand.

Deciding on your privacy settings

How widely you share other information you add to Facebook — profile elements, updates, comments, photos, and more — is up to you. Your first level of control is in deciding whether you post that information on Facebook in the first place!

You can also use privacy settings to manage which content posted by others can link *(tag)* directly back to your Facebook profile. Just know this: Preventing tagging doesn't stop someone from posting that content. The content is still on Facebook where it was originally posted. It's just harder for your network to connect that it relates to you.

Populating your Facebook profile

With your brand awareness strategy in mind, purposefully complete your Facebook profile to include information such as the following:

- Your work experience
- Your educational experience
- Links to your LinkedIn profile, website, blog, Twitter account, YouTube channel, and other sites

You may consider leaving blank (or limiting views to) personal information, such as relationship status, religion, and political affiliation. Of course, there are exceptions to this guideline. For example, a political candidate would likely want to include information about his political views on the profile.

Facebook, change, and sharing your brand story

Of all the popular social networking platforms, Facebook changes the most often, in ways both large and small, much to the chagrin of its many users. Expect these changes. Look for them both on your own profile and in places like `www.facebook.com/blog`. When change happens, refresh your original personal branding goals and then take advantage of new opportunities to showcase your personal brand. This was the case when the photo strip and profile appeared on your Facebook Wall in an earlier version of Facebook.

Also be sure to look out for new risks and adjust your settings to minimize them. (Remember when Facebook first added photo facial recognition in 2011?)

Take advantage of all the different ways you can share your personal brand on Facebook. Brainstorm ideas using the model in the figure.

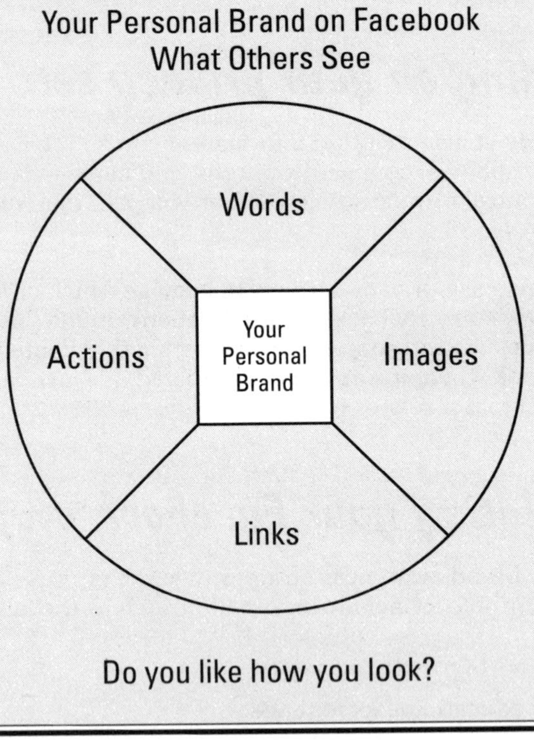

TIP

If you have your own Facebook page for your business, link it to your work experience entry so that your personal network can easily join you there as well.

The About Me section is your opportunity to tell your personal brand story in a more direct manner. You can highlight the solution you offer, but remember that it's not the place to hard-sell product and services. Instead, let your readers know what you do, as well as *why* you do what you do — your passion for the business. As with all things online, use keywords that will resonate with your readers.

Sharing your personal brand story one post at a time

After you've set up your Facebook profile to showcase your personal brand and added Facebook connections, you can work toward building better relationships with those connections. You do so by posting content consistent with your personal brand and participating in related conversations started by others, either on other personal Facebook profiles, in Facebook Groups, or on Facebook Pages.

People notice not only what you post but how you post it. Be sure to proofread everything you write before posting. Don't write important posts when you're tired, upset, or overly emotional (whether happy or otherwise). Let those thoughts simmer for a while before committing them to Facebook. Upon reflection, you may decide to keep some of those things off Facebook completely.

Getting Connected with Google+

As I write these words, Google+ is a fairly new social media site. Google+ is Google's attempt to rival Facebook. It integrates several social services, such as Google Profiles and Google Buzz, as well the services Circles, Hangouts, and Sparks. Google Buzz is a stream of posts much like that of Facebook.

A Google Profile includes

- Your introduction — personal overview
- Bragging rights — what makes you memorable
- Occupation — what you do
- Employment — where you work
- Contact information — work phone and e-mail
- Places lived — past and present

Here are some Google+ features that allow you to promote your personal brand:

- **Circles:** Enables you to organize your contacts into groups for sharing. You can essentially create your personal branding tribe with this feature, which replaces the friends list used by Facebook.
- **Hangouts:** Places used to facilitate group video chats.
- **Messenger:** A feature available to smartphones for communicating through instant messaging within circles. You can also share photos in Messenger between your circles.
- **Sparks:** A Google search allowing users to identify topics they may be interested in sharing with others.
- **Stream:** Where users can see updates from those in their circles. The input box is where users enter updates in their status or upload and share photos and videos.

Tweeting on Twitter

Twitter is an online social networking and microblogging web service that allows its users to send and read text-based messages of up to 140 characters, known as *tweets.*

Twitter is the great equalizer in that you can become a content expert without years of schooling and a prestigious job title. If you're prolific enough and get enough followers who are interested in what you have to say, you can rise to the status of content expert.

Kristen Jacoway, author of the book *I'm in a Job Search — Now What???* (Happy About), is a Twitter expert who advises that when you are on Twitter, you want to make sure that you're providing value to your target audience (your followers) by giving them links to articles, blogs, and more that offer good, useful information. Tweeting isn't about self-promotion (although you can use it this way from time to time). Most people agree that you want to tweet useful, helpful information 80 to 90 percent of the time. Consider why you are on Twitter and the strategy you need to employ.

TIP

One of Jacoway's favorite tools for collecting relevant information to tweet about is Google Alerts (`www.google.com/alerts`). A similar tool is TweetBeeps (`www.tweetbeep.com`). You can choose Google Alerts for once-a-day notifications as they happen or receive them once per week. By doing so, you get all the news about a specific topic via your e-mail. You can quickly glance through the titles of the articles in your e-mail and decide which ones to click through to read. If you feel like it's valuable information, you can share it by tweeting the link.

Most articles and blog posts give you the ability to share on Twitter or other social networks. Just click on the icon of the social network where you want to share the information, tie it with your Twitter account with a click of a button, and voilà — it's sent.

To find blogs in your area of expertise, visit www.technorati.com and start following blogs in your industry.

Extending your Twitter reach

EXPERT OPINION

The remainder of this section on Twitter was written by Kristen Jacoway.

Finding people to follow on Twitter is really easy to do and is one of the simplest ways to start getting followers for yourself. You can Google the term Twitter Directories, and you'll come up with several options. Many people want to find Twitter users in their local area. Consider this: Companies hire 1 in 10 referrals versus 1 in 100 applicants. Effective networking on and offline is the critical component in any endeavor!

Here, I introduce you to a few of my favorite ways to network using Twitter:

- **Twellow** (www.twellow.com) is a great place for you to list yourself in the Twitter Yellow Pages. I list myself under the following three attributes: personal branding, social media, and career consultant. Try to think of attributes to describe what you do to match what people will use in their own search to find people in those professions. What I love about Twellow is that after you've created your account and signed in, you can search and follow people all within the Twellow website.

  TIP

  You can do a specific search like "Healthcare Recruiters" to find industry-specific recruiters. You can search a particular company and follow not only the company but also employees of that company. You can also search for people in a certain geographic region.
- **WeFollow** (www.wefollow.com) is much like Twellow. You pick three *tags* (attributes) that describe you. When you click through to a Twitter user of interest, you can click the button called Follow This User and be redirected to that person's Twitter home page.
- **Twitter Grader** (http://twitter.grader.com) is a fun tool. You can enter your Twitter username and come up with a Twitter grade. It measures your "power, reach, and authority" on Twitter.

  The feature I like, located on the navigation bar, is called Twitter Elite. Here, you can search for the Twitter Elite by Top Users, Top Women, Top Cities, and Top Brands. Twitter Grader makes it easy for you to find some of the leading experts in specific industries.

Within Twitter Grader, another popular tool is Twitter Search, which works like a Google search within Twitter. You can search for keywords, topics of interest, trending topics, hashtags, people, and more. You can find people who are tweeting information that is of interest to you.

- **People Similar To You** is a Twitter feature that offers suggestions based on the keywords listed in your profile, keywords you use in tweets, people you are following, and other factors. To see this feature, you need to go to the Profile section of your Twitter page. The information is below your tweet/following/followers' statistics. Additionally, at the top of your Twitter page, you will see a link called Who To Follow.
- **Follower Wonk** provides you the ability to search Twitter bios for keywords, including location. When I typed Auburn, AL, I returned 109 results with some rich data, including the number of tweets (shows how active they are on Twitter), number of friends, number of followers, Twitter bio, and a hyperlink to their Twitter page (in case you want to follow a particular person).
- **Tweepz** is another Twitter user locator service. Here, I typed "Auburn, AL" again and returned an impressive 1,534 results. I appreciate the fact that the first hyperlink takes me to the Twitter Profile page, but it also includes a link to the Twitter user's website.

Following back your followers

After you start following people and writing helpful, compelling tweets, you will start getting followers. How do you follow these new followers? On your Twitter home page, you'll see the number of tweets you've tweeted, the number of people you are following, the number of followers you have, and the number of lists in which you appear. As you mouse over the word Followers, it becomes hyperlinked. Click the link.

The next page shows a picture of the page where you will arrive after clicking the hyperlinked text. To follow any new follower, simply click the +FOLLOW green button.

Creating a Twitter list

You can add followers to lists. For example, maybe you have lists for social media experts, career experts, recruiters, and more. As you begin to follow people, look at their profiles and their tweets. Determine whether they can add value for you. If so, add them to a list. Lists make Twitter easy to navigate and make engaging in conversations easy. Figure 10-6 shows where you find the option to add someone to a list.

Figure 10-6: Adding followers to a Twitter list.

Kristen Jacoway.

If you don't have a list to match a person's expertise, simply create one. Type the name of the list, click to make it a public list (meaning that anyone can start following this list) or a private list (which may be better if you're in a confidential job search and don't want others to see the companies or recruiters you're following), and click Save List.

Finding out who has unfollowed you

Twitter has a rule that applies to everyone: You can follow up to 2,000 people, but until your follower ratio is at just 10 percent less than your following, Twitter will not allow you to follow any additional people. Put another way, if you have followed 2,000 people, you need at least 1,800 people to follow you before you can continue to follow additional people.

I personally use a tool called Just Unfollow. You sign in with your Twitter account, and it looks at all the people you've followed who are not following you in return. I periodically use this tool because some people follow others only in order to get the follow back to increase their own number of followers. They almost immediately unfollow your account. Just Unfollow makes it incredibly easy to unfollow people on their website. You can pay a very small fee per year to unfollow large numbers.

Just Unfollow also has a feature called Show Inactive Following. Many people start on Twitter only to abandon their accounts, so this service is invaluable for you to identify inactive Twitter users.

Publishing an Electronic Newsletter (Or Not)

This section was contributed by Rachel Gogos, President of theBrandID.com ("Making the web more personal").

People are inundated with electronic information Be honest: How many e-mails do you get a day that you don't have time to read? What makes you actually click a content link? In other words, what makes something worth reading?

Before creating a newsletter for yourself and your business, you need to determine whether doing so truly has value for your target audience. Here are some considerations:

- **Do create a newsletter if you like to write and can use it as a way to communicate and engage your audience with meaningful information.** (If you're not blogging, a newsletter is a great tool.) Even if you're blogging, create a newsletter if you like to write and you have additional meaningful information to share.
- **Don't start a newsletter if you have only more of the same to say and won't create additional value.** Your readers may feel frustrated if you're just repackaging information. (However, the packages matter. For example, if you blog consistently and turn the posts into a newsletter that comes out weekly, you'll likely frustrate your reader. If you blog frequently but send a newsletter only every other month, and the newsletter consists of the posts that were most read, the newsletter could work well.)
- **Don't overcommunicate with your audience because you risk being unsubscribed.** Find the best frequency for your target market; you can do so by trial and error or by offering a short poll via blog post or e-mail.
- **Do use your newsletter to offer value, but don't just sell, sell, sell your products.** Your newsletter is best when you connect and provide information that your target audience finds valuable and makes it remember that you provide specific expertise.
- **Do keep newsletter articles tightly written and don't drone on in the copy.** Your readers are short on time and appreciate brevity.

Selecting a newsletter tool

Lots of excellent newsletter tools are available to help you produce a newsletter with ease. Some of the better known ones are:

- **Microsoft Outlook:** This tool is simple (and fairly inexpensive). Outlook provides a convenient way to build your address list while using your e-mail. Use a more sophisticated system if you plan on publishing newsletters often and really building your distribution list.
- **MailChimp (**www.mailchimp.com**):** This user-friendly system features strong analytic tools and, as of this writing, is free for a mailing list of up to 2,000 (and quite inexpensive for larger lists).
- **AWeber (**www.aweber.com**):** With strong analytic tools, this user-friendly system is great if you do a lot of e-marketing.
- **Constant Contact (**www.constantcontact.com**):** Although less user-friendly than MailChimp and AWeber, this system also boasts strong analytics and is fairly inexpensive.

TIP

Before you select a newsletter tool, think about your long term e-marketing goals. Moving your lists from one service provider to the next isn't always easy, and some tools require that your list re-opts-in when you transfer, so try to select a service that will meet your needs for the long-term.

Designing your newsletter's look and feel

What should your newsletter look like? You can create a custom template or (much easier) just customize an existing template from the tools listed in the previous section. Keep these details in mind when customizing your newsletter:

- **Masthead:** Create an imprint at the top of your newsletter that represents your brand. Include your logo and/or create a catchy name for your newsletter. If you create a new name for your newsletter, make sure that it's aligned with your existing brand. (A good example is the Reach Personal Branding newsletter, which is called *YOUnique.)*
- **Color:** Keep the colors of your newsletter consistent with your website, business card, and any other existing materials. (See Chapter 13 for a complete discussion of your visual presentation.)
- **Font:** Stick to the same fonts used on your website and other materials. Consistency creates a lasting impression, and you look put together and polished.
- **Contact info:** Always make it easy for a reader to contact you. Keep in mind that while you aren't necessarily hard selling through your newsletter, you do want to make yourself accessible to your readers.
- **Share and subscribe:** Make it *really* easy for readers to share and subscribe to your e-mail list. Definitely include the ability to like your newsletter on Facebook, Tweet the newsletter link or connect with other social media tools. Also, make it easy for a reader to simply forward the newsletter to a friend (and land a new subscriber for you!).

- **Review:** Constantly review and improve your template. Make it as user-friendly as possible.
- **Proofread:** *Always* proofread your content before you send it because misspellings reflect so poorly on your personal brand.

Posting Videos

William Arruda, founder of Reach Personal Branding, launched his own personal branding video resource at `www.Personalbranding.TV`. Arruda says video is the new frontier in personal branding; video may be the most powerful tool you can use to build an emotional connection with the people you connect with virtually. Video allows you to deliver a complete communication — something that is often missing in a world where most communication is electronic.

In building your personal brand, Catharine Fennel, founder of videoBIO, offers sage advice to show how video is an important media tool to help visualize and personalize your message. She says that when thinking of generating video, you need to look at it as a toolkit of videos that best represent your brand. Video is not a singular event; it is replacing the way people are communicating online. Therefore, you need to identify what parts of your message you want to translate into video on an ongoing basis.

A video bio should be the cornerstone video for your personal brand toolkit. The bio is the video that represents your overall story and profiles you and/or your business in general. Consider your video bio an opportunity to connect with your audience, establish trust and a connection, and build your credibility and expertise in your particular subject matter. Your personal brand and persona simply cannot be expressed only in the written word. Video fills in the blanks between the lines by giving your message the high-impact human touch that connects you with your audience.

Typically, a videoBIO includes a mix of the following:

- Introducing yourself, your role, and/or your company
- Storytelling or sharing a point of view on your area of business
- Identifying achievements
- Educating or sharing information about your industry
- Calling viewers to action — what do you want viewers to take away and do? How can they contact you?

In addition to a video bio, you may want to consider creating promotional videos, educational videos, how-to videos, or editorial-type blog videos that can become part of a regular communication schedule and be included on your website, blog, or social media channels.

You want to gain the widest exposure possible for your video communications. Videos should live on your website; be pushed to social media channels like Facebook, LinkedIn, and Google+; and be hosted on a YouTube channel. Video can also supplement your e-mail communications; video can live passively as a link in your e-mail signature, or you can generate video messages and send them out embedded in an e-mail message (no attachments necessary!).

In the next few years, I believe video will take over how society communicates, whether it be a recorded video, a live video chat via Skype or Facetime, or a new technology not yet invented. You'll no longer be able to hide behind a phone call, so your appearance (at least from the waist up) will begin to take on a larger role when communicating virtually. (Chapter 12 is full of tips for getting your appearance to align with your personal brand.) Video can help connect you with your brand audience in ways never before possible.

Podcasting

Podcasting is a great way to share your expertise. A *podcast* is an audio file that you can download into an iPod or MP3 player. A podcast can feature a lecture or presentation you give to a conference, group, special interest, or class. Most universities have a technology department that supports their professors in creating and uploading podcasts.

If you're looking to build your brand through your thought leadership, consider creating a podcast and uploading it to your blog or website. It adds the element of voice to your words and personalizes your knowledge. You can use podcasts to introduce a topic or as a value-added benefit for those visiting your website.

Measuring Your Online Reputation

You need to measure your online reputation in order to get a clear picture of what your online presence says about you. According to William Arruda, author of *Career Distinction* (John Wiley & Sons, Inc.), there are five measures of online reputation: volume, relevance, purity, diversity, and validation. Here, I explain each measure and how it impacts your online reputation:

- **Volume** speaks to how much content is on the web about you. Lots of content means "This person must have something to say." A higher amount of volume on the web helps you show up more prominently in a Google or other search.
- **Relevance** answers the question: "Is this content consistent with who this person says she is or who I need her to be?" If you were touting honesty and integrity as part of your brand but you showed up in a Google search as someone who had cheated others, your words and reputation would be inconsistent, and you'd lose your relevance.
- **Purity** focuses on how successful you are in standing out with your content when others share your name. Purity is a big problem if you have a common name. You need to work really hard in establishing your online profile if most of what is written online is about the *other* John Smith. A good friend of mine who works in higher education found himself combating a profile of a man with the same name who happened to be a porn star. This was not the reputation that he was striving for!
- **Diversity** addresses the increasing use of multimedia on the web and the blended search results Google reveals. As you work to increase your online presence, you may want to add video, photos, and a *slideshare presentation* (an application that allows you to show PowerPoint presentations) to add to your diversity of content.
- **Validation** is the newest and perhaps most important measure of your online reputation because it helps build credibility. If your validation score is high, it means you have positive feedback from others visible in your Google results. To increase your validation, it's helpful to work with charities or have community activities that support your personal brand and help you show up online in a positive and aligned way.

TIP

To understand what others are thinking about you when they Google you, use the Online ID Calculator (`www.onlineidcalculator.com/index.php`) that was developed by Reach Personal Branding. This calculator can give you an understanding of the areas you need to focus on when building your brand on the web.

Combating a Regretful Online Identity

On the Internet, your reputation often precedes you. So far in this chapter, I've been touting the many positive attributes of the Internet to use in building your personal brand, but what happens when something dreadful is written about you? The scary thing about the Internet is that it's very difficult to get rid of something after it's been posted.

Reputation management is a moving target and often out of your control, especially if someone publishes something about you that is less than flattering. It becomes more complicated when your digital dirt is true.

For example, I had a client who came to me in career transition. I Googled him — as I do with all my clients. What I found was a detrimental, white-collar criminal record prominent on page one of the Google results page. I brought up this subject early in our appointment, and he was unaware that so much news about his activities was on the Internet. He asked if it would impact his job search, and my answer was a resounding YES!

Many companies conduct social media background checks and are legally allowed to keep the records for seven years. Here are some of the things that they look for in a background check.

- Compromising pictures of you, including inappropriate sexually explicit pictures
- Offensive language
- Racial slurs or discriminatory posts
- Illegal activities, including drugs or excessive alcohol abuse
- Posts that badmouth previous employers
- Discrepancies in your work history or evidence of mistruths

You need to minimize your digital dirt. To do so, keep activity high with sites that you *can* control so that they show up on page one of your Google search. The more active you are online, the more it raises your search results. People often don't look beyond two or three pages of search results, so by taking the offensive and getting a lot of content on the Internet, a search of your name will show your positive sites first.

Some of the sites that often show up on page one are these:

- A blog or website with your domain name
- Your Google profile
- Your LinkedIn profile
- Twitter posts
- Your Facebook profile
- Google +
- Your Vizibility.com QR code profile
- Comments you've made on popular blog sites

Be cautious about what you post online. On social networking sites, establish your privacy settings to avoid letting everyone see everything about you. Limit the amount of personal information posted about you online. Delete any unwanted or inappropriate comments that someone makes on one of your personal sites. Remove your name on photos where you have been tagged and may not want to be identified. (This is especially true of pictures taken at parties where you may have had one too many drinks — or even appear that you did.)

My final words of wisdom are to engage a few Internet tracking tools to follow what is showing up about you online. Continually check all your sites, and periodically do a Google search on yourself to see what shows up. Create a Google Alert (`www.google.com/alert`) that communicates when you are being searched or when new content is added about you. Addictomatic (`http://addictomatic.com`) is a site that allows you to view online references about yourself across multiple platforms at the same time. These are just two examples of sites to help you stay on top of your online reputation.

Chapter 11

Planning Your Personal Brand Communications

In This Chapter

- Delivering your on-brand message to your target audience
- Communicating the three Cs of personal branding
- Claiming your expertise
- Customizing an experience to make a great impression

Power is the capacity to translate intention into reality and then sustain it.

— Warren Bennis

In this chapter, I help you organize all the communication ideas spinning around your brain so that you can launch your brand into action. I explain how to determine the best ways to reach your target audience; how to achieve clarity, consistency, and constancy with your brand message; how to use communication tools to position yourself as an expert; and how to create a customized experience for your audience that makes you memorable.

William Arruda from Reach Communications says "Be lazy!" when determining how you will communicate your message. By that he means that you need to figure out what you want to communicate and then do it over and over using different communication tools. You don't need to reinvent the wheel (or, in this case, the content message) each time you'd like to build your professional credibility. Speak about it, write about it, blog about it, and volunteer to support it — but first make a plan about how you are going to communicate that message.

If you've read Chapters 9 and 10, your brain is loaded (perhaps overloaded!) with information about communication tools and how to use them to promote your personal brand. If you haven't yet touched those earlier chapters, be sure to look at Chapter 9 for help developing your branded resume, cover letter, and bio. Chapter 10 helps you find out everything you ever wanted to know about communicating your message with social media.

Laying the Groundwork for Your Communications Strategy

Determining the best ways to reach your audience begins with a review of who you are trying to reach. You need to express your personal brand to your target audience, which may include your peers, your work colleagues, potential customers, or even your competitors. Chapters 5 and 6 look at your target audience and at your competitors, so feel free to spend some time with that information if you haven't already done so.

Identifying who you want to communicate to is the first step in determining how you should go about communicating your brand. When you have your target audience firmly in mind, you're ready to move toward a communications strategy, which is the focus of this section.

TIP

Constructing a communications wheel (see Figure 11-1) can help you be lazy (in a good way) and lays the groundwork for your communications strategy. The idea here is that you want to identify a content area that you know well or can develop some expertise in. Then you use a visual tool to help you see how to spread your expertise to your target audience via various types of communication.

To create your communication wheel:

1. **Determine your content area of expertise that you want to use at the core of your personal brand communications.**

   Your content area of expertise is your professional knowledge around which you want to build your personal brand communications. Remember to keep your target audience in mind! (For more on your this topic, see the next section, "Figuring out your area of expertise.")

2. **Draw a circle with another circle in the center.**
3. **In the center circle, write your content area of expertise.**
4. **Draw several slices in the outer circle, as if you're slicing a pie.**
5. **In each slice, write a specific communication method that you might like to use to convey your expertise.**

   If you're unsure what to put in each slice, see the section "Filling in your slices," later in this chapter.

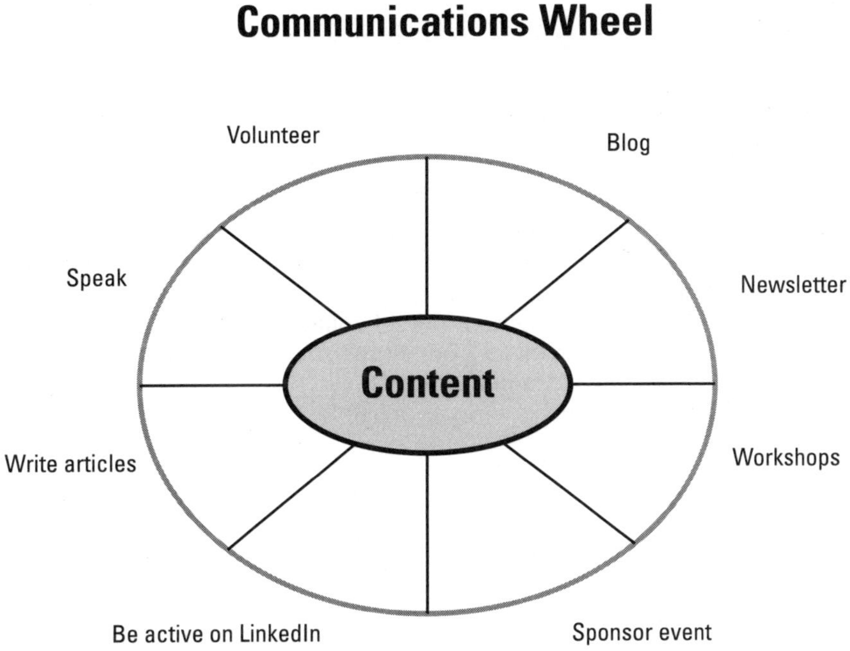

Figure 11-1: A sample communications wheel.

Communications Wheel inspired by William Arruda.

Figuring out your area of expertise

REMEMBER

Your content area of expertise likely will be a specialty area within your professional field. For example, if you're a dentist and want to specialize in pediatric dentistry, that would be your area of expertise. Having such a specific focus distinguishes you from all other dentists. You want to find something that is special enough so that you stand out and aren't competing with thousands of other people communicating about the same subject. Your specialty subject can be a narrow focus of your broader niche, as discussed in Chapter 6.

How do you get specific about your desired area of expertise? You likely need to do some research. First, brainstorm to create a list of subjects that you are interested in. Then, do some sleuthing to see how many people in your community consider themselves experts in those subjects. If you find a specialty that interests you and isn't too crowded with expertise, you've got a good fit! Discovering your message and delivering it over and over is how you make a name for yourself.

Filling in your slices

Within the slices of your circle, you need to specify how you want to communicate your message. The delivery of your content should be appealing to you (so that you enjoy what you're doing) and take into consideration the people you're trying to reach.

I encourage you to be creative and choose communications methods that you enjoy using and that fit your brand. For example, if your expertise relates to technology and you're a terrible public speaker, your methods of choice should be heavily weighted toward online communication. However, if you want to brand yourself as a hometown, hands-on expert (whether in baking or plumbing or any other field), you should plan to make yourself visible in your community in as many ways as possible.

The following starter list offers ideas on how you can deliver your content message:

- Be a community volunteer.
- Join professional associations.
- Create a blog.
- Start a Yahoo! group and moderate it.
- Create a website.
- Write articles.
- Conduct a webinar or teleseminar.
- Write a book or e-book.
- Write From The Expert articles in the local paper.
- Brand your e-mail signature.
- Write a newsletter or contribute to one.
- Interview others for case studies.
- Start a theme-specific book or movie group.
- Create networking events.
- Sponsor events that are important to you (such as a wine tasting, a sporting event, micro-financing events for entrepreneurs, or speakers of interest to your target audience).
- Record a podcast with your content expertise.
- Speak at events within your target market.
- Write a *whitepaper,* a report written for your target audience that helps solve one of their problems.

- Deliver workshops.
- Create videos and post them on YouTube.
- Post your profile on social media sites (such as LinkedIn).
- Issue press releases.
- Teach a college or adult school class.
- Comment on other people's blogs.
- Post book reviews online at Amazon or Barnes & Noble.

Setting the Strategy

It's not about being famous, it is about being selectively famous.

— William Arruda

Setting the strategy to guide your communication plan is like setting any good set of goals. You first want to think about the big picture of what you hope to accomplish in communicating with your target audience. The big-picture goal is best accomplished by then filling in your plan with details of how you'll implement that plan. By including details about the activities you want to use to promote your personal brand, you'll be more likely to follow the activities through to action.

Perhaps you're new to your field and no one knows who you are. Your goal may be to become more visible so that people in your field recognize your name when they hear it. Here is how one colleague achieved that.

I belong to a Yahoo! group for career professionals. One of the participants started posting career-related articles almost daily. She has brilliantly become known in a relatively short period of time as a resource expert. Everyone knows who she is, and she has achieved high visibility in her chosen field. She was quickly perceived not as someone new to the field but rather as someone who is an expert.

When you create your plan, think about pieces of information that you can duplicate, reuse, or point in a new direction. Is there a type of communication that you can create that can be used in different ways? Following is an example of a well-planned communication strategy.

Steven decides that his communication strategies should include writing articles, speaking, blogging, and joining a professional organization. For each month of the coming year, he determines specific details related to each of these strategies so that he can accomplish his goals:

- Steven's article writing strategy is that he will write one article every three months and submit these articles to his professional journals. On his communication plan calendar, he enters what month he wants to write the articles, the names of the associations to submit to, and subject ideas.
- His speaking strategy is to research the names of at least six organizations that he would like to speak to during the next year. He will contact all six organizations within the first three months of the year and offer to speak on the article topics.
- To build a blog identity, he considers whether he wants to create a blogging forum or contribute to other people's sites. He determines that his own blog forum should be his primary focus. He will blog about the same subjects that he plans to write articles about, and he decides that he will write blog posts twice a week, posting new information every Tuesday and Friday.
- Steven wants to join a professional organization, so he plans to conduct an Internet search for professional association meetings in his area and to read the local business publications to see what meetings are scheduled. He will attend at least three meetings within the first half of the year and will join the organization whose mission and activities seem most beneficial to him.

TIP

Remember to be lazy! You can write one article and break it down into smaller parts to use as blog posts. That same article can become the topic that you give a presentation on to a professional association, or you can use it inside your company to present as a brown bag lunch talk to your colleagues. Find something you enjoy and use it for each one of your goals, such as writing, speaking, blogging, and volunteering.

Considering a sample communications plan

After you write your goals and the details of how you plan to achieve them (a process similar to the one Steven went through in the preceding section), you should create a communications plan that looks similar to the one I present in this section.

The sample plan in Table 11-1 illustrates how you may put your plan into action within several different goal areas — in this case Personal Communications, Professional Associations/Community, Career Thought Leadership, and Inside My Company. The details are outlined monthly; note that something is happening each month in each of the categories. Putting together a plan helps you put your thoughts into action and move you toward building a more visible and credible personal brand.

Table 11-1 A Sample Communications Plan

Month	*Personal Communications*	*Professional Associations/ Community*	*Career Thought Leadership*	*Inside My Company*
January	Get a professional headshot taken.	Research groups and associations to join.	Research current topics in my area of interest.	Research current topics of interest in my company.
February	Set up LinkedIn and Twitter accounts with my new headshot.	Decide on two community/ professional groups to join.	Write an article about the most interesting topic.	Write an article and post it on the office intranet.
March	Build my LinkedIn account. Add 40 connections.	Join a group. Offer to volunteer.	Start a blog using the article topic.	Offer to do a brown bag lunch talk on the article topic.
April	Build my LinkedIn account. Add 40 more connections.	Attend a teleclass or webinar.	Write two blog posts, and comment on other blogs.	Put the article in the company newsletter.
May	Follow at least 20 new people on Twitter.	Attend a local meeting.	Write two blog posts and comment on other blogs.	Make a Top 5 list of my research topic to send to my coworkers.
June	Post updates to my LinkedIn and Twitter accounts. Update my profiles.	Offer to speak at a local group on my article topic.	Write two blog posts and comment on other blogs.	Find a new topic of interest to write about at work.
July	Post updates to LinkedIn and Twitter.	Participate in an online community meeting.	Write a new article and submit it to a professional association.	Write a new article.
August	Post updates to LinkedIn and Twitter.	Do some volunteer work.	Write two blog posts. Submit article to more sites.	Break my article down into short info bites for my coworkers.
September	Review my profiles and post updates to LinkedIn and Twitter.	Attend a local meeting.	Write two blog posts and comment on other blogs.	Offer to do a brown bag lunch talk on my new article topic.
October	Post updates to LinkedIn and Twitter.	Participate in an online community meeting.	Write two blog posts and comment on other blogs.	Put my article in the company newsletter.
November	Post updates to LinkedIn and Twitter.	Volunteer at a food bank.	Write two blog posts and comment on other blogs.	Organize a food drive in my department.
December	Send holiday greetings to my friends and contacts.	Attend a local meeting.	Send my article to my contacts.	Send holiday greetings to my coworkers.

Building word-of-mouth support

Every business owner knows that he has reached an important milestone when he begins receiving more word-of-mouth referrals than business from other means of marketing. It means that he has delivered an exceptional service or product that his customers are happy to talk about to their community.

You want to be what others are talking about — in a good way. For example, if you're a hairstylist, you want to be the first person who comes to mind when someone asks a friend, "Do you know where I can get a good haircut?" To achieve that goal, you need to be known for something. Do you offer the least expensive haircuts? The best quality haircuts? The craziest haircuts? The best coloring of gray roots in town?

What if you aren't a business owner? Word-of-mouth support is still crucial. That's because word-of-mouth-support is what's known as the *hidden job market* — it's where most jobs come from. When a company has a job opening, the person in charge of hiring is almost certainly going to ask friends and professional colleagues if they know of anyone who fits the bill. Building and keeping a network of fans and supporters can help you find the right opportunities and the right people.

To build a strong word-of-mouth network, you need to show that you're sharing information to help others and promote them as well. People always like to promote others who are promoting them! The clearer you are about your brand message, the easier you make it for people to spread the word about you and build your network. (You can explore how to build your network in Chapter 15.)

Achieving the Three Cs

According to William Arruda, founder of Reach Communication, all strong brands boast the three Cs: Clarity, Consistency, and Constancy. These brands deliver on their brand promise every day with everything they do, and they are constantly visible to their target audience — the people who are making decisions about them. The three Cs help you express your personal brand with confidence and energy, so you want to be sure to build them into your communications plan.

Clarity: Crafting a clear message

Strong brands are clear about who they are and who they are not. Achieving clarity is often the hardest part of the communications plan because you may have a hard time deciding what you stand for, especially early in your career.

Clarity comes from understanding and embodying your unique promise of value. Review your unique promise of value in Chapter 7 to help you form a clearer idea of what you want to communicate.

Often, the clearer your stand, the more enemies you will have. I think what holds many people back from taking a stand is knowing that some people will not like them or agree with them. But strong brands have a clear message, and you need to have the courage to communicate yours. Having a clear message doesn't give you permission to have bad behavior. It does mean that you clearly communicate your message and stick to it. Being clear about your message and living in alignment with who you are is a freeing way to live.

Consistency: Presenting the same message every time

When you are clear about your message, you want to deliver the message consistently no matter what communication method you use. Every time you send your message, it needs to be perceived in the same way.

For example, every time you see Kenny Chesney singing, he is wearing his cowboy hat. He is consistent in his brand. Your clothing, your words, your tone of voice, the graphics you use in your written communications . . . all these items can help you send a consistent message, so be sure you think hard about the message you're sending to your audience. (You discover the importance of clothing to your personal brand in Chapter 12, and I discuss your brand's visual identity in Chapter 13.)

If you're trying to brand yourself as a solid professional whom people can count on, you need to deliver that message with everything that you do and every message that you send. That means you need to save your flighty, indecisive self for private times and not tarnish your brand with inconsistency.

Constancy: Designing a plan so that people hear your message frequently

Strong brands are *always* visible to their target markets. This means that if you're trying to build your personal brand, you need to make sure that you stay visible regularly. You can't disappear for months on end and hope that people will still remember you.

Developing and implementing your communications plan helps you stay visible to your target markets. I have colleagues who send a monthly newsletter or chair an organization where they're seen by the people who need to see them every month. Others are weekly bloggers. Find the communication tool that you enjoy and constantly use it to remain visible to your people. Carve out a small amount of time, often as little as 15 minutes, daily or weekly to update your communication channels.

Establishing Yourself as an Expert

Being known as an expert provides credibility to your brand. Expertise establishes why people will initially want to engage with you and why they will think of you, and your brand, to solve their problems.

Tina Fey claimed her expertise as a *Bossypants* (Little, Brown & Company) in her autobiography by the same title. She pokes fun at herself in the book and plays the bossy pants role on her TV show *30 Rock* as well. Most people don't stand up and own their bossiness, but for Fey, doing so has certainly worked!

Throughout this book, I encourage you to examine your many characteristics in order to uncover your unique promise of value (see Chapter 7). That promise identifies what you want to be known for and the behavior you authentically demonstrate to achieve your goals.

To be known as an expert at something, you often just need to own what you do well. And if you aren't sure that you do anything particularly well (yet), take the initiative to read and study about an area of interest so that you can claim that area as your own!

TIP

Here are a few suggestions on claiming your expertise:

- Become very knowledgeable about your chosen area of expertise. Obviously, you need to know what you're talking about to be an expert!
- Find a *niche* (your distinct segment of the market) that you can claim for your area of expertise.
- Seek endorsements from your boss, coworkers, or clients attesting to your expertise. If you're in business for yourself, you may want to add these statements as testimonials to your website — but remember to ask for permission first.
- Dress like the expert that you are. Chapter 12 tells you how.
- Build relationships that support your area of expertise. Find more about building your network in Chapter 15.
- Exude confidence in your knowledge. In other words, act confidently. Even if you don't feel confident, fake it until you believe it!

Using your niche to find your uniqueness

Responding to the directive to "be unique" can be tough. What if you don't know how to stand out? How do you figure out your niche?

The best place to start is with what you know. What do you know how to do that few others know how to do? What segment of the population do you understand better than most people in your field do? Chapter 6 guides you further to discover your niche.

I often find that people overlook the everyday parts of their lives that they know and do well in. For example, maybe you really understand a specific group of people (such as senior citizens or teenagers or people who love to shop). Maybe you're the best person in your office at producing Excel spreadsheets. Maybe you shine when it comes to keeping everyone organized and moving forward. Maybe you're the office cheerleader who knows exactly when to lighten the mood and help everyone blow off steam. Your unique combination of work experience, life experience, and personal characteristics create the foundation for determining your niche.

When you're entering or reentering the workforce, pinpointing what makes you unique is especially hard. Take the case of Kate, a new college graduate with a business major looking for her first job. She had the same sort of education that thousands of other recent college graduates had. However, she had also traveled to 26 countries by the age of 22. When Kate was interviewed with the international division of a large retailer as an entry-level financial analyst, they were thrilled to find someone with her experience. Her interest in travel created a niche for her that she hadn't even considered.

To be known in a certain niche, you're wise to choose an area of expertise or market segment that isn't saturated. If you're a personal trainer, for example, you may get lost in a sea of generic personal trainers. If, however, you're a personal trainer who specializes in rugby players in a market with an active rugby league, you will create a powerful and distinctive niche.

Staying authentic

As you prepare to take your expertise out into the world, make sure that you walk your talk. You don't want to be someone who talks a good game and has no substance to back it up. Personal brands are built on authenticity. You need to be real and offer real expertise.

You don't need to be a Supreme Court Justice to claim your expertise as an attorney. However, you do need to know something well enough that you can build a communications plan around it and back it up with substance.

If you're just emerging as an expert, start small. Be an expert in a small arena before widening to a larger audience. You can gradually build your presence to a wider group of people after you've established yourself.

Preparing a personal press release

A *press release* reports an event or situation that someone wants to promote. It's designed to be sent to journalists (whether for print and online media sources) and encourage them to develop a story about that event or situation. What kind of things would a personal press release promote? It could announce a book you've just written or alert your target audience of your content-rich blog or a workshop you're giving. Make yourself newsworthy, and think about writing a press release to showcase your brand.

The following steps walk you through the basic formatting for a press release:

1. **Start by writing a header.**

   It should look like this:

   FOR IMMEDIATE RELEASE:
   Contact:
   Contact Person
   Company Name
   Telephone Number
   Fax Number
   E-mail Address
   Website address

2. **Write a headline.**

   Keep it to one sentence. Capitalize the first letter of all of the words, but DON'T USE ALL CAPS OR EXCLAMATION POINTS!!! (Doing so can be annoying to the reader.) Make the headline newsworthy.

3. **Write a strong introductory paragraph.**

   You want this paragraph to grab the reader's attention and contain the information most relevant to your message, such as the who, what, when, where, and why. It should give an overview of the press release as if the reader were only going to read that one paragraph. The first paragraph summarizes your entire message and includes a hook (which is usually a hard fact) to get your audience interested in reading more. (For example, if you're giving a talk about fraud prevention, your hook may be that more than 10 million Americans are victims of identity theft each year, and you offer five specific tips for avoiding their fate.) Also include the physical location of an event and the month, day, and year.

4. **Write the body of the press release.**

   These next two or three paragraphs contain more detailed information. Expand on the information offered in your first paragraph and include quotes from colleagues, customers, or subject matter experts.

   REMEMBER Keep in mind that you're writing a press release to attract the attention of the media. Therefore, you must be factually accurate and have an angle that will appeal to journalists. Always put your most important information first and let your less important information come last in the release.

5. **Write a final paragraph that restates and summarizes the key points of your release.**

   In that last paragraph, also repeat your contact information (your name, address, phone, fax, e-mail, and website address).

TIP Here are some additional tips for writing a release:

- Write your press release in the third person.
- Prepare a message that is newsworthy and has substance. Tie it into current news, a holiday, or an event.
- Ask yourself how people will relate to your release and tell your audience why this information is intended for them.
- Use correct grammar and spelling. Avoid excessive use of adjectives and jargon.
- Present the facts to make it newsworthy.
- Write like a journalist by avoiding assumptions or crazy promises.
- Try to keep the press release to fewer than 500 words total. Succinct and to the point work best.
- Submit your press release to free sites like `www.free-press-release.com`.

Creating an Experience for Your Audience

As you take your communications plan and your expertise into the world, you want to make sure that you allow for flexibility in your interactions with your target audience. In other words, use your communications plan and your expertise as tools to give you momentum and confidence and use that confidence to allow you to improvise. No matter what field you're in, you have to bring a human touch to your personal interactions or else your target audience may not feel comfortable doing business with you.

Keep this in mind: Your target audience wants an experience — not just a product or service. When someone reaches out to you for help with a problem, she takes for granted that you have the expertise to assist with that problem. (And she may not have the knowledge to judge your expertise anyway.) Therefore, the first impression you make is with the relationship you create and the human bond you establish. Assuming that you perform your job with skill (by delivering on the expertise you've promised), the job well done supports that first impression, and you become the go-to person the next time a similar problem arises.

REMEMBER

Living in a branded world means that you live in an experience economy. You engage your target market not just with what you can provide but with who you are. Something happens in the interaction between you and your target audience that changes the way your audience feels. When you customize an experience to each person you meet (while still being true to your personal brand), you make a memorable impression. That interaction becomes transformative in some way.

Experiences are personal; no two people can experience the same situation exactly the same way. If you can deliver your personal brand authentically, you will create an experience and a memory of who you are and what you do. Show the world how good you are at being you.

Part IV
Controlling Your Brand Ecosystem

The 5th Wave

By Rich Tennant

In this part . . .

This part covers how to work toward getting every component of your world as on-brand as possible. I show you how to dress the part of your personal brand and discuss how to create marketing materials that fit the bill. (The fonts, colors, and images you select are crucial.)

Your brand ecosystem depends on who you are (a college student? young professional? woman in the corporate world? entrepreneur?), so I discuss specific populations in this part as well. I also show you how to tweak your brand as needed when your career takes you overseas.

Finally, I explain how to build and nurture a professional network and how to promote your personal brand within your workplace.

Chapter 12

Fashioning Your Image to Match Your Personal Brand

In This Chapter

- Dressing and grooming for your brand
- Matching your clothes with your brand characteristics
- Mastering your body language and voice
- Smiling for the camera
- Taking an image quiz

Your personal image is a culmination of what you say, how you say it, your actions, body language, grooming, and the way you dress. Your image is all the ways in which you present yourself.

Have you ever wondered why some individuals seem effortlessly to succeed in attaining their personal and professional goals, while for others success doesn't come naturally? Consider what happens when someone doesn't look prepared to take on an opportunity: Most likely that chance passes right by. Success occurs when your preparation meets an opportunity. Being prepared with appropriate knowledge, skills, and resources (including those in your closet!) gives you the confidence to pursue your goals. This chapter helps you prepare your image so that it supports your personal brand.

Realizing How Much Appearances Matter

For years, I have been a Boy Scout counselor for the Communications merit badge. I work with 12- to 15-year-old boys on this badge. You can imagine what a challenging audience they can be! I like to start the training by asking the boys this question: If our total communication score is 100 percent, what percentage of our communication is

- **Verbal:** The content of what you say
- **Vocal:** How you sound when you say it
- **Visual:** How you look when you say it

Most of the boys know instinctively that how you look when you say something is probably the highest percentage, but they have a hard time guessing how much. They then begin to argue about whether the content of what you say is more important than how you sound. They're sure that content is really important.

A 1967 study done at UCLA established what's called the *Mehrabian rule.* The research found that in a very specific situation (where people were communicating about emotions and attitudes), 7 percent of what came across depended on the content of what was said; 38 percent depended on how it was said (the speaker's voice, tone, and accents); and 55 percent depended on how the person looked when communicating.

REMEMBER

I'm not claiming that these percentages hold exactly true for every situation in everyday communications. And I'm certainly not trying to encourage you to ignore the content of your communications! However, the study did drive home the point that visual (nonverbal) communication is hugely important. For example, if I'm trying to get across the message to a potential client that I want his business, I may speak the words "I'm really excited about the possibility of working with you." The words are my content, and they're on target. But what if I fail to make eye contact when I speak? And what if I'm slouching or (heaven forbid!) stifling a yawn when I say them? Is my potential client going to believe that what I'm saying is true? I seriously doubt it!

The take-home point is that what your listeners *see* in a face-to-face encounter is at least as important as what they *hear* from you, so don't neglect your nonverbal communication. Dress the part you want to play (using the tips in this chapter), pay attention to your mannerisms, and if you suspect that something in your visual presentation may be off-putting to your audience, ask a trusted friend or colleague for feedback. (Maybe you don't realize that you tend to scowl when you're listening intently or that you fiddle with your watch when you speak, for example. If you're really concerned, arrange to have yourself videotaped when you're speaking in public so you can see what others see.)

Have You Got the Look? Focusing on Clothes and Grooming

Diana Jennings, personal brand & image strategist and the owner of Brand You Image, is the chief contributor to this chapter. Diana is a successful image consultant who specializes in nonverbal communication.

Does your clothing represent the sum of who you are or a just a fraction of the whole you? Presuming that you're aiming for a position that includes greater responsibility, dressing for the life you aspire to means demonstrating attention to detail, particularly as it relates to proper fit. I'm not just talking about physical fit here; I'm talking about a *psychological* fit, which means that your clothing represents your values and personality, and a *situational* fit, which means your look complements your role and the occasion.

Everything you wear conveys information about you. For this reason, you need to understand the foundational details of a well-dressed individual. Be realistic and honest with yourself about what fits your body and what doesn't. Do your research by shopping without buying. Learn what brands and designers cut their garments in a shape most similar to your body. Successful people connect well with others through their writing, speaking, *and* nonverbal communication. They recognize that their clothing and grooming (as well as their body language, which I discuss in the "Recognizing That You Are Always on Display" section in the chapter) are nonverbal tools they can control to help them achieve their goals and ambitions.

What you wear and how you wear it has a domino effect. Judith Rasband, certified image master and director of the Conselle Institute for Image Management, refers to the *universal effects of image.* This phrase is appropriate because the way you look affects the way

- You think about yourself.
- You feel about yourself.
- You speak.
- You act or conduct yourself.
- Others react or respond to you.

Color is an important aspect of your personal brand in the clothing that you wear. You can find out more about color in Chapter 13. In the following sections, I offer specific tips to help you steer your clothing and grooming choices in the right direction.

Career dressing for men

In this section, Diana Jennings suggests essential criteria related to pieces in a man's wardrobe that can help you look your best and visually communicate your personal brand.

Suit jacket:

- The collar lays flat against your shirt.
- The fabric is smooth across your back (no wrinkles or bunching).
- The suit jacket is long enough to cover your buttocks.
- Each sleeve is hemmed to where your wrist and hand meet.

Shirt:

- It's pressed and lightly starched. (Heavy starching decreases the lifespan of your shirts.)
- The collar is comfortably loose enough for one finger to fit in the neckline.
- The shirt collar stands a half-inch above your suit collar.
- The sleeves extend a half-inch below your jacket sleeves.

Trousers:

- The waistband fits smoothly over your stomach and doesn't curve under.
- The pockets lay flat and do not pull open.
- The leg fabric hangs straight down from your buttocks.
- The legs are hemmed long enough to rest on the tops of your shoes, producing a slight break.

Shoes:

- They're leather.
- They fit comfortably.
- They're polished and in good condition.
- They match your attire in terms of level of dressiness.

Tie:

- It's a classic tie width (2¾"–3½").
- It's tied with a dimple or crease centered right below the knot.

- The tip of the tie brushes the top of your belt buckle.
- It matches your attire in terms of level of dressiness. (The larger the tie pattern, the more casual the message.)

Socks:

- The color matches or blends with your trousers.
- They're made of wool or cotton, which allows air to flow and reduces heat and perspiration.
- They're long enough to cover your calf.

Miscellaneous accessories:

- Your belt color matches your shoes or relates to your suit color.
- You wear either a belt or suspenders, never both.
- Your pocket square complements your tie but does not match it.
- Your watch matches the dressiness of your attire. (The thinner the watch, the dressier it is.)

Career dressing for women

EXPERT OPINION

In this section, Jennings gives suggestions to emphasize a polished branded look for a woman's wardrobe. Regardless of your shape or height, these are the basic rules of being well-dressed.

Jacket:

- It closes with ease at the bust and hip lines.
- It fits well under your arms and across your back.
- It's long enough to drape over wider hips.
- Full-length sleeves are hemmed to where your wrist and hand meet.
- You can substitute a sweater for a jacket to relax the look.

Blouse:

- Layer a sleeveless top under a jacket, sweater, or shirt jacket.
- The neckline is 2 inches above your cleavage. If it's lower than that, wear a nonlaced camisole under the blouse.
- The fabric is wrinkle-free and smooth across your bust and back.
- It's long enough to stay tucked in, or else it's hemmed at the hip bone.

Slacks:

- There's enough room in the waistband for you to insert two fingers.
- The pleats and zippers lie flat.
- The leg fabric falls straight down from the buttocks.
- The fabric across the front of your legs is smooth without visible stretching.
- They conceal your panty line.

Skirt:

- The pleats do not pull open.
- There is no crease or pull across the front or back of your legs.
- It's hemmed at the knee and does not rise up more than 3 inches above your knee when you're seated.
- It easily turns around your body.
- If it's a pencil skirt, it hangs in a straight line and does not curve under your buttocks.
- Its slit (if it has one) is a maximum 3 to 4 inches above your knee.

Dress:

- It's a coat dress, a shirt dress, or a two-piece matching top and skirt.
- The neckline is 2 inches above your cleavage. If it's lower than that, wear a nonlaced camisole under the dress.
- The fabric is a solid color or a medium to small print. Avoid floral prints if you want to be taken seriously.

Shoes:

- They're a neutral color.
- They have a closed toe or a minimal peep toe.
- They have a closed heel or a back heel strap.
- They have a conservative heel height. (Reserve stiletto heels for after work hours.)
- They're polished and in good condition.

Hosiery:

- It's neutral or a coordinated color that blends with your hemline.
- If you're choosing hosiery that matches your natural skin tone, it's either the same shade as your shoes or lighter — never darker than your shoes.

- Avoid bright colors, which draw attention down to your leg area.
- Keep an extra pair of hosiery on hand to replace a pair with runs or snags.

TIP

Wearing hosiery keeps the message professional. If you have bare legs, you're taking the message to a personal level. You can achieve a bare-legged look while still maintaining your professionalism by finding a brand of hose that's sheer and neutral.

Jewelry:

- Simple and understated pieces are best for most work environments.
- Larger pieces make a fashion statement and should be appropriate for the work environment and no larger than the size of a quarter.
- Avoid dangling or large hoop earrings that give an unprofessional look.
- Also avoid noisy jewelry or pieces that move.
- A necklace, in particular, should be simple in design and understated to avoid drawing too much attention to your neckline.

Accessories:

- Avoid wearing tinted lenses indoors.
- Wear a watch that is simple in design and understated.
- Carry your purse *or* briefcase into a meeting but never both.

Grooming tips

Like the clothes you wear, your grooming is a complex form of visual, nonverbal communication. Grooming not only includes keeping your body clean and odor-free but also caring for and maintaining your teeth, breath, hair, hands, and nails. Body piercings and tattoos are best covered up in the work environment.

Casual Fridays

Casual Fridays present another dilemma for the well-dressed personal brander. You're always on display, and even your casual clothing on Fridays, work casual functions, and off-site retreats should be on-brand for you. If your look is one of the professional, your casual clothes should not be too casual. You'll want to carry the same image into your casual clothing only with a less formal look. A rumpled shirt doesn't send the message of competence whether you're in the office or at the company retreat.

TIP

Sufficient sleep and rest also factor into the equation so that you can look your best and appear to be ready for the next opportunity.

Managing your grooming routine communicates an attention to detail that helps you create a positive first and lasting impression about you and your abilities.

For men:

- Opt to be clean-shaven or else wear a well-shaped and closely trimmed moustache or beard. Even a 5 o'clock shadow needs to look intentional and groomed.
- Keep your nose and ear hair trimmed and your eyebrows neat.
- To maintain a polished look, see your barber/stylist every three to five weeks. The easiest way to stay on top of your appointments is to schedule several months out at a time.
- Invest in a small hair trimmer. It's the best tool for keeping the back of your neck groomed between appointments.

For women:

- A light and natural application of makeup enhances your appearance and shows that you put thought into your head-to-toe appearance.
- Shape and regularly maintain your eyebrows.
- Choose a hairstyle that is current and easy to keep up. Very long hair is best worn up to be distraction-free.
- Keep nails well manicured.

Styles for your body type

Be realistic and honest with yourself about what fits your body and what doesn't. Not all designers cut for the same figure type, nor are all styles suited to all body shapes. Do your research. Discover what brands and designers cut for a figure type most similar to your own.

Find a style that highlights your best assets and diminishes those parts of your body that you would rather not emphasize. All you need to do is to take a walk downtown to see what people *shouldn't* be wearing! You don't want people thinking those same thoughts about you.

REMEMBER

Personal branding takes your best self out into the world. The look that you present speaks to that. Let the best parts of your image be seen and let the right clothing cover the rest.

Branding Your Attributes to Look Like You

Having a personal brand means that you know who you are and what you stand for. As I say throughout this book, your brand must be authentic because pretending to be someone else can be painful and exhausting. When it comes to creating a style that boosts your personal brand image, your goal is to wear clothes that you feel good in and that help you visually express the real you. When your style matches your brand, your best self can shine through.

In Chapter 4, I help you identify your personal brand characteristics. These attributes have visual characteristics as well, which translate into certain looks. In this section, I help you get specific about how to convey your brand by making certain style choices.

Choosing clothes based on your personal brand characteristics

The more you understand what clothing details convey, the easier it is to consistently and precisely manage your nonverbal communication. These tips help you convey your brand characteristics by choosing the right wardrobe:

- **Cheerful:** Try to develop a wardrobe that features colorful accents.
- **Conservative:** Aim to be neatly dressed in coordinated outfits, modestly buttoned up, with a haircut that is simple to style and easy to maintain.
- **Creative:** You can wear an eclectic mix of garments, patterns, and textures.
- **Organized:** Pay close attention to the details of your image and appearance. An organized person pays attention to the details. This person is neat, and each piece of clothing is in place.
- **Modest or religious:** Wear garments that do not call attention to your body.
- **Refined or sophisticated:** Invest in quality clothing and accessories. Your look should be well-coordinated and your grooming impeccable and flawless.
- **Helpful:** Focus on styles and fabrics that are approachable, a more relaxed fit, softer fabrics, and softer colors.

Aligning your style with your work goals

After you define your personal style, you need to consider what works and what doesn't work for your company, your desired position, and your personal goals so that you can harmoniously and authentically blend them together. Every workplace has a certain look that represents the company. In some companies, that look is written into the dress code. Other companies have unwritten rules about what to wear. You need to dress the part for the role you play, the work you do, and the company you do it with.

Certain clothes, fabrics, and styles help you create certain looks. In this section, I offer suggestions for achieving three looks that have been adapted from Judith Rasband at the Conselle Institute of Image Management.

Serious, authoritative, distant, and demanding

Men want to wear straight lines, dark or dull colors like black or gray, firm or stiff fabric, small patterns, pinstripes, point or snap tab collars, long sleeves, tailored plain or reverse pleat pants, matched suits with minimal trim, a small to medium pattern tie, and conservative accessories to achieve the look.

Women should wear the female version of the man's straight lines, restrained curves, dark or dull colors like black or gray, stiff fabrics, small patterns, pinstripes, high or buttoned collars, long sleeves, straight and A-line skirts, matched suits, coatdresses, minimal trim, and small to medium conservative jewelry to achieve a serious and authoritative look.

Energetic, fun, friendly, approachable, and outgoing

Men can wear clothing with curved lines, brighter colors, knits, plaids, checks, stripes, or prints, soft fabrics, loose fits, bold contrasts, polo, crew, henley, or mock turtle necklines, open collars, short or pushed-up sleeves, casual style belts, socks, or shoes, hats, or gloves for this look.

Women can enjoy full-curved lines; bright colors; gathers or pleats; knits; plaids, prints, or polka dots; soft fabrics; bold contrasting colors; scoop necklines or open collars; short, puffed, or pushed-up sleeves; colorful trim; and casual larger jewelry for this look.

Calm, quiet, gentle, and supportive

Men need to wear solid colors, subtle color contrast, small patterns, small floral or paisley print ties, softly tailored styles, soft or fine fabrics, soft pleats, natural shoulder lines, and simple and sophisticated accessories to exude this style.

Women should wear solid colors, subtle color contrast, small and floral prints, soft and delicate sheer fabrics, fitted styles, soft gathers and flair, bows, and small or delicate jewelry to exude this style.

Recognizing That You Are Always on Display

You are your personal brand every time someone interacts with you. Your personal brand is more than what you wear; it's the image you project with your entire being. How you carry yourself, your facial expressions, and how you sound all matter. Do you send the same message with a 39-cent pen as you do with a nice quality pen? Each item you carry adds up to your brand image.

REMEMBER

Video and voice recording devices embedded right in cellphones make it hard to hide bad behavior! Living your authentic brand means that you need to embody who that is in all that you do. Act as if you are always on display — because you are.

Getting your body language to be on message

I try to live by the axiom that actions speak louder than words. Your actions and how you conduct the tasks of the day give others insight into who you are. Body language consciously or unconsciously communicates your feelings or psychological state and consists of facial expressions, body posture, and movement.

Facial expressions

Your facial expressions communicate mood and a willingness to connect with others. A smile is a smile in all languages and, when genuine, opens doors for others to connect with you. A returned smile shows that you've had a moment of connection and creates a safe space between you and the other person.

REMEMBER

Eye contact demonstrates your level of interest in the person or the topic at hand. When quality eye contact is missing, it's likely that your interaction will not be perceived positively. I can think of many situations when I didn't trust someone who wouldn't look me in the eye. In the American business culture, eye contact is associated with trust, and in order to have a positive personal brand, people must trust you.

Some people are so transparent that you can tell how they feel by the look on their face. If this is you, be aware of how your emotions are reflected by your facial expressions and how others receive your expressions. It's a good lesson to begin to observe how your facial expressions impact others' reactions to you.

If you aren't sure what other people see when they speak to you, ask a friend to videotape you during a casual conversation. You may be surprised by what you see!

Body posture

When you were a kid, maybe your parents or teachers reminded you to stand up straight or sit up in your chair. But as an adult, you likely don't get those reminders anymore. That's why I'm here: To remind you that standing and sitting up straight are still important.

Body posture plays a big role when sitting in a group, when you are at an interview, or whenever you meet with someone one-on-one (including when you're on a date). In other words, your body posture matters in *every* situation where you're meeting with someone in person, in a videoconference, or on Skype via webcam.

How you carry yourself speaks to your level of confidence and communicates the attitude you have for where you are at that moment. For example, if you are at a table and are slightly leaning forward toward the other person, that position shows an interest in what the person is saying. In contrast, if you're leaning back in your chair with your legs stretched out and hands behind your head, you send a message of arrogance and disinterest.

You can use your clothing as a tool to help you maintain better posture. The more structure a garment (such as a jacket) has, the more it reminds you to stand or sit a little taller. If the attire is too relaxed, baggy, or sloppy, it allows you to unconsciously slouch.

The best way to start improving your posture is simply to observe yourself. Take a moment to notice how you walk, stand, sit, and interact with others. Notice whether your posture and body movements are on or off brand.

Handshake

A handshake is an offering to connect. It is a greeting that, properly done, says "I am pleased to meet you" and conveys your confidence. A handshake greets the other person with an extension of your energy and sets the tone for your interaction.

You don't want to offer either a hand-crushing grip or a hand masquerading as a limp fish. The hand-crushing grip conveys domination and competition, while a limp fish handshake sends a clear message of low self-esteem and weakness. This advice goes for both men and women. If you aren't sure whether your handshake passes muster, ask a friend or family member to help you find the right firmness that conveys confidence.

Movement

How you move communicates either confidence or insecurity. Without consciously thinking about it, your movement can deliver a greater sense of clarity of who you are and what you represent. The way you walk down the hall can signal your level of calm, stress, enthusiasm, or aggression. How you pass an item to another person can reveal the level of respect you show for the situation, item, or recipient. Hand gestures can indicate whether you're annoyed with someone or being patient and understanding.

TIP

I can't possibly list every type of body movement and how it could be interpreted, so I offer this advice: Pay attention to your movements when you're feeling calm and confident, and the next time you get really upset about something, try to notice how your body movement changes. Maybe you'll discover that you walk very quickly or use more hand gestures when you're angry or insecure. Maybe you crack your knuckles when you're under pressure, or you put your hands on your hips, or you massage your temples. Whatever movements emerge during those unpleasant times are cues to the people around you that you aren't on your game. When you become aware of your actions under pressure, you can make an effort to control them going forward.

Voicing your brand

Obviously, your voice is a crucial communication tool. In the "Realizing How Much Appearances Matter" section, I explain that studies show your voice accounts for a significant percentage of your overall communication — a higher percentage than the content of your speech! The quality of your voice is crucial to the quality of your communications. I can remember my mother commenting about someone that "She is such a pretty girl until she opens her mouth."

If you master your voice, it can be a positive part of your image and brand.

Pitch, pace, enunciation, and volume

Some people (as diverse as Vincent Price and Gilbert Gottfried) build an entire career out of a distinct voice. You likely don't need to base your entire career on your voice, but you do need to consider how you sound:

- **Pitch:** Is your pitch very high or very low? While you can't radically change the voice that you were born with, you *can* practice changing your pitch. A high-pitched voice can come across as screeching or whining, which usually doesn't serve you well. If your tone falls outside the normal range, practice changing your pitch. (Sometimes just slowing down your pace can help you lower your pitch.)

- **Pace:** *Pace* is the speed at which you talk. Are you a New York–type fast talker? A southern-style slow-talker? Yes, I'm dealing in stereotypes here, but pace is important if you want to connect with your audience. A perfect pace doesn't exist; instead, you often need to pick up your pace or slow it down to mesh with your audience. In other words, try to mirror (to some extent) the people you're speaking to and match the pace at which they speak. Don't exaggerate this effort, or else you'll end up sounding and feeling foolish, but practice altering your pace slightly in order to connect with your listeners.
- **Enunciation:** Are you clear when you speak? Do you enunciate your words? Obviously, it's important to speak clearly so that people can understand you. I have seen brilliant scientists held back in their careers because no one could understand them when they spoke. Poor enunciation is especially problematic when English is a second language. If you're hard to understand, work with a linguistic coach to learn to more effectively communicate your brilliance.
- **Volume:** You want to speak with a moderate volume, neither too softly or too loudly. The volume of your voice, like the radio in your car, needs to be at the right sound level. Observe yourself and notice whether people ever comment that you're speaking too softly or that you could turn it down a notch. If you speak too softy, you can be perceived as weak. If you speak too loudly, you can be perceived as a bully. Have your volume match your brand.

Telephone tips to enhance your brand

I predict that in the near future, most phone calls will have a visual/video component, such as Skype. But until that transition occurs, your voice carries the weight of your phone communications.

When you're speaking on the phone, you need to paint a picture of the missing visual components for your listener. In other words, you need to practice your phone voice. Determine in advance whether your audience responds better to a bubbly, friendly, fast-paced voice or a more serious, reflective, slower paced voice.

And even though you aren't in the same room with your audience, don't stifle your facial expressions while you speak. If the other person says something that would prompt you to smile in a face-to-face encounter, go ahead and smile! Do your best to imitate that face-to-face encounter, and your voice will paint the necessary picture.

Having good phone manners can boost your personal brand score. Let your natural enthusiasm come through in your phone voice and try not to sound flat and monotone. If you're nervous before you make a call, practice what you're going to say. Be confident and practice good pitch, pace, enunciation, and volume to let your brand ring through.

When a call goes through to voicemail, make sure that you follow the same advice. In addition, I appreciate when a caller leaves a clear, understandable message by doing the following:

- Speaking clearly so that I understand what's said.
- Speaking at a pace that allows me to write down a message.
- Saying her name at the beginning and the end of the message.
- Saying the phone number twice and saying it slowly enough for me to write it down.

Having Headshots and Other Photos Taken

Headshots used to be only for chief executives who needed photos for the annual report. But thanks to online media (see Chapter 10), headshots have gone mainstream. Anyone on LinkedIn needs a good headshot — and yes, you should be on LinkedIn, so this means you! You can use your headshot on your professional biography, on all your social media sites, and possibly in the signature of your e-mail.

To take the best headshot possible, keep these points in mind:

- **When you sit for a headshot, *you* should be the focus — not the setting.** Look directly at the camera as if you're engaging in a conversation. You should look natural and comfortable, and you should have a warm, friendly expression on your face.
- **Your photo should be in color, but be careful of having too much vivid color in the background.** If you use a stronger color, make it a solid color.
- **The photo should appear to have natural lighting on a solid, simple background.** You don't want to stand in front of your bulletin board or by a striped wall. Avoid distracting backgrounds.

Think about the audience that you want to attract with your headshot. If it's a business audience, take a few shots with a jacket on and a few without a jacket. When you relax the business dress yet still look professional, a photo has a more open and inviting feel to it. Make sure that you feel good in the clothes that you choose and that you feel successful and aspirational for what is going to come into your life. Keep your look current and don't wear clothes that are out of date.

Here are additional tips for creating your best on-camera look:

- Make sure that you look rested and are feeling well.
- Wear your hair styled in your best look. Wait at least one week after a haircut. Make sure that your hair is clean and that no differently colored roots are showing.
- Men, be aware of your facial hair. Shave before a photo. Be aware that a two-day growth isn't always perceived as professional.
- Women, apply makeup over a good moisturizer so that your skin doesn't appear dry. Wear more makeup than usual, but no frosted makeup. Know how to use makeup to contour for effect.
- Choose clothing that projects the image you want to project. Stick with solid colors; avoid solid white, polka dots, distracting stripes, or wild prints. Don't wear anything that will reflect the lights too much, like a shiny silk blouse.
- Choose a neckline that enhances the shape of your face and neck but is not too low cut.
- Keep in mind that light to medium-dark colors are more flattering to the skin. Avoid dark green, black, or navy.
- Because glasses can reflect the light and cause a glare, take pictures with your glasses both on and off.
- Keep your jewelry simple to keep the focus on your face.
- Don't look straight at the camera. Turn to show the best profile of your face.
- Smile and have a pleasant expression.

Quiz: Your Image Is Showing

EXPERT OPINION

by Valerie Sokolosky

On any given day in various parts of the country, people are hurrying on their way, and each, through clothing, projects a special message to the world: administrative assistants, perfect in their company chic; modern executives in their corporate code; and high-tech programmers in comfy casual. Take this quiz and see what image you're projecting.

1. **Clothing language is an important visual code that projects your talents, needs, personalities, dispositions, and destinations. It lets others know what you're**

    A. Thinking

    B. Feeling

    C. Doing

2. When deciding what image you want to project, you should first decide what the image is

A. That is expected and respected in your organization.

B. That it will take to earn you to the next promotion.

C. Of your peers.

3. As you grow older or simply move through different stages of your career, keep in mind that you should

A. Adapt your outward appearance to project who and what you are

B. Keep a conservative appearance

C. Get more fashion conscious

4. The business-casual dress-code definition means

A. Any type of sportswear

B. Clothing that is comfortable

C. Clothing that is more casual but definitely says "I'm here to do business."

5. Consistency in your image has an impact on the message you give to the world. It means you

A. Like to have things done in a certain way

B. Have a strong sense of self

C. Are analytical in your decision-making style

6. In order to develop trust and believability, it is critical to

A. Take into consideration not only clothing, but also verbal and nonverbal messages

B. Be a trustworthy person yourself

C. Invest in sophisticated clothing and quality fabrics

7. A great deal of your image comes from your

A. Attitude and stance

B. Body shape

C. Wardrobe choices

8. If you're in sales and want to package yourself to help you get more customers, consider the

A. Attitude you want to have

B. Way your competitors look

C. Product or service you sell

9. If a sales professional travels to many parts of the country, it is wise to heed

A. What image the customers project

B. What image the locals project

C. Your own consistent appearance

10. By considering the concept of impression management, you can package yourself to

A. Get more sales and promotions

B. Predict the response people will give to you

C. Show others your level of success

Answers

Give yourself 10 points for every correct answer.

1. **B.** You likely have experienced better treatment when you look especially good, and you also know what it's like to be treated badly when you don't look so great. Your clothing can say, "Hey, I feel beautiful" or "I'm important" or "I'm not so sure of myself" or "I'm feeling aggressive." By overlooking the importance of your image and style, you're apt to convey uncertainty, awkwardness, or low self-esteem.
2. **A.** Don't forget that other people form an opinion of you the first time they meet you, and that impression can take a long time to change. It's important, then, that the first meeting be positive and accurately reflect your occupation and the organization in which you work.
3. **A.** Your image will, and should, change through the various stages of career growth. A first-line supervisor would not want to dress in a power suit every day. A senior executive can do that and be appropriate. Stop and decide what message you want to portray and dress accordingly.
4. **C.** Companies that want a more relaxed atmosphere to foster team cohesiveness and interaction use business-casual as a way to create that environment. What's acceptable varies from company to company and industry to industry but never includes sweat suits, tennis shoes, tights, or sleeveless or see-through anything.
5. **B.** The person who constantly affects different roles through clothing may indicate a search for identity. Important clues can be gained not just from the clothing itself but from the context in which it is worn. Someone who wears bright, colorful accessories one day; dark, somber clothing the next; and the latest fad the next day may likely be unsure of what is representative of himself or his job. Having a sense of personal style creates the image of self-esteem and power.

6. **A.** According to Dr. Albert Mehrabian, your image is reflected this way: 7 percent by what you say, 38 percent by how you say it, and 55 percent by how you look.

7. **A.** A model knows what attitude and stance can do for an outfit. Good posture and self-confident carriage give the illusion of power and positive self-esteem. You can wear a $1,000 suit and sabotage the image by slouching and walking with your head down. The person who stands out from the crowd is one who has a sense of personal style and projects self-confidence.

8. **C.** The product or service has a very important influence on the role the direct sales professional should play. In general, the more directly a product or service influences the customers' money, future, or family, the more serious a role the sales professional must present. Luxury items, recreational products, and novelty products allow the sales professional to be packaged more casually. The more serious the selling situation, the more serious the clothing should be.

9. **C.** You should be consistent in your appearance, even if you're in Florida one day and California the next. Traditional, quality clothing is acceptable everywhere. Although you should not change your image by dressing like the natives, you should remember that some areas of the country are more formal than others. Therefore, your appearance should vary in formality depending on where you are.

10. **B.** It is important to control the image you project to people so that you can predict their response to you. People will respond to the image you present in a predictable way by buying your product, your ideas, or yourself; in other words, look successful, and you will become successful.

Scores

80–100: Whatever you're doing in your career, you're projecting an image that others perceive as positive, credible, and professional. Stay updated and crisp in your personal packaging.

60–70: Whatever your career, pay attention to the impact of your personal style and how clothing affects your total personal presentation.

Below 60: Maybe you've wondered if what you wear makes a difference. After taking this quiz, I hope your awareness has been raised that it makes an impression that can make or break a deal. And if you have this score, you need to pay more attention to your image.

Chapter 13

Your Visual Identity: Making Your Mark on Your Brand Environment

In This Chapter

- Writing your design goals
- Designing an on-brand logo
- Looking for fonts and colors that represent you
- Setting the look of your brand environment

In Chapter 12, I share lots of ideas about why your physical appearance matters and how to make sure that your appearance communicates your brand. In this chapter, I also focus on appearance — this time illustrating how to get the rest of your brand environment (your printed and online marketing materials, as well as your work space) to visually represent your brand.

I give all this attention to appearance not because I'm shallow (or because I have a grudge against ears, noses, tongues, or fingers), but because people make so many consumer decisions based on what they see. You can't smell a website, and you can't hear a brochure. But you certainly can see colors, fonts, and images that either attract or repel you.

If you want your personal brand to soar, you need to figure out what visual elements attract your target audience and use those elements consistently. In this chapter, I offer lots of specifics about how to select colors, fonts, and images that jibe with your brand and set you up for success.

Writing an Effective Design Brief

EXPERT OPINION

Before I jump in to discussions of specific visual elements, I want to assume for a moment that you're putting your brand identity into the hands of a professional designer. The following information, written by Kirsten Dixson of Brand Yourself Online, explains what homework you should do to make sure that the designer accomplishes what you want and need.

Even if you're a do-it-yourselfer and plan to tackle all the design chores on your own (with the help of this chapter), I encourage you to read this section and consider Dixson's suggestions. You may find that drafting a design brief jump-starts your creativity and gets you moving quickly toward your design goals.

Your personal brand identity system provides a powerful layer of communication for your brand. When well executed, it can help to create a strong first impression that compels your target audience to want to learn more.

I highly recommend that you work with a professional designer to identify a color palette, font(s), and other imagery that convey your brand message. You may have a logo designed for your name in the fonts and colors you choose with or without a symbol. You can use this brand identity system everywhere — your e-mail signature, your personal website, your business cards, and the social media profiles that allow for customization, such as Twitter. (For more on social networking sites, see Chapter 10.)

TIP

To ensure that your designer understands both your personal brand and design preferences, it's helpful to write a *design brief* — a document that helps the designer align the business needs of the client with the design to ensure the client's desired outcome. Include information about the standout qualities you'd like to convey and/or the primary message you'd like to communicate with the design alone. Keep this brief focused because you can communicate only so much with the design.

Here's a sample design brief for Mark Johnson.

- **Project Scope:** Blogsite banner for Mark Johnson. His objective is Senior Manager of Information Security at a big-four professional services firm. It's important that he comes across as an information professional rather than a tech guy.
- **Copy:** Insightful business strategies that reduce the risk of breach and secure company information (emphasize "secure company information" in the layout). Mark Johnson will write the draft of his copy.
- **Colors:** He prefers blues and purples. Blue works to convey business, trust, and technology. Purple conveys wealth and high end. The background of his headshot is navy.
- **Fonts:** Mark specified a font called Bladerunner (he describes it as a computer font, yet he's trying to get away from being seen as a CIO), and he's open to recommendations. His target audience, professional services firms, is conservative. He wants a strong, modern font to convey security and innovation.
- **Images:** He wants to use his headshot in the banner. Other imagery could communicate a stable structure/risk management/corporate compliance/global.

TIP

It's helpful to provide your designer with a lightbox of stock photography you like from services such as iStockPhoto and Veer and let your designer know if you have a preference for photography or illustration. Sometimes you can combine several images to create a custom image or alter images to fit.

Leading with Your Personal Logo

Personal branding is about making connections, and the logo you choose should connect with your audience. A logo creates awareness. It can be a symbol, text, a graphic, or a combination of these things. (Keep in mind that people recognize images more often than they remember text.) It symbolizes your brand and provides an image that gives you a memorable identity. Many people associate logos only with company brands, but you can have a logo made just for you as an individual.

You want to keep your logo simple and clean. Here are some other tips for creating a great logo:

- **Shape or symbol:** Symbols are powerful. Create your logo so that it's easy to understand and see without glasses.
- **Color:** Use the color(s) that you consistently employ to represent your personal brand. (I discuss color selection in "Creating a Color Palette," later in this chapter.) Use colors that attract the people you want to attract. Most logos use vibrant colors in order to have the greatest impact.
- **Size:** When you place your logo into your materials, it should be large enough to see clearly and small enough that it doesn't dominate. (Make sure that you have your logo in a file format that allows you to resize it for various projects.)
- **Brand connection:** Think about how you want people to emotionally connect with you. Find a symbol that you care about and use it to connect with others.

REMEMBER

If you love your logo and feel good about it, you'll feel great about putting it on display, so take your time and design something wonderful. And don't be a copycat; you want your logo to be unique.

If you struggle to create a logo yourself, I encourage you to spend the money to get professional help. A great logo pays dividends by attracting business, and (ideally) you want a logo that you can use for years. If you don't know any designers, you can find one online at a design sites like www.elance.com, www.logomojo.com, or www.logodesignguru.com.

Choosing Fonts for Your Personal Brand

Your personal font is very much like your personal handwriting. The typeface you choose for your written materials (including your online materials) makes a strong impression — an impression that occurs before your audience reads a single word of what you've written. A font can show professionalism, a casual attitude, authority, or a creative flair. The fonts you choose to use in your materials need to reflect your personal brand qualities (a topic I cover in Chapter 4).

Think about some handwriting stereotypes for a moment. Pretend that you're playing a word association game, and I'm naming different professions. Your job is to describe their handwriting. Your responses may look something like this:

- **Doctor:** Illegible scratches
- **Architect:** Structured and neat
- **Accountant:** Small and precise
- **Romance novelist:** Curlicue letters with lots of flair

While not even a doctor wants to use a font that mimics illegible scratches, an architect or accountant creating a website may want to consider associations like "structured and neat" and "small and precise" when considering what fonts to use. If an architect or accountant chooses fonts with curlicues and lots of flair, the target audience may not quite know what to make of that presentation. Ditto with a romance novelist who chooses a small, precise font (or a square, chunky font); the people looking at that person's materials may be confused instead of impressed.

At a site like `http://new.myfonts.com`, you can peruse font options and look for those fonts that create the impression you want. Consider the following tips when making your selections:

- **Message and feeling:** Fonts show mood and emotion. A rounded font makes a somewhat casual and relaxed impression. Fonts with straight lines in the serif format feel reliable and trustworthy. A heavy font shows boldness, confidence, and strength, whereas a lighter font presents a softer message. Open fonts give the impression that you are an open, accessible person.
- **Clarity and readability:** Above all else, your font must be legible in both online and printed documents. All the time you spend considering a font's mood and emotion will be wasted if the reader can't quickly and easily figure out what you've written!

When choosing a font for a website, simpler is better because you want the site to open easily across all computer platforms.

- **Less is more:** Choose no more than two or three fonts to use in your materials. You'd never want to mix that many fonts in one document, and you want to use the same font(s) consistently in all your materials. Also, be careful to keep the font size fairly consistent within a given document so that the reader's eye isn't jumping back and forth between large and small text.

Fonts fall into two basic categories:

- **Serif:** Serif fonts have tops and tails at the ends of the letter strokes. These fonts are often used for print documents and are considered more classic style fonts. Most books are printed in a serif font because it lessens eye strain.
- **Sans serif:** Sans serif fonts have a cleaner feel because they don't feature any extra marks at the ends of the letters. These fonts tend to have a more casual feel, and they have become the standard for online copy because they're easier to read on a screen.

Figure 13-1 shows some examples of serif and sans serif fonts.

Serif	*Sans-serif*
Times New Roman	Arial
Century	Calibri
Garamond	Helvetica
Palatino	**Impact**
Calisto MT	Verdana
Georgia	Comic Sans

Figure 13-1: Examples of serif and sans serif fonts.

Creating a Color Palette

Color sends a powerful message and is key to representing your brand. Your brand color is the most important element of your visual brand identity. People remember color because it stirs up emotions. Therefore, you want to choose colors that best represent your personality and your brand.

Spotting color in the corporate world

Corporate brands (which I discuss in Chapter 2) rely heavily on color. Consider an example that's close at hand: The *For Dummies* books are consistently yellow and black. These books are references that are both friendly and smart. They're marketed to people looking to figure something out by themselves — people you might label *independent*. In a minute, when I explain what various colors represent, you'll see that yellow is associated with independence and is, therefore, the perfect color for a *For Dummies* book.

Consumers identify company logos and almost everything that they purchase by the brand color. McDonalds is red and yellow. WalMart is blue and white. Coca-Cola is red and white. Pepsi is red, white, and blue. These colors don't change when the company starts a new ad campaign; they remain consistent through the years because customers identify the products so closely with these colors.

A 2011 study by PPG focused on consumer opinions regarding the importance of color as it relates to new car purchases. Here's what the study found:

- Of automotive consumers, 48 percent who responded said they generally choose products based on color.
- Of automotive consumers, 77 percent said exterior color was a factor in their automotive purchase decision.
- About 31 percent of the automotive consumers said they are willing to pay extra for a vehicle that expresses their personality through color.

A similar study by The Color Marketing Group shows that

- Color increases brand recognition by up to 80 percent.
- Color improves readership as much as 40 percent.
- Color accelerates learning from 55 to 78 percent.
- Color increases comprehension by 73 percent.
- Color ads are read up to 42 percent more than similar ads in black and white.
- Color can be up to 85 percent of the reason people decide to buy.

The Red Hat Society, a society of women that supports and encourages women in their pursuit of fun, friendship, freedom, fulfillment, and fitness, has built an entire brand based on the colors of red and purple. Robin's egg blue is so important to Tiffany and Company that it's protected by a color trademark — in other words, legally it is only its to use. Mary Kay Cosmetics awards its top sellers a pink Cadillac knowing that the pink car will advertise its products wherever it is driven.

Choosing colors that suit you

You are a brand, and you need color recognition as well. Your color choices for your marketing materials may or may not reflect your personal favorites. If you're drawn to a particular color, that's a good place to start when considering options for your brand materials. However, you need to know that colors have meanings and make bold statements. You must consider those meanings and statements before you can determine that your favorite color will be your customers' favorite as well.

When choosing a brand color, also be sure to look at what colors your competitors are using. If everyone in your industry uses blue, use another color so that you stand out and are differentiated from others in your industry.

REMEMBER

Not everyone has an eye for color. If you're certain that you don't, ask a friend for help making your selections or — better yet — invest in the services of a professional designer. Like your logo, your color selections should remain the same (or at least similar) through the life of your personal brand. Isn't it worth the up-front expense to make sure that you get those choices right the first time?

Considering the meanings of colors

When considering which colors best represent your personal brand attributes, you may want to take a look at the Reach Communications video found at this website: `www.personalbranding.tv/what-color-is-your-personal-brand`. This site gives you a basic overview of the color meanings. Then, consider these associations:

- **Blue:** Intelligence, wisdom, integrity, leadership, authority, truth, peace, loyalty, reliability, confidence, hope, clarity, communication, imagination
- **Green:** Growth, rebirth, nature, optimism, spring, change, fertility, relaxation, youth, luck, healing, environment, prosperity, safety
- **Yellow:** Sunshine, joy, warmth, happiness, caution, warning, vision, intellect, creativity, light, self-motivation, independence
- **Orange:** Energy, optimism, enthusiasm, determination, encouragement, humor, informality, success, competition, force, productivity, strength, vitality with endurance
- **Red:** Power, attention, love, activity, potency, energy, desire, action, passion, determination, courage, vitality, motivation, playfulness, enthusiasm
- **Purple:** Royalty, ambition, wealth, competition, mystery, spirituality, mysticism, inspiration, magic, dignity, luxury, personal power, self-worth
- **Brown:** Solid, grounded, earthy, orderly, plain, not luxurious

- **Pink:** Love, warmth, friendship, children, affection, femininity, softness
- **Black:** Protective, strong, luxurious
- **Gold:** Riches, wealth, fame, the sun
- **Silver:** Mystery, intuition, the moon
- **Gray:** Elegant, classic, well-established
- **White:** Purity, cleanliness, spirituality, openness, truth, refinement

Using your color(s) everywhere

Applying your brand color(s) consistently will help others recognize and associate materials with you. You can brand materials that you use every day with your personal color(s). Possibilities include

- Your clothing and/or accessories
- Stationery
- Business cards
- File folders
- Cellphone case
- Coffee mugs or giveaway items
- Your office walls

Selecting Images That Tell Your Story

You are the brand in personal branding, and you may want to think about using an image of yourself in your marketing materials. A picture of yourself can build trust with your target audience members before they even meet you. Your picture is an important feature on your LinkedIn profile (see Chapter 10) and can have the same effect on your website. People like being able to connect a face with the name or service.

As I explain in Chapter 12, your professionally taken headshot can be the primary image that you use on your website, LinkedIn profile, Twitter account, and even your e-mail signature.

Unlike a logo or brand color(s), you can build your brand using multiple images on your website or marketing materials. Think about the image(s) that you want to take the dominant role and use other images to reinforce the message of the primary image(s). You want all the images to evoke the feelings and emotions that appeal to your target market.

You can place images or textures in the background of your website as well. If you're looking to emphasize stability, you want a calm image of trust in the background. For activity and movement, think about images that show movement, including the use of flash media or pictures that cycle in and out of your site.

Building Your Brand Identity System

Your brand identity is carried through all of the items that your target audience touches. It incorporates your logo, fonts, colors, and images into one look and feel. Each item should reinforce the unique promise of value that your brand stands for (see Chapter 7). You want to apply your brand look in everything that you do to create a set of coordinated materials.

Figuring out how to use a logo, fonts, colors, and images all at once may feel overwhelming, so think about one item at a time as it relates to the core marketing materials: your business card, brochure, and website. Just keep in mind that you want to be consistent in all your applications so that when someone sees your visual identity items, she recognizes the look as yours.

Creating business cards

Your business card is a brief business communication that you leave behind to create an impression of who you are and what you stand for. All over the world, business cards are exchanged in meetings and as reminders of conversations. Done well, your card communicates not just its written and visual message but also your unique personality.

A business card should be able to answer these questions for the person receiving it:

- Who are you?
- What do you or your business do?
- Who do you do it for?
- How do you differentiate yourself from your competitors?
- Is it clear how to contact you?

Your business card may be the only visual tool that your target audience sees from you. Your card has one purpose, and that is to get noticed by those receiving it. It helps you stand out and be remembered by someone you just met.

When you design your business card, evaluate it by asking these questions:

- Is it visually appealing enough to catch someone's attention?
- Is it specifically appealing to your target audience?
- Does it send the message that you want it to send?
- Do you look like a professional with high-quality standards (and not someone who whipped out cards on his printer right before an event)?

Following are the design elements to consider for your business card:

- **Direction:** Most people have horizontal business cards, but vertical cards are gaining popularity.
- **Position:** The focal point of a business card is the center, and this position is the best place for your name to be seen and remembered.
- **Size:** Obviously, the reader sees the largest item on the card first and considers it most important. The larger the item, the more important the reader will perceive it to be.
- **Theme:** Carry your concept throughout the card using your logo, font(s), color(s), and perhaps image(s).
- **Content:** Use words that are interesting to your reader. Don't clutter your card with too much content, or it will just look messy.
- **Back of the card:** The back of your business card gives you more room to highlight what you do or how you can serve your audience.

Generating stationery

Printed letterhead stationery and envelopes serve as primary branding tools for most businesses. As a savvy personal brander, you, too, want stationery that aligns with your brand. All your correspondence should show your brand colors and logo so that it conveys to the recipient the personal brand message that you have crafted.

It's important that all your written correspondence be properly branded. If you've engaged a designer to design a logo or website for you, have that person also design the stationery to show continuity of your brand.

A less expensive option is to use your logo and selected colors at a website like `www.vistaprint.com` where you can design your own stationery and still use your consistent theme.

Designing brochures

In recent years, a lot of marketing has moved online. But including a personally branded brochure in your marketing tools is still an effective way to connect with your target audience. Your brochure fulfills two purposes: It gives your target audience a chance to know about you and your business, and it helps that audience trust you. A brochure is another touch point to assist you in connecting with your audience. Your brochure's primary objective is to be a relationship builder, not a sales closer.

To create a great personal brochure, consider the following tips:

TIP

- **Highlight your unique promise of value.** Make sure that you convey your personal brand in a way that shares your emotional attributes. Use your biography to help the reader feel like she knows you.
- **Tell your story.** Think about the stories that make you interesting. Tell them in the third person so that they don't sound like bragging.
- **Use excellent design elements.** Make sure that your cover is eye-catching and makes the reader want to open it to discover more about you.
- **Experiment with an unusual size.** Square brochures feel like invitations and are opened more often than rectangular brochures.
- **Invest in quality.** Spend the money and print your brochure on quality paper with full color.

Printing postcards

You may want to get postcards that match your brochure. You want to design the cover but leave the back blank. Having a blank back side permits you to print timely notices when you want to send a reminder or announce an event. This strategy lets you take advantage of bulk printing rates.

As with your brochure, use high-quality, heavy-stock paper. Produce a large quantity of postcards to use for different occasions. Keep your messages short and make them calls to action. You can also use your postcard to send personal notes to your clients.

TIP

If you're not in business for yourself but still want to reinforce your brand to your target market, have personal postcards printed using your personal brand identity system: your logo, font(s), color(s), and perhaps image.

Preparing PowerPoint slides

Perhaps you haven't yet thought about creating a customized design to bring the consistency of your logo, font(s), and color(s) to your presentations. You can customize your PowerPoint slides with your logo and your color palette so that your look appears on each slide regardless of what the presentation is about.

TIP

If you've worked with a designer to create a logo, for a few extra dollars, that person can create a PowerPoint template for you to use in your presentations. By doing so, you'll look professional and coordinated. Having templated slides can give the appearance that you're a professional presenter, which only reinforces your brand.

Applying Your Visual Identity Online and with Media

Your online look is as important as the look of the hard copy materials that you create. You'll be carrying a consistent theme from the printed materials through to your online visual identity, although you may opt to use different fonts (for better readability) and more images online. You want to apply your branded logo and colors to your e-mail signature, website or blog, social media sites, and any video that you add to your sites.

WARNING!

I want to offer a word of caution about creating your online materials. Some people develop fabulous websites and online communications, but when I meet them in person, I'm disappointed because they've presented an inflated picture of themselves. Even as you're trying to sell your brand, you need to authentically represent your best self — not create a persona that you cannot live up to. If you know that your website has stretched the truth, best not to go down that path as you'll disappoint who you're trying to influence. Personal branding is based on authenticity.

Securing the right online addresses

You want to use your name to build brand recognition. You can reinforce this element every time you send an e-mail or connect with someone on a social media site.

If you haven't yet secured your website name, do so right away by purchasing your vanity name (meaning *yourname.com*). You can buy your name at `www.godaddy.com` or `www.hostgator.com`. Even if you don't plan on using it right away, a website name is relatively inexpensive (less than $20) and worth securing.

Social media sites like LinkedIn, Facebook, and Twitter should use your name as well to build your brand. For example, my Twitter name is **SusanChritton**. Having a common name makes using your name more difficult, but with a little creativity you can secure an identifiable name.

TIP

One place to find out who else is using your name is at `http://knowem.com`. This site looks to see who uses your name at the various social media sites. You can visit `www.howmanyofme.com` to find out how many people online have your same name. The website `www.visibility.com` creates a scannable code and allows you to point people to your sites even if you are not using your name. If you're still having difficulties, make yourself identifiable by using a professional credential in your name. Or, if you are in business for yourself, add your company name.

Piecing together your e-mail signature

Your *e-mail signature* is what follows the content of your e-mail. You can reinforce your brand with every e-mail you send by paying attention to your signature. Start to observe other people's e-mail signatures to see what you like. Notice what feels like the right amount of content and see whether they use logos.

WARNING!

Don't make your signature too content heavy by filling up the page with everything that you do. Do use your logo and contact information to strengthen your brand. After you've gathered ideas from other people's e-mail signatures, design your own to reflect your brand. You may want to include

- Your name or your company's name
- Brand logo
- Phone number
- E-mail address
- Website address
- Personal brand tagline (see Chapter 7)
- Social media addresses

Carrying your identity into your website

You want your website to communicate your brand and connect with your target audience. Use the logo, font(s), color(s), and images that you've already determined speak to who you are.

The secret of branding your website is being clear so that others understand who you are, what you can do for and with them, and how they can reach you should they need your service. Making the effort in designing a well-branded website helps prepare you for future opportunities. Here are some fundamentals:

TIP

- Invest in a well-designed logo and design for your site; they strengthen your professionalism.
- Make absolutely certain that your website is easy to read and navigate.
- Have a professional headshot taken. Using your headshot on your website gives the viewer a sense of trust.
- Make sure that your hyperlinks work and are current. Link to good resource sites that support your viewer.
- Have links to your social media sites easily accessible on your website.
- Update your website frequently so that it stays fresh and shows you are current.
- Continually question whether your website aligns with your promise of value.

Personalizing your social media sites

You make a first impression online in much the same way as you do in person, so you want to personalize your social media sites. Ask a friend to give you her first impression when she looks at your social media sites; if that impression doesn't align with your intentions, make the necessary corrections. Your social media sites often act as the hubs of your online identity, so make sure that they represent you well.

Of the three major social media sites, Twitter allows for the most visual personalization; with a bit of research, you can customize your background page on Twitter. You can personalize LinkedIn with your headshot and with the content that you share. Facebook allows for visual personalization through the pictures that you post and videos that you share. Whenever possible, add your personal logo and use the colors and images that convey your brand.

Building a video library

Video is the next major tool on the verge of becoming mainstream to support your personal brand. If you're in business for yourself, you might look at offering a series of videos to encourage your target market to look to you as an expert.

Mastering the use of music in your media

Not everyone associates music with a personal brand. But if you love music and it's a big part of your life, consider adding some music clips to a presentation, to your website, or as part of a talk you're giving. You may even entertain clients by inviting them to a concert!

Music can set the tone for who you are and what you like. I have an executive client who loves music. She has more than 50,000 songs on her three iPods. She pondered how she could incorporate her love of music into her brand in a fairly conservative organization. She decided that she would start taking her clients to dinner and a concert and share her interest in music. It set her apart, and her clients loved being invited to one of her events.

When I do workshops on change management, I have a certain group of songs that I play in the background, including David Bowie's "Changes" and Jimmy Buffet's "Changes in Latitudes, Changes in Attitudes." The people in the group connect to change in a much more personal way when they hear that music.

Don't be afraid to incorporate music into your brand where appropriate. Play something with a universal appeal and be cautious that you aren't playing music that is offensive or invading someone else's work space. Have some fun and test the boundaries!

A colleague of mine in the branding world uses the backdrop of cycling to promote his brand. He brilliantly has come up with the ten speeds of building your personal brand. He produced ten videos shot on a bicycling trip where he explains the phases of branding.

You can place your videos on your website or put into one of your social media sites to show more of your personality. People trust you when they know you're human, and video puts your humanity on display.

Branding Your Workspace

Your brand extends into your physical office workspace, as well as your portable workspace (the equipment you use). Everything that someone sees around you is part of your brand environment. Your next step in the branding process is to align your office to fit your brand.

Aligning your office environment to fit your brand

After you determine your personal brand color(s) and image(s) that speak to you, taking those elements into your office further aligns your personal brand with how you operate on a day-to-day basis.

TIP

Color is one of the best ways to bring your brand into your office. If you're a bold personality and red is your color, use red to show your brand in your office. If you're in a cubicle where painting a wall would not work, consider covering one wall of the cubicle in a high-quality red paper.

If you've worked through Chapter 4, review your brand persona and personality characteristics to get other ideas. If you fancy yourself a world citizen, think about how you might reflect that fact in your office. One of my clients who handles international accounts brings in small souvenirs from the destinations that he visits to adorn the upper shelf of his bookcase.

You also want to look at what makes your target audience (the people who visit your office) comfortable. If you're selling expertise, having books showing your knowledge supports that brand. If you're in the healing professions, a key goal would be to make your patients feel comfortable by having a quiet, calm waiting room.

Personalizing your workspace

Is your office the cubicle nation that the Dilbert cartoon makes fun of? Are you allowed to show some individuality in your workplace? When someone walks into your office space, would he know that it's your office?

A study conducted at Eastern Kentucky University shows that up to 90 percent of Americans personalize their workspaces. When you're able to make your office space your own, you're more likely to have higher workplace satisfaction and an improved morale. Being able to decorate your office makes you feel like you belong and raises productivity.

Further studies have shown that impressions that you get by looking at someone's office are often correct. If you're an extrovert, you're more likely to have items in your office that invite others in, such as a candy dish or a comfortable chair. As an introvert, you may not want to be interrupted, so your office may not look as inviting to anyone other than yourself. (I had an introverted client who actually wore headphones with no music playing so that people would be less likely to interrupt her.)

A conscientious person likely has an organized desk with pencils sharpened, a calendar neatly filled out, and books displayed on a bookshelf. Someone who places high value on family would have a few family photos placed in her office.

Clutter or a chaotic office sends a message as well. A cluttered office gives the first impression that this person is scattered and disorganized. For certain occupations, such as artists, a messy workspace may not be a problem, but for most people, it creates a very poor first impression.

Items to help bring your personality into your workspace include

- Art or photographs
- Plants or flowers
- Motivational sayings or posters
- Small memorabilia from trips you've taken
- Books that support your work

Never display offensive cartoons or anything sexually explicit in your office. Be careful about pictures of yourself downing a bottle of alcohol or doing other serious partying. Also, filling an office with stuffed animals makes you look juvenile. Don't bring *anything* into the office that compromises your credibility.

Messaging your business tools

Using smart business tools sends a message. If you're casting yourself as a cutting-edge expert, you need to have current equipment (smartphones, iPads, laptops) that people see you use. You can take the extra branding step of customizing your laptop with a skin to put on the surface. You can follow your branded color theme and images. Likewise, you can create a customized case for your phone. People always comment on my colorful images that mark my laptop and phone. They're on brand for me and draw attention to the equipment that I use. They send a subtle message that I know how to customize my tools.

If you regularly present at meetings, invest in a laptop, a remote, and perhaps even your own projector. You'll look professional. Don't take for granted that your host will provide these things for you. Make an inventory of the equipment that supports you in your business and align it with your visual marketing. Doing so shows attention to detail and helps you appear up to date.

I once had a client who was worried about being perceived as old. My response was this: Don't act old. Learn to use the latest technologies. Get a smartphone and find cool applications. Carry an electronic tablet to a meeting and take notes using a portable keyboard. Being up to date on technology is one of the best ways to appear ageless.

Everything you use is part of your visual identity. Take a day to observe yourself and look at each item that you use. Make the changes that you need to make to align with your brand.

Chapter 14

Focusing on Special Populations

In This Chapter

- Branding during different phases of your career
- Taking action as an executive, service professional, or entrepreneur
- Considering specific steps for women
- Exporting your brand

This chapter looks at the nuances of personal branding by examining characteristics of groups of people with similar issues. I'm not trying to deal in stereotypes; I'm well aware that you are the only *you* around. (Personal branding wouldn't work if each person weren't unique.) However, the groups I discuss have certain commonalities that may include values, life circumstances, or professional experience and goals.

If you're aligned with any of the populations I cover here — whether you're a recent college graduate, young professional, midcareer professional, executive, service professional, entrepreneur, woman, community volunteer, or international worker — I encourage you to consider the advice I offer to your peer group. You may find that these tips help you bypass some stress and head straight for success.

College Students: Getting on Brand Straight Out of the Gate

Once upon a time, young people in the United States who went to college had their futures mapped out for them before they even graduated. The hard work was getting into college (and paying for it); after the degree was earned, a career pretty easily fell into place. Those days are gone.

Today, recent college graduates face competition from other college grads with experience, noncollege grads with experience, and older people in the workforce. Therefore, I consider it crucial to figure out what makes you unique when you're first entering the workforce.

You may ask, "How will I look unique when I am an average student with a business major from an average school?" Well, now is where you need to employ the principles of personal branding to help you stand out and stand for something. Here are some places to look to find your uniqueness:

- Internships you had in college
- Travel experiences, both foreign and domestic
- The network of people that you know, including your parents' friends, your friends' parents, past employers, coaches, and other adults who know you well
- Languages you speak
- Special projects you've done that you're proud of
- Your attire and self-presentation at your interviews
- Your social and communication skills

After you identify unique qualities, don't hide them or assume that they aren't important. Make sure that these qualities are prominent in your resume (see Chapter 9) and that you highlight them in interviews.

TIP

Build your confidence by having meaningful conversations with people during informational interviews. Set a goal of meeting with at least three people who are willing to talk to you about the work they do and ask you about your interests. Each time you talk about your brand, you're building it. Own your uniqueness, and you'll find the right place where it will be appreciated.

Young Professionals: Conveying Energy and Professionalism

As a young professional, you've worked for a few years and have some experience to support you. Ideally, you have found work that you enjoy. These are the years of establishing yourself. You are in a self-driven time of your life, and moving ahead is up to you. Your goal should be to shatter the label of "entitled" that has been affixed to your generation and to prove that you have the brains and talent to move forward in your profession on your own merit.

You want to solidify your personal brand by taking these steps:

- **Set career goals.** Write them down and work toward gaining accomplishments and building your skill level.
- **Expand your expertise.** Just because you're young doesn't mean that you can't be an expert. Take courses to boost your knowledge. Offer to speak to a group or write a thought paper.
- **Continue to build your network.** Find people with whom you can have meaningful and long-lasting relationships. Offer to assist others, and make sure that you're worth having as a network contact (see Chapter 16).
- **Manage your image.** Look the part of the young professional. If you haven't ditched your college clothes, now is the time to do so. Look like the professional that you are. (Chapter 12 is full of tips for how to dress the part.)
- **Expand your communication skills.** Make sure that you're not only up to date with your social media communication but also that you have learned to communicate well in the workplace using both your written and oral skills.

The Middle Years: Strategizing for Success

Personal branding done well requires an implemented strategy to guide your success. It keeps your career fresh and exciting at a time when many others, during the middle years of their career, are happily hanging out in routine. Setting a strategy to continue to grow in your career and continually evolve your personal brand takes courage and vision.

To begin, evaluate your current position and set both short- and long-term goals. You may have an idea that you'd like to create in your current workplace, or you may find that you need to look beyond your current workplace. Your personal brand is developed from your authentic self. Don't be afraid to let your differences begin to show as long as those differences are appropriate for the arena you're working in.

Creating a buzz around your brand can take place with a variety of strategies. Take a look at some of these strategies you can use to give presence to your personal brand and think about which ones may work for you at this point in your career:

- **Be the go-to expert.** Find a niche of expertise and then learn all you can about that subject. Build a communications plan (see Chapter 11) around that expertise. Become known for what you know about something that few others know.
- **Lead a project.** Look at your situation and see where you can take on a leadership role that would make you and your personal brand more visible. Perhaps it's time for you to step up and lead your professional association or a service project others have avoided committing to. Leadership gives you visibility and a chance to inspire others.
- **Build your brand on one of your unique characteristics.** Communicate that characteristic in all that you do. I've heard people introduce themselves with a tagline touting that characteristic, and pretty soon, it becomes what they're known for. An example would be, "I'm David, and I make the best banana muffins in the Northwest."
- **Develop the best clients.** Understand who your target market is (see Chapter 5) and actively go after key clients. You can build your brand based on the clients you serve. The more specialized the client, the more in demand you'll be. The more in demand you are, the more your fees can reflect your specialization. Be known through your clients.
- **Risk being the first one with a new idea.** If you're creative but always wait to be assigned a project, take the risk and present your new idea or project. If you're in business for yourself, think about what you can do that would be the first in your industry. Being first is a brand builder.
- **Build your brand on your pedigree.** I have seen clients become known as the "Russian lawyer" or the "UC Davis dentist" because they attract people with similar pedigrees to their businesses. You can create a stronger brand by aligning yourself with something in your background that others are attracted to as well.

REMEMBER

During the middle phase of your career, it's important to re-examine your brand on occasion and look at what you need to do to spice it up a bit. Don't let your brand get stagnant or else you may soon be forgotten. Keep it fresh and keep it evolving!

Branding a Second Career

These days, the likelihood that you'll need or want to reinvent yourself professionally is high. Your personal brand can help ease the pain of reinvention by reminding you that at your core, you're still you and need to be your authentic self. Your reinvented self may be wearing a new outfit, but in all that you do, no matter what you call yourself, you are still you. Your personal brand helps you identify those core pieces of yourself that you want to express and use in the world.

This rest of this section was written by personal brand strategist Maren Finzer.

Your biggest obstacle in launching a second career may reside in your own mind. Shift your mindset and build your confidence. Head into your second career knowing it's a new season. Start out expecting great things. Turn your negative thoughts into the positive actions you can take to get to where you want to be.

Here are tips to prepare yourself for the necessary changes:

- Starting now, think and talk differently about yourself and your future.
- Don't use age as an excuse not to get the job you want.
- Focus on what you've gained from your wealth of experience and what you have that younger applicants don't.
- Target companies that value the skills and experience of seasoned professionals by seeking out industries known for hiring older workers.
- Research smaller companies in your area, which may be more open than larger companies to hiring mature workers. Reach out to the owners and managers directly.

Accept the fact that you're competing in a marketplace very different from what existed in the past. Learn about today's workplace, accept it, and leverage it to your advantage. Work to better understand generational differences. For example, keep in mind that mature workers are generally seen as loyal, dependable, hardworking, and honest. Also know that mature workers are considered *not* to be tech savvy and energetic. Use the positive assumptions to your advantage and be proactive about addressing the negative assumptions. For example,

- **Are you current with technology and social media?** Update your skills and education where needed. Show your prospective employer that you're a lifelong learner.
- **Are you current in your appearance?** Yes, it matters. If you think you're not, meet with an image consultant and follow that person's advice.
- **Does your energy come across, or have you put a few extra pounds on that slow you down?** Now is the time to join a gym and get the help you need.

You may have to do something you've never done — personal sales and marketing. You can be an amazing talent, but if nobody knows about you, it doesn't matter! Especially if you're starting over in a new industry, you have to raise your visibility as an expert in your new niche. Convince the people you meet that you're an undiscovered source of talent. Expand your own thinking about your capabilities, and announce your abilities to the world.

Make sure that you're communicating your unique personal brand value in everything you do by

- Crafting your online profile and identity (see Chapter 10)
- Reconnecting with and/or building your network (see Chapter 16)
- Connecting with local groups and associations
- Seeking out volunteer opportunities
- Speaking, writing, teaching, and consulting

Here's the great news: Studies show that most workers who change careers at older ages say they enjoy the new job more than the old job. So look at this time of change as a new opportunity to follow the dream you've always wanted to achieve. Ask yourself how can you combine your wealth of experience, knowledge, and personality to deliver something that the younger workforce can't. Brand yourself to stand out, regardless of your age.

Reinventing yourself

If you're facing a transition into a second (or third or fourth) career, here are some tips on easing the pain of reinvention:

- **Take responsibility for your life and work.** Life is an adventure. Embrace your role in the creation of your new self.
- **Don't be afraid to learn new things.** If you're behind in learning how to use online social media, take a class or ask a friend for help. Start with a beginner's mind. Embrace the idea of starting from scratch. Most people have to learn new things all the time; it's just a fact of life.
- **Set up a daily schedule to give you structure.** Having a schedule provides a sense of stability.
- **Stay social.** Be open about your reinvention. Share your stories with your friends. Don't isolate yourself.
- **Maintain your sense of humor.** Remember to laugh often and to be able to laugh at yourself.
- **Ease up on your perfectionism.** You need to start somewhere, and you may not be very good at it in the beginning. Believe in your ability to learn and grasp new concepts.
- **Examine your finances.** Cut back where you need to and give yourself the gift of time to try out your new role without the financial pressure. Now may be the time to sell an extra car or drop a club membership.
- **Remember your core values and stay true to your personal brand.** You may feel less sure of yourself during transition, so believe in yourself and live your values.
- **Seek help from a counselor or coach to support you in your changing identity.** This is a good time to get the support that you need to help you get clarity on your path.
- **Be inspired and trust the process.** Allow a sense of wonder and divine timing to enter your life. Remember all of the times when you've heard someone say, "That was the best thing that ever happened to me."

Executives: Presenting Confidence and Control

The executive population was the first to embrace personal branding. The people occupying the chief executive offices recognized early on that if branding worked for a company, it could work for them as individuals. During the formative years of personal branding, forward-thinking executives knew that in order to differentiate themselves, they needed to work on their public image and guide that image instead of being wholly associated with the companies they worked for.

According to the Conference Board's 2011 CEO Succession report, the average CEO tenure has declined from approximately 10 years in 2000 to 8 years in 2010. Given the volatility and political nature of positions at the top, personal branding gives an executive portability. It does so by helping that CEO to develop an individual reputation that can be transported to other positions and to separate his or her association with a particular company.

Service Professionals: Selling Your Personal Brand to Each Client

Personal branding was made for service professionals. Doctors, lawyers, accountants, consultants, and other professional service providers sell their expertise, usually as an intellectually based service. Selling something that you can't see or touch is always harder than selling something tangible. In order to survive, let alone thrive, you must learn to sell your intellectual expertise and sell who you are.

REMEMBER

In the professional services, you exist to serve your clients. If you don't perform, your clients will go elsewhere. In order to get clients, you must be able to clearly articulate your unique promise of value (see Chapter 7). That requires not only communicating what you can do for a client but why you are the person that client wants to do business with.

As a service professional, even if you work for a large firm, you have a lot in common with a small business owner. Essentially, yours is a business within a business, and you must think of yourself in an entrepreneurial way. That's because your clients do business with *you,* not just your firm, and it's up to you to keep the client happy. You are there to solve problems, provide expertise, and have a positive professional relationship with each client. Your brand is highly visible at all times.

If you have not carefully dissected the components of your personal brand, I suggest going back to Part II, as well as to Chapter 8. Having a well-positioned personal brand sharpens your focus on how you can best grow your business and serve your clients.

Twenty-one ways your executive brand can drive your career

Meg Guiseppi, a C-level executive branding, job search, and online identity coach and the creator of Executive Career Brand (`www.executivecareerbrand.com`), offers the following list for an executive brand:

1. Helps you reconnect with your values and passions so that you can move toward the kind of work you love doing.
2. Empowers you to gain clarity about your authentic self and the combination of personal qualities and qualifications differentiating the unique promise of value you offer over your competition in the job market.
3. Forces you to be introspective and reflective and to examine the weaknesses that may be holding you back.
4. Helps you identify your competition and target audience so that you can create differentiating personal marketing communications designed to resonate with them.
5. Beckons you to solicit feedback from those who know your value best (peers, management, staff, employees, clients, mentors, and so on), helping you understand the true measure of your brand — how you're perceived by the external world.
6. Makes your personal marketing documents (resume, bio, LinkedIn profile, and so on) a more interesting and powerful read. Compared to a traditional executive resume, communicating your brand on paper or a web page casts a richer and deeper impression of who you are, compelling people to want to meet you.
7. Helps you take control of your real-life and online identity and the way you're perceived by others.
8. Generates chemistry for you when networking and helps decision makers assessing you more readily determine whether you're the good-fit candidate they're looking for.
9. Empowers your interviewing finesse. You're pumped by what differentiates you from the others being interviewed, what unique value you bring, and how you'll best add value at that company.
10. Helps you position your value proposition directly in front of your target audience and stay top of mind with them (via your strategic brand communications plan — expressed clearly, consistently, and constantly across all channels).
11. Helps you establish yourself as an industry subject matter expert and thought leader within your area(s) of expertise.

Guiseppi notes that your executive brand is like career management insurance. For the long term, knowing your brand and consistently communicating it accomplishes the following:

12. Helps you transition seamlessly because you were hired based on the authentic "you" and the understanding that you'll fit in with management and your team.
13. Helps you know your limitations so that you lead with your strengths instead as you progress through your career.
14. Precedes you and reinforces your reputation. Your brand can be the deciding factor in advancing your career to the next level and matching you with good-fit opportunities.
15. Establishes you as the go-to person for your areas of expertise. People know that they can always rely on you for certain things.
16. Empowers you daily, as you deal with people and go about your work day, with that same brand chemistry that defines the way you operate.
17. Boosts your confidence. Understanding what is authentically you, your value, and what you're capable of delivering leads you to embrace business opportunities that positively impact your company's profitability, growth, and reputation.
18. Compels you to use your strengths to help your teams achieve their own career goals and benefit the company.
19. Guides you to make the right career decisions for you and the right business decisions for your company.
20. Keeps you top of mind with key decision makers when they need to select the best people to lead future projects and initiatives.
21. Attracts opportunities. As your brand reputation gains traction and visibility, internally and externally, more people with opportunities will be naturally drawn to you, leading you to career advancement and fulfillment.

Entrepreneurs: Connecting Personal Brand with Your Business Plan

As a small business owner, entrepreneur, or solopreneur, your personal brand is the heart and soul of your business. Your brand is intertwined with the business; it's how people experience both you and your business. The image, energy, and expression of your business are how others perceive you.

REMEMBER

Personal branding shares a lot in common with creating a business plan. As you work through the personal branding process to reveal your authentic self, I encourage you to align your personal brand to your small business plan because everything you do becomes important to the business.

If you're in business for yourself, I assume that you've created a business plan either formally or informally. Much of the process that you use to develop your personal brand is mirrored in the business planning process, as I show in Table 14-1. A smart entrepreneur aligns the two processes to make the business and the personal brand congruent.

Table 14-1 Components of Your Business Plan and Personal Brand

Business Plan Components	*Personal Brand Components*
Executive summary	Personal brand statement (see Chapter 7)
Company overview: mission, vision, values	Defining who you are (see Chapter 4)
Competitive analysis	Knowing your niche and target market (see Chapters 5 and 6)
Marketing plan	Communications plan (see Chapter 11) Building your network (see Chapter 16)
Strategies: people, operations, network	Communication toolbox (see Chapter 9) Social media (see Chapter 10) Visual identity (see Chapter 13) Image (see Chapter 12)
Action plan	Goal setting (see Chapter 4) Personal branding in the workplace (see Chapter 17)

Women: Highlighting Strengths

Women want to be just as successful as men are, but often they want to succeed in a different way. If you'll allow me to generalize for a moment, women (more than men) tend to embrace the desire to want to live more authentically, and that translates into being more of who they are in the workplace.

Personal branding is about living your authentic self and building on natural talents and strengths. In general, I have found some of the following characteristics to be more true for women as a group than for their male counterparts:

- Collaborators
- Connectors
- Socially oriented
- Focused on community
- Natural multitaskers
- Awareness of visual identity
- Strong verbal communicators

- Empathetic and intuitive
- Engaged in stories
- Builders of deeper relationships

When a woman works on her personal brand, she needs to let go of the fear that these characteristics are bad things in the workplace (especially if she's in a male-dominated work environment). Often, male coworkers don't see these female qualities as intellectual or as worthwhile as the more male characteristics of individuality, facts, and logic.

These are the complex subtleties that women face every day in the workplace. As you refine your brand, you continually need to be true to yourself and to know how to play the game in your particular workplace.

In rapidly changing work environments, the rules aren't as clear for women about how to be who you are, what you should wear, and what qualities are acceptable. Building a female personal brand means focusing on your best self within the variables that you can control and not being afraid to be seen for your uniqueness.

Community Volunteers: Merging Mission and Meaning with Community

Volunteers are a noble bunch, and you can tell a lot about a person's character by how she gives her time in service. Personal branding encompasses all aspects of your life. Therefore, how you volunteer your time, as well as which community you serve, becomes part of that brand.

Be confident in what you know

A few years ago, I was at a dinner with a group of partners in a professional services firm. The event was comprised of 75 percent men, but somehow eight of the ten people at my table were women. One of the two men at the table was a senior leader in the firm. The first thing I noticed was that our table was much more social than others. We had a lot of talking, laughing, and sharing of stories. One of the women was telling a work story when the male senior leader said, "Do you know what is wrong with women?" The table gasped and all turned to him. He continued with, "You are at least as smart as the men, maybe smarter, but you wait until you know how to do something at least 80 percent before you say, 'I can do that.' We men will say we can do something when we know it 25 percent. We are confident enough to know we will figure it out. If you want to get ahead in business, you need to have the confidence to say that you know how to do something much sooner."

If you identified your values, purpose, and mission in Chapter 4, you've already pinpointed what has meaning for you and know where you want to put your time. Working your personal brand means that you align your life so that what you do and how you communicate make sense for you. Giving your time and money in service can become part of that alignment plan.

Consider the example of a woman in her fifties who has a personal brand as a strong leader. She has pioneered women's programs in her workplace and has struggled to obtain a professional status. Her community service efforts both as a volunteer and in how she donates her money follow her brand. She volunteers at a low-income women's entrepreneurial training program and gives money to Planned Parenthood. She supports other causes as well, but these are her signature projects, and everyone knows her for her efforts here. Her volunteer work is on brand for her.

WARNING!

You need to volunteer with the same standards as you would have in the workplace. You can damage your reputation and your brand by behaving badly as a volunteer by being lazy, complaining, or having poor follow-through.

Overcoming a personal branding stereotype

People are often branded to be a certain way because of their age, race, gender, nationality, or religion. But personal branding allows you to redefine what you think about yourself and what others think about you. When you're combating a stereotype, you need to be extra mindful of what others may think about you just because of the group that you fall into.

You first need to be aware of what that stereotype is and how you may be judged. When I have been in that position, I often mention what I think the perceptions may be to bring the issue out into the open. It's a gutsy move and not appropriate for every situation, but it sure sets up a good dialogue. At that moment, you have taken control of your brand and can guide the conversation to why you should be viewed differently.

When you must overcome a stereotype, you need to work extra hard to have your personal brand be known. You need to display your unique gifts and challenge the stereotype.

One of my heroes is a woman named Helen Harkness. She is an octogenarian who is at the top of her field in career development. She debunks the myth that she should be retired by being an active thought leader in her career. She exudes a vibrancy of someone half her age. Her spunk lights up a room. When you see Helen, you don't think of a senior citizen. The stereotype you may have of an older woman becomes irrelevant because she has such a powerful and authentic personal brand that you see her radiance shine through.

If you feel that you may fall into a stereotypical category, get very clear about who you are and what you stand for. Know that you will need to overcome an initial impression someone may have of you. Put thought and energy into your personal brand and be very deliberate in how you build it and what you do to maintain it.

Instead, you want to become known for your character, for the good deeds you do as a volunteer, and/or for the causes you support. Volunteering is one of the best ways to build your brand, widen your community, expand your network, and serve the greater good.

Kim McAtee is a realtor in the east bay of San Francisco. She sells family homes in an affluent community. Kim believes in serving the community that her business is in and looks for volunteer opportunities that deepen her roots and have a direct impact. Kim joined the Junior League in her geographic area and became a stellar volunteer. Everyone knows that they can count on Kim. She does what she says she'll do, takes on enough for two or three volunteers, is overly generous, and attends every event. If you've volunteered with Kim, you naturally assume that she handles her business like she handles her volunteer work — as a complete professional. (Hence her reputation as a top realtor in the area and someone whose business is driven by referrals.)

Here's one example of the way Kim conducts herself as a volunteer: When the movie *The Help* was released, Kim rented a local movie theater and offered all Junior League members and their friends free admission. Before the film started, she said a few words about being a local realtor and thanked everyone for coming. She mentioned that donations would be accepted at the theater for her favorite Super Stars literacy charity but made donating optional. Everyone had a wonderful time, appreciated her generosity, and remembers the fun event.

Having a Personal Brand around the World

Your personal brand isn't universal. That's because your target market (which I discuss in Chapter 5) is part of the equation in determining your personal brand. When you work globally, your target market changes. You need to take the concepts of personal branding and overlay them with the cultural nuances of each country, taking into consideration the specifics of each target market.

After you discover your unique promise of value (see Chapter 7), your personal brand is challenged with these questions:

- Are these characteristics seen as positive in the country or culture I am living in?
- How do I communicate my brand with the cultural specifics of my market?
- What are some of the ways I could offend people with my brand?
- What factors must I consider when making my brand visible in this country?
- Will my brand be accepted in this country?
- How much will I need to modify the American version of my brand so that it works internationally?

EXPERT OPINION

What's faith got to do with it?

By Winnie Anderson, Reach personal branding strategist

According to personal branding guru William Arruda, the process of developing a strong personal brand has three steps

1. *Extract,* which involves uncovering your brand attributes.
2. *Express,* which looks at how you communicate your brand.
3. *Exude,* which asks you to look at your environment to ensure that it fully communicates your brand.

There's a fourth *E* in the personal branding process — one that I believe has been overlooked: *essence.* Creating a brand that's truly authentic requires you to embrace your brand essence.

Your *brand essence* is the foundation of your personal brand. If you've lost it along life's highway, you must reconnect with it before building your brand, or you'll be forever out of alignment. You'll feel out of sync with work and with virtually all you do because your very soul will cry out to you in sadness as it tries to express itself. Your essence is truly the ultimate nature of the real you.

To build a truly authentic, strong personal brand requires getting in touch with your essence, connecting it with your beliefs, and making sure that they're both so in sync that they're represented in your actions. Your beliefs and your essence must come to truly personify your brand.

Whether you align yourself with a specific faith denomination or simply consider yourself spiritual, religious principles are often at the core of your brand essence. Would people recognize these principles in your daily actions at work, at home, and in social situations? If you're not sure about that, here's a simple process to get some clarity about how well your essence is demonstrated in your actions:

- List the five core principles that guide your spirituality or faith.
- For the next day, list all of your actions that demonstrate these principles. Put a plus sign (+) next to each one.
- For the same day, list all your actions that are inconsistent with these principles. Put a minus sign (–) after each one.

At the end of the day, review the list. If you have more pluses than minuses, celebrate and reflect on how you can eliminate one negative from your actions the next day.

As you work to shine a light on your essence and embrace your brand, you'll discover one principle that connects all the others in your heart. Fertilizing it and cultivating it are perhaps the greatest challenges we have as faithful beings in a material world, yet they offer magnificent rewards.

The greatest teachers of our time, including Jesus of Nazareth, the Dalai Lama, and those famous 20th-century philosophers John Lennon and Paul McCartney, have all shared the secret: "All you need is love."

This section walks you through the basics of adjusting your brand to meet the needs of a different culture.

Relocating abroad: Doing initial research

Maybe you're being offered what feels like the opportunity of a lifetime to work abroad, and you're excited about the adventure. Don't let yourself be caught in the fantasy of a new life in a different country without doing your homework! Before you take an assignment overseas, visit the country and the work situation first. Assess whether you're making the right decision before you pack your belongings and relocate.

TIP

Some companies offer assistance to help you understand the culture and the way of life before you go. If your company doesn't provide that service, ask your human resources department for help to locate an expatriate who can assist you in your new city. (If you work for a large company, it should easily be able to connect you with a coworker or other peer living in the new location.) If that person has made the same move you're considering, he can help you understand the practical challenges ahead, from how to find schools for your children to which neighborhoods to live in. He can also be a great resource regarding protocol, etiquette, and the cultural nuances of doing business in that country.

Also, be sure to search online for information about the business and social culture in the city and country you're moving to. You'll likely find at least anecdotal information that can help you better understand what to expect. (However, take any horror stories with a grain of salt. Remember that people love to share the worst of the worst online! Use such stories as a source of questions to ask your contact in the new location.)

Assimilating your style across cultures

After doing some homework to learn about the culture you'd be moving into, closely examine your personal brand to determine what would need to change in order to adjust. Consider the characteristics of a successful person in your new country to understand which of your characteristics translate and which ones may need to be de-emphasized.

WARNING!

The biggest mistake an expatriate can make is to think that what works to succeed in business in one culture works in all cultures. The fundamental work to be done may be the same in every situation, but the way you do it and your interactions with coworkers may be completely different.

Consider just a few ideas that vary from country to country:

- **Tradition versus change:** Although most people don't like change, Americans give the appearance of being more adaptable than people from some other cultures. That's largely because the American culture doesn't have centuries of tradition. Also, because the United States is a cultural melting pot, Americans are exposed to various ways of doing things.

  REMEMBER

  Many countries revere tradition over change. If part of your personal brand involves promoting your success as a change agent, give some serious thought to how that attribute may be perceived in a culture outside the United States.

- **Age awareness:** You can't change your age, but you can recognize that age is perceived differently by different cultures. Some cultures, such as the Dutch culture, appreciate the energy of youth. Other cultures, such as the Japanese, appreciate wisdom and have much respect for an older person. Knowing a culture's perspective on age and tempering your appearance and attitude to respect that perspective can help you succeed.

- **Personal assertiveness:** Your outward personality is a major piece of your personal brand. If you're an assertive person, you may do gangbusters business in one culture and be seen as offensive and overbearing in another culture. Be aware of how you're perceived by others and notice the general tone of the business people in the country where you're working. Monitor the emotions you display and the nonverbal messages you send (see Chapter 12).

- **Time and organization:** Any traveler quickly realizes that each culture has a different perception of time. Germans are known for being on time and being efficient organizers. Southern Italy runs on a more laidback time schedule and isn't known for its organizational systems. You must adapt your expectations and your habits to the time perception of the country you are in.

- **Perceptions of gender:** The perceptions of men and women are changing rapidly in a global environment. However, there are still many do's and don'ts related to gender in almost every culture. Spend some time reading about the culture; find out what is appropriate for men and women to do, say, and wear; and respect the boundaries whether you agree with them or not. Be careful not to touch anyone inappropriately or to show disrespect of the opposite sex. Before you leave home, be sure you know what to wear when you arrive in that culture.

Giving the appearance of being global

If a man be gracious and courteous to strangers, it shows he is a citizen of the world.

— Sir Francis Bacon

Today's business climate is such that companies are asking their employees to be citizens of the world. Many companies conduct business globally and have a diverse population. You don't need to have traveled the world to be a global citizen. However, you need to walk through your life with a certain awareness of what is happening in other parts of the world.

If you aren't terribly well-traveled, what can you do to look like a citizen of the world?

- **Watch CNN, BBC, or read the international section of a large newspaper.** Knowing what is happening in the world gives you the appearance of being worldly.
- **Try different foods.** Be conversant in foods from different countries and the traditions around dining. Figure out what is considered inappropriate to eat in any culture you're visiting and what the proper etiquette is for the foods you're eating. How do you learn? Ask for help! When I'm in an unfamiliar dining situation, I ask for guidance and laugh at my own naiveté at not knowing what to do. Someone always steps in to teach me.
- **Find out how business cards are presented in different cultures.** I've seen people toss cards across the table in the United States. In Japan, the exchange of business cards involves a degree of reverence; tossing a card to a Japanese peer would be rude.
- **Decorate your office with mementos from your travels.** Let your office display your travel interests, especially international ones.
- **Discover the etiquette of using a person's name by culture.** Ask questions or read online to discover whether people use the familiar form of a name in a given culture or whether it's more proper to use titles to show respect. (You wouldn't want to use a first name or nickname prematurely when meeting a colleague from another culture.)

When you do have the chance to travel, being courteous, friendly, and humble to others will buy you some grace even as you make mistakes. Most of the time, a friendly stranger will help you if you are polite and nice. A smile and genuine warmth of character are appreciated across cultures.

TIP

When you're traveling, be sure to let your e-mail recipients know where you are. I recently received an e-mail from a client of mine that started with "Greetings from Osaka!" I thought that was a brilliant way to get the point across that he is a true global citizen.

Crafting your international bio

EXPERT OPINION

Megan Fitzgerald, expat career and personal branding coach at Career By Choice (www.careerbychoice.com), wrote this section to show you how to "internationalize" your professional bio. Megan has lived and worked in more than 40 countries and helps expatriates build personal brands to support their careers and success abroad.

An *internationalized* bio is a powerful tool that will help you build a personal brand to support you in realizing your goal of living and working overseas.

In an increasingly competitive and global marketplace, even if you're not looking for a job abroad, having a more international profile and personal brand will help you stand out and get noticed regardless of where in the world you want to work.

Here are a few tips on how to internationalize your bio:

- Highlight your international experience, including volunteering, study and work overseas, and relevant international travel.
- Demonstrate qualities and skills necessary to succeed abroad, including language skills, adaptability, resilience, and creative problem-solving.
- Express your desire or passion for working in international settings and multicultural environments.

In addition to highlighting skills and strengths necessary to work well in other cultures, it is critical to convey your unique value in a culturally appropriate fashion. Cultural fit is an important part of evaluating a job candidate. Be sure that the values communicated through your bio are aligned with the culture in which you'd like to work.

For example, team achievement is more celebrated than individual achievement in Japan. So if you're pursuing jobs in Tokyo, be sure that your bio reflects your team orientation (if, in fact, you have it).

You should also be sure to use the right keywords in your bio. Because up to 85 percent of employers and recruiters search online to find and research job candidates, the right keywords can increase your chances of being found and considered for work abroad. Examples of keywords include *cross cultural, global, bilingual, multilingual, fluent,* and *emerging markets.*

Internationalizing your bio is critical to being successful in your international job search, as well as giving you a competitive edge in today's global marketplace.

Chapter 15

Building and Nurturing Your Network

In This Chapter

- Deciding who belongs in your network
- Knowing what to say
- Getting the most out of conferences
- Taking your networking efforts online
- Building a network in your office
- Looking for referrals and mentors

This chapter employs the golden rule in networking: Give more than you get. Some people have the misconception that networking is something you do in order to *get* something. That attitude usually isn't too successful. A skilled networker *gives* to her network by sharing information and introducing people to each other.

To be a savvy networker, you need to genuinely enjoy learning about the people you interact with. Your goal is to build two-way relationships with people you want to be part of your circle. In this chapter, I show you how.

Defining Your Brand Community

I seriously doubt that you need to build your professional network from scratch. Unless you're going through a radical career change (such as moving from auditing to acting or vice versa), chances are that you're already connected with a number of people who can help you professionally. But when you begin to develop your personal brand, you assign a new level of importance to networking. You want to include your target market in your networking efforts and be more strategic in how you get to know other people who can support your brand and your goals. It's time to go beyond developing your network by chance.

Sharing your interests

The easiest place to meet people and build your network is through shared interest groups, such as professional association meetings, clubs, social groups, classes to learn about a hobby, parenting groups, exercise classes, or on the sidelines of a child's sport. Some of my favorite people are those I met when my children played on sports teams. Often we parents spent hours watching practices and games in order to see our kids play for a total of a few minutes. Meeting some of the other parents became the bonus of that space between watching the sports action. These fellow parents hold a special place in my network.

If you're on the shy side, attending activities with others who share your interests is much easier than meeting people at other functions. Begin with the person sitting next to you and build your network one person at time. The process feels more comfortable and less intimidating that way.

In this section, I help you determine who should be the focus of your networking efforts. I begin by asking you to consider people you already know and then show you how to expand your network to include others you haven't yet met.

Identifying who you know

For years, I taught networking classes for people going through job searches. The topic of networking was frightening to them because they didn't understand that networking really just involves meeting people and engaging in conversations. Even introverts can enjoy networking if they find the right people to talk to. The best way to begin is by having conversations with people you already know.

What scares people about networking is that they often neglect their contacts. When they realize that they need to tap in to their network, such as during a job search, they feel like they're using people that they've neglected for years. The best time to build a network is when you don't have an immediate need for it.

With social media tools like LinkedIn, Facebook, and Twitter (which I discuss in detail in Chapter 10), building a network is sometimes easier than calling a stale contact and reintroducing yourself. The place to start is with your immediate sphere of influence. To begin the process, take a look at the following list and think about who falls into these categories. Make a list of who you know in each of these areas and begin building your network with these people:

- Coworkers
- Friends
- Relatives
- Neighbors
- Vendors
- Former employers and coworkers
- Business owners
- Common interest associates
- Professional association members
- Local community leaders
- Salespeople
- Bankers, attorneys, and medical professionals
- Club members
- School or college acquaintances
- Faith community members

Getting out of your comfort zone

If the list of people you know seems too sparse to support your goals, your next step is to consider how to meet more people. Simple, right? Well, for some people, it's simple. For others, meeting new people may require a serious effort. Which category do you fall in?

The following quiz, provided courtesy of William Arruda, founder of Reach Personal Branding, can help you figure out how skilled you are at going beyond your comfort zone in the effort to meet new people.

1. **Do you take an active role in at least one professional or philanthropic organization?**
2. **Do you burn bridges when you leave jobs or assignments and never look back?**
3. **Do you attend functions where you know you'll meet people you need to know?**
4. **How many people do you typically meet at networking functions?**

5. Before going to a networking event, do you stress out, or do you identify your objectives for the event?
6. Can you state what you do, for whom you do it, and how you are different from your peers or competitors in 1 minute?
7. When you find a contact who would be perfect for friends or colleagues, do you connect them or instantly forget about it?
8. Do you know how to end conversations comfortably and when to end them?
9. When attending events, do you bring business cards or just your smile?
10. At social and business events, do you recognize faces/forget names or remember the people clearly?
11. When people ask you about what you do for work, do you tell them what you do and how you do it or just your job title?
12. Are you clear to others about who your ideal contacts would be?
13. Do you return voicemails and e-mails from network contacts?
14. Do you belong to a virtual network like LinkedIn or Google+?
15. Do you feel comfortable calling people who were referred to you by someone you know?
16. After meeting someone new, do you hope to see that person again or follow up with an e-mail or phone call?
17. Do you find clever ways to reconnect and/or stay in touch with contacts?
18. When you receive new contact information, do you put it in the contact pile or enter it into a contact system?
19. When following up, do you provide value or ask for something?
20. Do you send thank-you cards for business referrals or for career opportunities?
21. Do you talk to members of your professional network?
22. Do you have an e-mail list of your professional contacts so that you can easily send them a mass e-mail?
23. Do you send birthday greetings or e-greetings cards to members of your professional network?
24. Do you connect members of your network for their mutual benefit?

I assume that you can figure out what the ideal response to each question would be. If your honest answers are less than ideal, note which questions you need to improve on and add those improvements to your list of professional development goals.

Here are some specific tips that can help you begin to step out of your comfort zone:

- **Join groups.** Join professional or special interest groups where you can meet new people.
- **Participate.** Become active by taking on a board position. Attend the chapter meetings or events offered by the group.
- **Volunteer.** Volunteering exposes you to people you may not otherwise meet. You can build your skills, serve the community, and meet new people.
- **Speak at events.** Share your expertise about your career or interests to not only build your network but also become known for your brand.
- **Be active online.** Begin by crafting your profiles on key online sites (see Chapter 10). Post updates, share books, or identify interesting articles to your contacts.

Nurturing your contacts

As you build your network, you need to nurture your contacts so that you can be a valuable network resource. To give your networking efforts momentum, try the following suggestions:

- **Stay in touch.** Don't expect that just having someone's name on your contacts list is enough. Make an effort to stay in touch with your contacts by sending personal e-mails, going for coffee together, or making some other personal connection.
- **Connect your contacts.** Share your connections with other people. When someone asks you whether you know anyone who can help with a specific task, search your list of contacts for possibilities.
- **Ask how you can help.** When you meet with a member of your network, ask that person how you can be of service to him or her.
- **Share resources.** If you find a valuable resource or service, let your network know.
- **Include and collaborate.** Invite people in your network to attend events with you. When you have a project that is bigger than you can handle, ask members of your network for help.

- **Attend social events.** Say yes to social events. You cannot build your network easily if you do not socialize.
- **Pick up the phone.** Occasionally pick up the phone and call people to say hello and reconnect.
- **Update your social media sites.** Stay current with posts on LinkedIn, Facebook, and Twitter.
- **Send a newsletter or blog post.** A monthly newsletter or weekly blog post ensures that your network remembers you. You're providing value by delivering information that is helpful to them.

Plan to connect with the people in your network on a regular basis, but keep in mind that not all contacts are equal. For example, you may decide it's best to contact your closest contacts every two months, the next layer of contacts every six months, and your acquaintances once a year.

Whatever you do, don't let yourself disappear. Stay top of mind!

Choosing a networking group

If you look, you're bound to find lots of opportunities for professional networking in your community. Many organizations sponsor networking events for people looking to make contacts. But if you attend them all, you may have no room for anything else on your calendar!

How do you decide which events and which networking groups are worth your time? Start by considering these tips, provided by Wendy Terwelp, author of *Rock Your Network* (`http://rockyournetwork.com`):

- Ask yourself who needs to know about you and whether a specific event will likely attract your target audience.
- Consider how often a networking group meets, how much time membership in that group would require from you, and how committed you feel to the group.
- Pick at least three types of groups to consider:
  - A *peer group* for brainstorming, education, and commiserating
  - A *group of prospects* that includes your ideal target market — or people who interact with your target market
  - A *professional business group* where you can boost your credentials through certifications and your online presence via the membership's website

Networking for ideas

Networking doesn't have to be focused just on meeting people for professional growth. Networking can also be about sparking new ideas. To do this, you need to think creatively and stretch your comfort zone to try new things. Julia Cameron in her book *The Artist's Way* (Penguin Group) suggests taking a weekly artist date where you explore a new place, meet people outside your normal crowd, and do something that challenges you to think differently. New experiences promote new ways of thinking. Take a cooking class, listen to a speaker you haven't heard, eat lunch in the park, or travel to an interesting location. I often meet the most fascinating people when I go outside of my daily routines. Where might you meet people in your community who will spark your new ideas?

Starting the Conversation

Finding the people and groups that you want to network with is usually not the hardest part of building a network. For most people, the difficulties can be summed up this way:

- What will I talk about?
- What do I want to know from my network?
- What do I have to share with my network?

When you meet someone new, sometimes knowing what to say can be a challenge. Here are some simple conversation tips that can help:

- **Say hello to others and introduce yourself.** Confidently say your name, shake hands, and say "It's nice to meet you."
- **Make an inquiry.** Ask open-ended questions to encourage the other person to talk, such as "What are you enjoying most about the conference?"
- **State a fact.** Something as simple as "Wow, this is a really nice hotel, and the view is great" encourages small talk, which you can try to steer into more interesting subjects.
- **Identify common interests.** Tell a short story about one or two things that you like and see whether the other person has an interest in those things.
- **Share news or make a positive observation.** Mention something that you heard at the event you're attending or say something positive about the event.

- **Read about current affairs before you attend an event.** Comment on something that is not too controversial with this audience.
- **Talk about an article you read.** Ask for the other person's thoughts on the subject.
- **Introduce another person.** Try to mention something interesting about each person during the introduction.

TIP

As I explain in Chapter 11, becoming a content expert can give your personal brand a tremendous boost. Bonus benefit: That expertise can also give your conversational skills a boost. When you know a subject backward and forward, chances are you can speak about it with confidence.

Hitting the Conference Circuit

A conference is like a networking gold mine. Presumably, every person at the conference is (at least somewhat) committed to the professional or special interest community in question. And everyone in attendance has something in common — attending the conference! — which makes opening a conversation relatively easy. Most conferences have breakout sessions, so you likely have many chances to meet new people in small group settings. And breaks between sessions offer time to survey what the vendors have to offer and engage in further conversation.

To get the most out of a conference, do some planning and be a savvy networker by following the tips in this section.

Making the most of a conference

Here are some easy steps to take to make sure that your conference experience leads to new contacts:

- **Prepare before you go.** Read the conference brochure and choose sessions to attend that you find most useful. (Keep in mind that the most useful sessions may be those that will be attended by the people you want to meet.)
- **Plan on staying for the entire conference.** If you must leave early, try not to leave more than an hour or two before the end.
- **Sign up for extracurricular activities.** That way, you can get to know people in a more relaxed atmosphere.

- **Attend with a friend.** If you know someone going to the conference, the two of you can help each other by introducing contacts and sharing information from different sessions you each attend.
- **Try to stay at the hotel where the conference is being held.** Doing so allows you to take short breaks in your room and to meet people for meals.
- **Remember that you are never off duty.** Watch what you say and how much you drink.
- **Participate in the sessions.** Ask questions and join the conversation.
- **Show your gratitude.** Thank the people who worked on the conference and let them know how much you appreciate the opportunity to attend.

Giving out business cards

What would conference networking be without the exchange of business cards? Handing out business cards is a time-honored tradition, and you need to know how to do it right.

TIP

Don't be tempted to use your smartphone to collect contact information for each person you meet at a conference. Even if you manage to collect phone numbers or e-mail addresses, you'll likely fail to collect the complete information that a business card provides (and typos may undermine your efforts). Instead, take lots of business cards with you and follow these guidelines:

- **Carry business cards with you at all times.** Keep a backup supply in your purse or briefcase.
- **Make every business interaction an opportunity to connect.** Try to create a strong and positive impression and offer your card when appropriate.
- **Generate a positive connection first.** Before you give your card, shake someone's hand, make eye contact, and engage in conversation.
- **Keep your cards with your nametag.** Your conference nametag may have an opening on top. Put your business cards in that space behind your nametag for easy access.
- **Make sure that your cards are clean.** There's nothing less professional than a worn-looking business card.
- **Make sure that your cards aren't bent.** If you carry your wallet in your back pocket, place your business cards in another case holder so that your cards won't crease.
- **Wear an outfit with at least two pockets.** Keep your cards in one pocket and collect other business cards in the second pocket.

- **Write a note, if possible.** If time allows, write a personal note on your card to make your connection memorable.
- **Follow up with the people whose cards you collect.** Ask them to join your LinkedIn group or send them an e-mail to let them know that you enjoyed meeting them.

Working your brand into the conversation

The secret to a good conversation at a conference is to try to veer away from the standard questions (Who are you? What do you do? Where are you from?). Of course, sometimes you need to answer these standard questions before the conversation can flow into something more interesting.

Ideally, the "something more interesting" you talk about should relate to your brand. Without pushing too hard, try to work your professional interests, goals, and expertise into as many conversations as possible.

Conferences are the perfect place to use your personal commercial, which I describe in Chapter 8. Before you leave home, practice your 30-second commercial (otherwise known as your *elevator pitch).* Also, develop a shorter version that allows you to make a quick introduction and a longer version that you can use during more in-depth conversations.

Using Social Media to Build Your Network

Introverts, rejoice! These days, social media is the fastest way to build and maintain your network. LinkedIn is the most used tool for professional networking and needs to be in your toolbox. It is dynamic, interactive, and current. It is the primary networking hub to expand your presence and find people and groups you want to be associated with.

I devote Chapter 10 to an in-depth discussion of how to use social media to build your brand. Here, I illustrate how your online efforts can specifically build your network.

Minding your manners online

First, a quick etiquette refresher. Every good networker knows that good manners extend to all communications. Here, I offer some tips to follow when sending an e-mail or participating in an online networking group to make sure that you are courteous:

- **Slow down.** Pay as much attention to what you are writing as you would when writing a letter.
- **Think before you write.** Knowing what you want to communicate in advance helps clarify your message.
- **Keep it short and simple.** The more simply you present your message, the more likely you'll receive a prompt reply.
- **Be courteous.** Use "please" and "thank you," even in short messages. Note that depending on the recipient, "thanks" may be too informal.
- **Use the subject line effectively.** To make sure that your message is read, use specific keywords in your subject line.
- **Don't include confidential information.** If your message is in any way sensitive or confidential, think carefully before sending it to a networking group.
- **Send to the intended receiver.** Avoid Reply All disasters! Never send an e-mail or a response to an unintended recipient.
- **Proofread.** Apply the same business style you use in any written materials and check carefully for errors.

REMEMBER

Choose your words wisely and don't say anything negative about another person or company. Things live on in infamy on the Internet, so make sure that you won't mind your words being repeated or read by someone who does a Google search about you.

Establishing your professional network on LinkedIn

LinkedIn is the primary networking hub for professionals. To use it, you need to first complete your profile (see Chapter 10). Then, connect first with people you know well. LinkedIn will then suggest other people as possible connections.

TIP

Import your e-mail connections to LinkedIn to see who is already a member. From some e-mail domains (Gmail, Yahoo!, AOL, and Hotmail), you can easily transfer your address book to LinkedIn by entering your e-mail address and password.

To expand your network, join groups on LinkedIn that relate to the industry you work in, your interests, your alma mater, and so on. You can search for groups in the groups directory, or you can use the advanced search features to narrow your focus to groups that would be beneficial for you.

Supporting your efforts on Facebook

If you're serious about networking, you need to be on Facebook. As long as you approach your posts with your professional image in mind, you can reap great benefits. (Recently, I posted the same message to Facebook, Twitter, and LinkedIn. On LinkedIn, I received one comment on the post. On Facebook, I got 12 comments. Facebook is definitely worth your time.)

Facebook makes posting pictures, comments, and videos easy, which can be a blessing and a curse. Make sure that you think twice before you post anything to your Facebook page that you wouldn't want a recruiter to see.

Extending your reach on Twitter

Twitter allows for networking in real time. When you tweet, your message goes out to your contacts instantly.

You can use Twitter to connect with your network in an authentic way that supports your personal brand. To build your network on Twitter:

- Be interesting.
- Become a worthy resource (by sharing worthwhile information).
- Begin by following other people. Send a note and hope that they follow you as well.
- Follow already established network contacts and retweet their Twitter messages. Show your generosity by helping your contacts become better known.
- Educate yourself. Use Twitter to learn more about your areas of expertise.
- Get in the habit of tweeting something every day.

Networking within Your Workplace

Apply the same best practices of networking inside your workplace as you do outside it. After all, you're connected to your coworkers on a daily basis, and you need to nurture those relationships to be effective at your job.

Playing politics

Office politics are a part of your career. Whether you choose to participate in them or not, they come into play in every work environment. A savvy networker knows to be aware of political relationships in the workplace. The person who ignores them risks becoming irrelevant or ignored.

Treat office politics as a game of strategy. To accomplish your goals, you need to build the right relationships and steer clear of people who will take you down. However, don't slip into the role of the office gossip. Doing so can come back to hurt you. (See Chapter 16 for more on personal branding in the workplace.)

Early in my career, I carpooled with three other employees in my company. We had positions in different divisions of the company. My carpool knew so much about what was happening with the people in the various parts of the company that my boss's boss would talk to me weekly to find out what was really happening. She was too removed at her level to know the details in other areas of the company. Even though I was in a junior position, my information was valuable.

Being meeting savvy

You may have the chance to meet new people — and expand your network — in workplace meetings. Bring out your best manners at meetings so that you shine the most positive light on your personal brand. Here's how:

- Start and end the meeting on time.
- Follow the meeting's agenda.
- Don't send text messages or e-mails during the meeting.
- Turn your phone to vibrate and disarm the ringer.
- Conduct your personal grooming in the restroom, not in the meeting room.
- Allow the person leading the meeting to choose a seat first. If you arrive first, choose a less important place to sit.
- Avoid interrupting or speaking out of turn.
- Don't chew gum or crunch ice.

Amassing Referrals That Can Sell Your Brand

Building a strong network often leads to referrals, which are by far the best way to grow your business and shape your reputation. Personal referrals come from providing great service and being someone people can count on. In this section, I explain how to gather and use your referrals.

Building your brand ambassadors

Brand ambassadors are your fans — the people willing to spread the word about your personal character and/or your business. They are your cheerleaders. Your brand ambassadors build your credibility and support your trustworthiness, which solidifies your expertise.

Some of my friends send e-mails anytime they need to hire someone. Before searching online, they reach out to each other because they trust a friend's opinion more than an online ad. As a brand ambassador, my opinion about which dentist or tree service to use is valued.

TIP

Don't be passive about building your reputation through brand ambassadors. When you find out you have fans, ask them to help build your business. One way they can help is by providing *testimonials* — stories that focus on your character, skills, and talents. Testimonials build your credibility and highlight your accomplishments. When someone is looking to do business with you, a testimonial shows that you are trusted.

Ideally, you want to gather testimonials that drive home the following points:

- Working with you is a great experience.
- You provide excellent service.
- You treat people with respect.
- You are a pleasure to work with and are not difficult or demanding.
- Your work (product or service) is exceptional.

If you have zero testimonials at this point, consider writing a testimonial for a colleague and asking that person to do the same for you. If you know that someone thinks highly of you, ask for a written recommendation; send that person a short list of your accomplishments and let her know how you plan to use the recommendation.

Believing in reciprocal action

What goes around, comes around, so get in the habit of referring and endorsing other people. This is the spirit of networking: You give to your network in order to receive.

TIP

LinkedIn has a great feature that allows you to provide a recommendation to someone in your network. When you have a positive experience with someone, send him an unsolicited recommendation. Chances are he'll appreciate it so much, he may do the same for you.

Give to the people in your network, and when the time comes to ask something of them, you won't be embarrassed to ask for their help.

Expanding Your Network with a Mentor's Help

A mentor doesn't need to be older than you — just more experienced. A mentor is a trusted supporter who is interested in guiding you on your chosen path. You want a mentor who genuinely cares about you and wants to see you grow. Mentoring can be an ongoing process or a shorter term process that focuses on a specific teachable moment. With the right mentor, you can make contacts and build your network in ways that aren't possible on your own.

REMEMBER

Before you seek out a mentor, make sure that you're prepared to play your role well. If you want someone to devote time and energy to helping you build your brand, you need to approach the relationship seriously. You don't want to make a bad impression on your mentor, or else your network could actually shrink.

Here's how to make the most of a mentoring opportunity:

- Set goals for the mentorship that you both agree on.
- Ask good questions.
- Work hard, take initiative, and follow through with any assignments.
- Be willing to learn! If you spend your time trying to prove what you already know, you won't get much from your mentor.
- Communicate openly and express concern if you're feeling overwhelmed.
- Be willing to improve and to accept constructive criticism.

A mentor can help you build your brand and your network by

- Giving you feedback about your behavior and skills
- Identifying your strengths and areas for improvement
- Informing you about options, barriers, and office politics
- Sharing personal opinions and experiences
- Referring you to others who can help you
- Encouraging you to focus on attainable goals
- Providing reality checks
- Modeling workplace conduct

Chapter 16

Personal Branding in the Workplace

In This Chapter

- Shifting away from an employee mindset
- Showing your boss and coworkers what you're made of
- Getting in synch with your company's brand
- Using your brand to improve your current job — or succeed at a new one

One of the key factors boosting the popularity of personal branding is the changing landscape of the workforce. In the 1980s and early 1990s, U.S. companies laid off a lot of people. Certainly, such layoffs weren't completely unprecedented, but what happened in that period was something new. Previously, a company that laid off workers during a slow business cycle was likely to increase its workforce when business picked up again. As a result, a laid-off worker's hard times were almost certain to improve when the health of the industry he worked in improved. But in the 1980s, companies started closing departments, sending work overseas . . . in general, taking steps to ensure that they would never again require the number of people they had previously employed.

These days (unlike in the early 1980s and prior), most people realize that they'll have many jobs during their careers and must continually train to prepare for the changing workplace landscape. As a result, applying personal branding in the workplace is not a trend; it's a survival strategy. In this chapter, I focus on how personal branding helps you in the workplace, whether you've been on the job for two days or five years or are between jobs. I also show you how to build on your personal brand on the job so that you have a truly satisfying and financially rewarding work experience.

Moving Toward a Personal Branding Mindset on the Job

In the days of factory jobs and typing pools, fitting in was critical to keeping your job. These days, times have drastically changed. Personal branding experts agree that it is important to *stand out:* You need to be visible so that people know you have something unique to offer on the job. Standing out doesn't mean that you don't get along with coworkers or that you don't fit in. But standing out means that your let your skills and personality — your uniqueness — shine through.

Renowned business author, futurist, and speaker Tom Peters says in "The Brand Called You" in *Fast Company* magazine, August 31, 1997:

> *You're hired, you report to work, you join a team — and you immediately start figuring out how to deliver value to the customer. Along the way, you learn stuff, develop your skills, hone your abilities, move from project to project. And if you're really smart, you figure out how to distinguish yourself from all the other very smart people walking around with $1,500 suits, high-powered laptops, and well-polished resumes. Along the way, if you're really smart, you figure out what it takes to create a distinctive role for yourself — you create a message and a strategy to promote the brand called You.*

The *employee mindset* is all about fitting in; the *personal branding mindset* is about standing out from the crowd and more closely resembles how an entrepreneur looks at her work. These mindsets are outlined in Table 16-1 and explained throughout this chapter. When you initially peruse Table 16-1, it may be scary to think that the ways of the workplace are changing so quickly. The Chinese character for crisis is a combination of the symbol for danger and the symbol for opportunity. By being proactive in the self-management of your career, you can charge forward with opportunity.

Table 16-1 The Employee Versus Personal Branding Mindset

The Employee Mindset	*The Personal Branding Mindset*
Blending in	Having a distinct personal identity
Seeking job security	Seeking *employability* security (the ability to find work)
Sticking to a linear, predictable career path	Looking for the next career opportunity; being open to alternate paths

The Employee Mindset	*The Personal Branding Mindset*
Emphasizing company loyalty	Focusing on loyalty to a project, to your profession, to your coworkers, and to yourself
Striving for career success	Aiming for work/life balance (holistic life success)
Being a "company person" (merging your identity with your company values)	Understanding how you and your personal brand fit in with your company's work culture
Relying on academic degrees to open doors	Building on lifelong learning
Seeking a particular position or title	Showcasing your competencies
Depending on full-time employment	Embracing fluid, "gig" employment — Hollywood style
Hoping for a single job to carry you through your career	Knowing you'll have multiple positions in your work life
Creating an externally driven career	Creating a self-driven career
Waiting for annual reviews to see how you're succeeding	Gauging success based on your own personal career strategy
Playing office politics to get ahead	Building relationships on trust and authenticity
Holding a labeled, stagnant title	"Labeling" yourself with an ever-evolving personal brand
Fitting in to a boss/employee hierarchy	Understanding the complex web of ever-changing reporting relationships
Working on a project that someone else owns	Taking personal ownership of everything you do

The following sections offer detailed discussion of several of these table entries: embracing "gig" employment and lifelong learning, shifting your loyalty away from a single company and toward yourself and the projects you work on, creating a personal career strategy, moving away from a boss/employee hierarchical model, and proving your worth based on your competency.

Casting for the Hollywood gig model

Are you ready to be cast in the workplace as you would be cast in a Hollywood movie? A huge workforce trend is the movement toward a gig economy, one that resembles how the movie industry works. Think about how a film is made:

1. **Someone wants to make the movie and finds the money to fund it.**
2. **The key players are secured: the director, producer, and lead actors.**
3. **Everyone else is hired, each person bringing special skills to the set.**
4. **The whole crew works on the movie for as long as it takes to complete the project.**
5. **All the people hired for the movie say their goodbyes and move on to look for their next gigs.**

Many workplaces now function this way, and many more workplaces will do so in the future. As a result, workers need to be agile and able to clearly communicate what they can do and who they are.

Having a strong personal brand will serve you well in the gig economy. Instead of hoping that someone notices you and offers you steady, long-term employment, you must be prepared to take your personal brand on the road and leverage your skills. Chances are, you may not be an employee in the future; you may be a free agent.

The workplace has become project-oriented. More and more work is being organized into smaller segments that are facilitated by project teams. Projects are a great way to grow your brand because they have a beginning and an end, have specific deliverables, and often have measurable results.

The expendable worker

For decades prior to the 1980s, employees had come to trust that if they were loyal to their companies, the companies would take care of them. The business culture was somewhat parental: The ideal workplace operated much like a benevolent father taking care of the family he employed.

All of a sudden, that familial relationship was gone. Take IBM, for example. For many decades, IBM had been known for its job security. As in many companies, it was not unusual to find several generations and multiple family members working for the company. When IBM's business began to falter, first came company reorganizations, and then came employee layoffs. The ripple effect across businesses around the world was enormous.

With so many workers laid off and uncertain how to transition into new types of careers, one industry that boomed was *outplacement:* consulting and counseling services to help laid-off workers deal with job loss and move from one job (or career) to another. Outplacement services encouraged transitioned workers to become empowered as individuals and to think about what skills, knowledge, and abilities they brought to the table as they sold themselves to new employers.

One result of that empowerment was that people began to recognize they must take responsibility for directing their own careers.

Start thinking now about how you can take on more project work, and you'll be taking a crucial step toward becoming more employable. Toward this end, stop thinking like an employee and start thinking of yourself as a company of one offering your clients the best service that you can provide.

Consider an example of how a project gig may work: You join a project team and work on a project for two years. That project ends, and you take what you have learned and join former coworkers at a start-up business. You work really hard to build the company, and it's sold to a larger company. You leave and go to work for a competitor where you settle in for three or four years. That company merges with another business, and you leave to set up your own consulting firm. This type of transition goes on until you work fewer and fewer hours — not necessarily retiring, but at least modifying your work to fit your older lifestyle.

Engaging in lifelong learning

Proponents of higher education argue that you need to be an educated person to make it in the world. Proponents of vocational education say that you need to develop a specific skill to be useful. These days, most employers realize that both arguments are true — and neither type of education is enough on its own.

In decades past, having a college degree ensured your employability. But as recent college graduates are well aware, that degree doesn't ensure employment any more — especially if the student hasn't developed a special employable skill set. In fact, many college graduates are now enrolling in vocational programs, such as bookkeeping, veterinary technician, or cosmetology, to learn specific skills.

On the other hand, a vocational student who hasn't learned to think more broadly may plateau at a certain career level with no possibility of promotion.

You always need to be learning and figuring out more about the niche that defines your personal brand. Your learning options may include university extension programs, community college courses, weekend management courses, online skill-building courses, and self-study. You can never, *ever* think you're finished learning, or your brand (and your career) will stagnate.

Adjusting your loyalties

Generally speaking, working for a company for 20, 30, or 40 years is a thing of the past. For previous generations, company loyalty and job longevity were one and the same. Not so anymore.

Humans can be very loyal creatures, but career loyalty has been redefined. Here's the twist: Instead of being loyal to one company, today you can expect to feel loyalty to a project you're working on, the team you work with, your customers, and your profession. Everything you do should focus on your own growth and development, serving others, and serving your personal brand. The people you work for may change, but the loyalties to the relationships you build and the work you do become the portable gift you offer to everyone you interact with.

A study in brand loyalty: Sarah's change of heart

Sarah was an executive with a large global financial company when she began to develop her personal brand. She could see the political changes in the company and was worried that she would find herself in transition with the economic downturn. She was in her fifties and had worked very hard for just a few companies in her career. Like her Baby Boomer peers, she was extremely loyal to the companies she worked for.

Sarah believed in showing her company loyalty by wearing company logo polo shirts on her weekends, carrying the company logo computer case, and even using the company logo on her credit card. Her first priority was always her work, to the detriment of her health and often her relationships. She was a company person through and through.

One day Sarah was called into Human Resources and told her services were no longer needed. She was lucky to receive a severance package to give her time to transition and find a new position. After she worked her way through her anger, she vowed never to devote so much of herself to a company again. She continued the journey to develop her personal brand.

Sarah worked through all the steps to develop her personal brand and moved forward in her job search. She determined that she stands for intelligence, integrity, the ability to turn around large messy systems, and a genuine warmth in her character. She was able to articulate her strengths and qualifications, but more than that, she enjoyed having networking conversations.

Sarah interviewed and found that she didn't want to settle for a company that didn't value her attributes or one where human relationships were kept to a minimum. These companies were off brand for her. After a number of interviews where she held true to her brand, she landed a position that she is very happy with.

Sarah says that she learned so much about herself in developing her personal brand. She is still a superb employee, but she thinks about work differently. Now she keeps an objective distance and works to produce an outstanding work product because it enhances her sense of herself and her reputation. She develops relationships differently by thinking about how she can contribute to a team member's success, not just how that team member will perform for the company goals. She has changed from someone trying to please the people she works with to someone who views work as a forum for building her brand.

Sarah realizes that her work accomplishments are part of her brand. Sarah now wants to partner with a company and share her brand qualities with those she leads but never again give her soul to a company. Personal branding for her has meant that she gets to keep her soul and share her talent.

Exercising your personal brand career strategy

In the past, workers depended on others to manage their career advancement; they often did little more than hope for a promotion or raise. The thinking was that if you worked hard and did what was asked, someone would notice and reward you for it. That still happens — sometimes. But if you choose to take that route, you hand over a huge component of your life in hopes that someone else will take care of it.

TIP

Your better bet is always to be thinking ahead of what you need to do to learn, grow, and improve your work and continually monitor your situation so that you don't miss any opportunities. Most people don't take this proactive approach, and that fact alone gives you an advantage.

Exercising your personal brand career strategy means that you don't rely on someone else to hand your advancements to you. It means you *partner* with others so that they invest in your career and help you with your career goals. (See Chapter 4 for guidance on setting those goals.) It means taking personal responsibility for your own path in life, of which a huge piece is your work.

In Chapter 7, I show you how to craft your personal brand career strategy plan. To do so, you pull together discoveries from Chapters 4, 5, and 6 that include

- Needs
- Values
- Interests
- Personality
- Mission
- Work experience
- Strengths
- Education
- 360° feedback
- Goals
- Target audience
- Competitor analysis

Your plan isn't just an exercise; you should strive to fully engage it in your work. The fun part is using what you've been planning and putting your brand into action.

Identifying your boss(es)

"Who is my boss?" may sound like a silly question to ask, but in some cases, it's a tough question to answer. As you start to do more and more project work, you may end up reporting to one person for one project, to several other people for another project, and to customers (who are the ultimate bosses in most situations) — often all at the same time. So the answer to "Who is my boss?" becomes complicated.

How does a personal brand help you find the answer? Remember that personal branding is all about knowing what you stand for and what work you do, expressing who you are clearly, and being authentic. In Chapter 5, you can identify your target audience that highlights characteristics in a boss, client, or workplace. Through the development of your personal brand, you recognize that what you bring to the table is different than what others offer through their personal brands. In this crazy world where it may not be obvious who exactly you are reporting to and who your "boss" is, it is important to treat each person respectfully and uniquely deliver what you've promised to each of them. These qualities help you move from situation to situation and boss to boss.

Choosing your own job title

When you're in business for yourself, you can call yourself just about any title you'd like. (There's even a website that thinks of a title for you: `www.bullshitjob.com/title`.)

Here are a few titles listed on one person's LinkedIn profile: Communications Strategist; Chief Storyteller; Speaker Coach; Public Relations Pro. Who do you think gave that person his titles? I would bet he gave them to himself based on his abilities and goals.

If you're working for a company, chances are that you won't be able to give yourself a title. However, you may have the option to give yourself a tagline that you can add on to the company title — for example, *Administrative Assistant ~ Taking organization to a new level.* The tagline (see Chapter 7) becomes a way to differentiate yourself among all the other Administrative Assistants in your company and add your individual brand to your title.

The goal isn't to let your past job titles limit or fully define you. Personal branders try to innovate with new job titles that showcase who they are, what they do, and what they stand for. You don't want to get too esoteric (potential employers may not be able to decipher what a Dynamic Implementation Engineer or a Global Paradigm Administrator is), but definitely do some brainstorming to discover creative ways to communicate your abilities.

Thriving in a competency-based world

While your job title(s) may help you get an interview, to be hired you need to make sure that you can deliver quality work. Obviously, when people hire you, they want to know what you're competent to do.

What exactly is a competency? A *core competency* is fundamental knowledge, ability, or expertise in a specific subject area or skill set. The *core* part of the term indicates that you have a strong foundation from which to build the additional competence to do a specific job.

Being able to explain your competencies and demonstrate your skill sets are aspects of how you differentiate yourself from your competitors. Understanding clearly what you can do and being able to express it clearly to potential employers are keys to selling yourself in the job market.

Selling Your Brand to Your Internal Market: Your Boss and Coworkers

You live in an *experience economy* where your success is based not on your years of service but on what you deliver and how you deliver it. Other than you, the person who has the most control over your brand and can influence how that brand is perceived at work is most likely your boss. This means that the person that you most want to influence with your brand is your boss. Your coworkers are almost as important because they, too, must support who you are and work together with you on projects. If you haven't partnered with your coworkers in a mutual show of support, they can turn their attention to sabotaging you instead.

To be successful in the workplace, you must understand the needs of your boss and coworkers because they are your audience. If you're unsure what they need, ask them. Build the strength of your brand by providing excellent service to them and making yourself indispensable. Go beyond the "that is not my job" mentality and show your audience what an asset you are.

Throughout this book, I encourage you to look at your strengths, skills, and talents. You need to find ways to use all of them at work. You'll always be better at improving your strengths than trying to improve your weaknesses, so find projects that highlight your talents. What do you want to be known for at work? What are you already good at? What do you need to learn to develop the niche that can help your boss and coworkers the most? Learn to be a resourceful problem-solver.

Building credibility

Here are some suggestions for building your credibility in the workplace:

- If you read an article, take a course, or participate in a seminar that addresses issues that affect other people in your department, take the initiative to write a brief overview of what you learned that may be useful to your coworkers.
- Volunteer for a project that no one else will take on and make it look interesting to those observing you.
- Even if your boss doesn't request it, submit a short status report once a week, on the same day each week, so that you establish a pattern of proactively communicating your successes and ongoing efforts.
- If communication with your boss or coworkers needs improvement, ask your boss if you can implement a regular (weekly, biweekly, or monthly) breakfast or lunch meeting for your entire department to share success stories, concerns, and ideas.
- Create a how-to or resource manual for your workplace that can help others in your department.
- Be a person with integrity. Make sure that your words and actions are congruent. You build a stronger brand when people know that they can count on you to do what you've promised. If you're a leader, integrity is an especially crucial quality because people will want to work for you.

Building a strong relationship with your boss

Here are a few specific tips for creating an excellent relationship with your boss:

- **Communicate your goals and understand your boss' priorities.** Start by building the best working relationship with your boss that you can. If necessary, adjust your communication style to match her style so that you're communicating according to her preferences. For example, I once had a boss who liked receiving a Friday report where I listed what I had done during the week and what my goals were for the upcoming week. I didn't particularly like this task, but I got very good at communicating the way this boss wanted me to.

  Along those same lines, don't assume that you understand what your boss's priorities are. Ask him to outline for you what work is most important to him and how you can best deliver that work.
- **Be a problem-solver, not a problem-creator.** Be known as the person who solves the problems, not the person who creates them.

- **Get results.** Talk about stating the obvious, right? But I can't tell you how many times I've watched people expect to be rewarded when all they've done is show up to work. ("Great job, Joe — you didn't call in sick!") One of the best ways to build your brand is to be excellent at what you do and to get results. I promise you that bosses like results.

REMEMBER

Your boss can help you build your brand or tear it down. Do what you can to make the relationship work or work to find a situation where you can grow into your better self.

Aligning Your Brand with the Company's Brand

When you know your personal brand, you can figure out how to use it within the corporate culture where you work. It becomes an authentic exchange of assets. Developing a personal brand is more than insurance in a volatile workforce; it establishes a clarity of career goals that allows you to chart your career course by taking assignments to help you grow and develop. In most cases, that action serves your company well.

Most companies have a corporate brand or a set of company guidelines that all employees agree to buy into. Often, the company brand is part of its allure to workers. For example, workers at Google buy into the idea that Google is a company on the cutting edge of innovation and has a reputation for being a cool place to work. Someone chooses to work at Google because he believes he's the kind of person who fits that corporate brand.

Intertwining your brand with your company

TIP

As you build your personal brand, you can identify areas of growth that overlap with your employer's goals. One place to begin is to look at the company's annual report where the mission, vision, and values are stated. Ask yourself if you can see how the personal brand you're developing overlaps with your company's mission, vision, and values.

A wise employer will encourage you to align your values with company values and find this "sweet spot" of personal buy-in. You'll have greater satisfaction with your work and fill your employer's need for increasing job performance and greater productivity.

Personal branding can appear to be a self-centered approach to work, but in fact, it's an avenue of self-empowerment. Having choices gives you a feeling of control over your destiny by taking away a feeling of being a victim (feeling like you have no choices) in your work. When you develop a strong personal brand, you demonstrate a pro-activity that can help you grow over the course of your career. Your dedication to self-improvement ultimately serves the people you work with as well.

William Arruda, Reach Communications founder, gives this description of personal branding in the workplace:

> *When I started my personal branding business over a decade ago, companies were skeptical about personal branding. Today, companies understand that corporate brands and personal brands work well together. Your company needs you to deliver on its brand promise in a way that is authentic to you. You must leverage what makes you exceptional in support of your company's mission. If you conform to a set of standards without integrating your greatest strengths and passions, your company does not benefit from the unique ingredient you can contribute.*

Being authentic in what you do

At the core of personal branding is this question: How do I get to be authentic in what I do? Most people don't feel they can be themselves at work. Here are some key questions to ask to determine whether your personal brand aligns with your work:

- What does the company stand for? What are its mission, vision, and values?
- What is your personal brand? What are your mission, vision, and values?
- How do the two compare? Are there places where they match? Where are they in conflict?
- Do you feel proud to work for this company? Can you identify with the work that your company does?
- Are you motivated to go to work? What do you most enjoy doing?
- Do you feel like this company can use your unique contributions? Are you able to engage your unique promise of value?
- Do you have an opportunity to add value that is remarkable, measurable, and different?
- Are you doing the right job for who you are and what your skill set is?
- What have you accomplished in this work that you can brag about?
- Do you see yourself and your personal brand being able to grow in this company? Can you build your brand here?
- Do the company's ethics align with your sense of right and wrong?

Finding the ideal situation

The ideal situation is when your values (see Chapter 4) align with what your company values. When that happens, you're likely to feel engaged and committed to the work you do. I'm talking about something different than company loyalty; the goal here is a day-to-day good fit and a genuine interest in the work.

When your personal brand and the company brand align, here's what you get:

- Higher motivation resulting in greater self-direction
- A happier employee (you!) who is connected not only to the task of her work but also to the company and fellow teammates
- Less stress because there is a better fit
- An increasing willingness to take on more work
- More passion and creativity, and less burnout
- Excitement and a renewed enthusiasm

Growing things

Ben was an attorney and partner at a law firm with a reputation for giving solid, trusted advice. His firm commanded top dollar and provided some of the best legal advice in the state. The attorneys were self-assured, very smart, and won most of their legal arguments. Ben fit in very well with the firm and loved being part of it. He fit in so well that when he was asked who he was, he realized that he described himself with the same qualities that the firm was known for. Ben discovered that he had no individual differentiators other than the firm's reputation as providing self-assured, smart, and solid trusted advisors. He wanted to feel more connected to his work and feel like he had an individual identity. As a result, he began working on his personal brand.

Ben looked at all aspects of his life, including what he did outside of work. Ben loved to garden. He took great pride in his organic vegetables and enjoyed sharing his bounty with his clients and coworkers. He even made labels to go on the paper bags he brought the vegetables in. Ben looked for ways to merge these seemingly different aspects of his life and realized that he loved to grow not only vegetables but also his legal business.

Gaining a better understanding of his love to grow things helped him come up with a new strategy to better represent the law firm. He was able to stand on the company brand of being a solid trusted advisor with a track record of winning cases and use his personal brand of growing things to strengthen his reputation both in the firm and as a leader in the community. He built a plan around growing his business and began mentoring other attorneys in how to grow their business. The win-win was that Ben was enjoying his work more than ever, and the firm became more profitable.

Standing Out in a Likeable Way

Marketers measure *brand likeability*. You may not need to use specific metrics to measure your own likeability, but you do need to pay attention to your behavior on the job to make sure that you don't tarnish your personal brand. A personal brand helps you stand out in the workplace rather than simply fit in. Here are some common-sense ways to make sure that you shine when you stand out:

- **Make yourself attractive.** As I detail in Chapter 12, appearance matters. No matter how long you've been on the job (a day, a year, or a decade), don't slack off on your appearance; it influences the way your boss and coworkers perceive your performance every single day.
- **Find common ground.** If you're new on the job, find opportunities to talk to coworkers about their personal lives and identify things you have in common. If you've been on the job for a while and haven't taken the time to get to know your coworkers, it's never too late to make an effort.
- **Be authentic.** No one likes a phony! This is the cardinal rule of branding. And trust me: Your coworkers will eventually see through any pretenses. Be honest from the start, and you'll feel more comfortable and confident.
- **Be interested in others.** Even if you've worked with the same team for years, don't assume that you know everything about them. Strive to be an active listener and to show genuine interest in their stories and ideas.
- **Practice empathy.** Develop the habit of trying to understand something from another person's perspective.
- **Mind your manners.** Even if you're struggling to connect with a certain coworker, strive to show that person respect and treat him with common courtesy. Your efforts won't be lost on the people around you.

Poor behavior and a bad attitude will take you down no matter how hard you work on your personal brand. One truly bad moment on the job can sink your brand, as well as your prospects with that company. Make sure that you avoid these common causes of on-the-job failure:

- A lack of self-discipline (which shows up as poor impulse control)
- An absence of ambition (which leads you to expect the world to deliver every opportunity to you)
- Failure to follow through
- A tendency to gossip
- The assumption that your level of education is sufficient and you don't need to learn anything else
- Poor time, money, or resource management

- Narcissism (assuming that everything is about you)
- Failure to cooperate
- An unwillingness to do anything extra (because "That's not my job")

Should You Stay or Should You Go?

Many people who make the effort to develop a personal brand are in the midst of a transition. Some people start the personal branding process after losing a job. Others do so because they know they have the potential to move higher in their careers. Still others are considering whether to make a bold move in a new vocational direction.

In this section, I offer advice for using your personal brand in three distinct work situations: when you're employed and want to convince your boss to make improvements to your existing job; when you're negotiating either for improvements to your current job or for a new job; and when you've just begun a new position.

Redesigning your current job

Assuming that you aren't being forced out of your current job — you haven't been laid off, and you aren't having serious problems with your boss or coworkers — you should think twice before searching for the next best thing. Jumping ship to look for a better job is often the first reaction to wanting a change in career. After all, the grass may be greener at some other workplace, right? Maybe — or maybe not. The first place to look for a better position may be right where you are, and your personal branding efforts can help.

When you're limited by an employee mindset, you can easily get stuck with a narrow perspective of your work environment; you may find it hard to look around and think about what could be different or how you could redesign the job you already have. When you begin expanding your perspective by adopting the personal branding mindset, you realize that (very likely) your employer wants you to succeed because your success makes the company and its managers look good as well. If you can demonstrate how the company would benefit by giving you new tasks and by transferring tasks that are more difficult for you, you may be surprised to see the changes that can happen in your current workplace.

Here are a few ways you may be able to improve your current job situation:

TIP

- **Go back to school.** Seek additional training so that your skills better match those demanded by the position or responsibilities you really want. For example, if technology is a weakness for you but a certain level of tech savvy is crucial to your career growth, take courses to get up to speed. If your writing or public speaking skills are poor and you want to work up to an executive position, take the initiative to improve those skills.
- **Lobby for telecommuting.** Spell out for your employer the benefits of allowing you to work from home on certain days. If making this type of change will reduce your stress level and increase your productivity, say so. If your boss has concerns about telecommuting, ask whether she's willing to give you a one- or two-month trial so that you can prove you're able to produce effectively at home.
- **Adjust your schedule.** Consider how you can revise your work schedule to better fit the life you want to create for yourself and think about how you can pitch that change to your boss. For example, maybe you know the only way you'll commit to exercising regularly is to do so midday, which will increase the amount of time you need to take for a lunch break. Explain your health goals to your boss and ask for his buy-in. If you're willing to come in earlier or stay later each day to make up for the lost work time, chances are you'll get the schedule flexibility you desire.
- **Get involved in new projects.** If you've been on the job for a while and feel like your work is stagnant, take the initiative to ask for new responsibilities or for the chance to work on new projects. Even if doing so causes your workload to increase temporarily, the extra effort can lead to greater excitement and engagement. And assuming that you work hard and demonstrate your skills to everyone involved, it may also lead to a chance to redefine your position in the company.

TIP

Too often, a professional who wants to improve her skills or her career prospects feels compelled to move to a new company. For a mid- to senior-level manager, that departure means six months to a year of learning the new company culture before she can understand her new position in depth. If possible, the first place to consider implementing your personal brand should be right where you are. If you're willing to speak up and to learn some new tricks, you may find that your company is willing to grow along with you.

Highlighting your personal brand when negotiating

Whether you're trying to alter your current work situation or have decided that moving to another company is your best option, you need to know how to negotiate to get what you want.

If you've worked hard on your personal brand (see Parts II and III, as well as the preceding chapters in Part IV), you can walk into a negotiation with detailed knowledge of your values, skills, and abilities. You have studied your competitors and target market so that you know what other opportunities may be available to you. You can also communicate your expertise effectively. All these pieces add up to the fact that you have positioned yourself as a person of value; you are aware of what you have to offer.

Personal branding clarifies what you bring to the table. You are a strong brand, and strong brands are paid more than commodities because they are special.

As any good negotiator will tell you, you need to enter a negotiation with as much information about yourself and the situation as you can. This gives you the advantage of knowing what you really want and what you are willing to compromise on. Good negotiations represent give and take in an atmosphere where there is open communication that is friendly, relaxed, and businesslike.

In addition to knowing yourself and knowing what you need, here are steps to a successful negotiation:

1. **Research what the company (or the individual in the room with you) needs and wants.**
2. **Ask good questions to clarify what the company (or the individual) needs.**
3. **Listen carefully to the offer being made and identify the many factors that can be discussed.**
4. **Express any areas of concern or disagreement.**

   You may need to confront issues that do not work for you. (Just be sure to do so professionally and creatively so that you don't shut down the process.)
5. **Consider what you're willing to compromise in order to get what you really want.**

   What can you offer in exchange for something else? (Less pay but more vacation days?)

For more tips on how to master the art of negotiation, check out *Negotiating For Dummies* by Michael C. Donaldson and David Frohnmayer (Wiley).

Succeeding During the First 90 Days of a New Job

Whether you're new to the job market or making the transition from one job to the next, building on the foundation of your personal brand is crucial. In most cases, you can assume that you have about three months to be fully contributing in your new position. To make sure those three months go smoothly, you want to craft a plan for success before you walk through the door on your first day.

Here are specific ways to demonstrate to your new employer that the decision to hire you was a great one:

TIP

- **Create a plan and solve problems.** During the interview process, you probably learned of key areas of concern or problems that needed solving. Make a list of those issues and consider projects that can be easily implemented. Create a plan that engages other people, shows your skill set, and solves a problem. Tackle the easier problems first and choose ones that show you know what you are doing and build credibility among your peers and with your boss.

  Pulling in other people to help accomplish these first projects shows that you are a team player.

- **Find an ally.** In fact, find several allies. These people can show you around, help you with company procedures, tip you off to office politics, and (hugely important!) help you with the copier. These people are often found in the support staff or in different departments (where they aren't threatened by a new employee). Finding someone to show you this kindness is critical to your success.

- **Define what you need to learn.** If you're in a new company or have been promoted, you probably have a lot to learn. If you've been promoted, don't mistakenly assume that you already know what to do.

  To make effective decisions, you need to learn not just the technical aspects of the position but also the more subtle information, including the company culture, unspoken strategies, and the politics of the organization. Ask your coworkers some key questions:

  - What are the biggest challenges this department is facing?
  - What are some key things you think I should be working on?

  Don't be arrogant; assume that you have much to learn.

- **Get in alignment with your team.** If possible, meet with your team or peers in the weeks before you start your job. This way, you can begin your position before you walk through the door on your first day. Building relationships isn't emphasized in a job description, but poor relationships can make you fail. Let your coworkers know that you are interested in them and that you want to work as part of a team. For specific tips on getting along with them, check out the earlier section "Standing Out in a Likeable Way."

- **Track your early successes.** Keep a record of what you have accomplished to share with your boss at your 90-day review session. (If possible, try to accomplish an early win that is especially meaningful to your boss.)

REMEMBER

In the first weeks of a new position, you're being sized up by your coworkers. Those judgments form the basis of what people think of you; it can take months to turn around a poor first impression. You have developed your personal brand and have much to be proud of. Walk with confidence into your new job.

Part V

The Part of Tens

The 5th Wave By Rich Tennant

"I added a bunch of new people to my network today. They were standing behind me in the express check out line at the grocery store."

In this part . . .

This part offers four short and sweet chapters chock full of great advice. I highlight the benefits of developing your personal brand and then warn you about ways you can quickly sink that brand if you aren't careful. I offer hints for how best to demonstrate your brand, and finally I suggest steps you can take to continue to build your brand even after the fundamentals are in place.

Chapter 17

Ten Key Benefits of Personal Branding

In This Chapter

- Reaping the rewards of a more authentic life
- Showing the world what you can do

Personal branding is about deciding to take an active role in the direction of your life. You benefit from creating a personal brand because it allows you to self-manage your life and stop depending on others to do it for you. Your personal brand helps you make the most of what you've got to offer. In this chapter, I describe ten benefits of personal branding.

Granting Permission to Be Yourself

The personal branding process assures you that it's okay to be yourself. If you've built your life on pretenses — on attempts to be someone you are not — this assurance is a huge relief. Personal branding is about expressing your authentic self by allowing you to be the person you are meant to be.

The strategic process of personal branding (which I outline in Chapter 1) makes you an active partner in creating the direction of your life. You get to decide what your unique promise of value is and who you want to share it with.

Gaining Confidence

You develop confidence as you develop your personal brand. That confidence comes from looking at your strengths and knowing that you have many positive qualities to share. When you know that you have something of value to offer, your self-esteem soars. Your personal brand done well highlights your strengths and gives you a direction in which to use them.

As an added bonus, personal branding also minimizes your weaknesses. It's human nature to want to improve your weaknesses, but by crafting your brand, you can determine whether you really need to use your weakest skills at all. Chances are they don't need to play a huge role in your life's plan. If those skills are required to create the product or service you want to create, consider whether you're the best person for the job or whether you can outsource those tasks so you can focus on what you do best.

Building Credibility

Your target audience (see Chapter 5) wants to know that you can do what you say you're going to do. You build credibility not through your words but through your actions. If you live your personal brand and keep your brand promise to your target market, you are automatically on the path to credibility. Your actions, which align with your brand, validate that you can be trusted and show that you are credible.

After you build a track record with your target audience, *their* words — in the form of testimonials and references — can then become tools supporting your credibility. While your own words may not prove your worthiness to anyone, their words will.

Showcasing Your Specialty

You need to specialize and have an area of expertise. When asked what you do best, your answer can't be "everything." No one knows what that means. To develop a specialty, the best place to start is with what you know. What can you do that few others know how to do? What segment of the population do you understand better than most people in your field do?

You have a unique combination of work experience, life experience, and personal characteristics that create the foundation for determining your niche. To be known in a certain niche, you are wise to choose an area of expertise or market segment that you know well and that you enjoy. Chapter 6 can help you figure out how to develop your niche.

Leaving Your Mark

Part of the branding process is becoming known for something. Chapter 3 gives you examples of people who have left their mark on the world, and you can do the same. Your first step is to identify your best characteristics so that you know what to build on.

In a way, developing a personal brand is a means of ensuring that you leave a legacy. People will remember you through your actions, your expertise, and the emotional connections that you make.

But keep in mind that strong brands often repel as much as they attract; not everyone belongs in your target audience. Defining who you are means that you need to be brave enough to let your true self be visible. (Chapter 5 gives you tips on identifying your target audience.)

Connecting You to Your Target Audience

Personal branding success requires communicating your message to the right people — not necessarily to the entire world. And it requires communicating in a way that creates emotional connections with your target audience. You simply cannot build a solid brand without building relationships, which are based on emotional connections.

In Chapter 2, I explain that even corporations build their brand successes by connecting emotionally with consumers. The stores you shop in, the products you buy, the restaurants you eat in . . . all of them are branded in ways designed to tap in to your emotions.

Building a strong personal brand helps you interact with your target audience in a clear, consistent way that quickly becomes familiar. That consistency builds trust in your target audience, which allows those emotional connections to form.

Distinguishing Yourself from the Competition

You are hardwired to notice what is different. You notice the person dressed in red in a sea of black clothing. Differentiation is crucial to your personal branding success. If you are like everyone else in the market, you are a commodity, and you look the same to the customer as all the other options. If your target market discerns nothing special about you, it's easy for the customer to pass you by.

You need to recognize and develop your unique talents. You also need to uncover your niche by identifying what your target market `needs` and `wants` and understanding what your competitors are not providing. Study the competition (Chapter 6 shows you how) and deliver something that it does not.

Getting the Support You Need

I am an optimist and believe that people genuinely want to help you. The problem is that if you are vague about what you need, no one is going to jump in and try to figure your life out for you (except perhaps your mother). You need to be clear about who you are and what you need so that you can ask for support with clarity. If you know what you need, you know what to ask for. Defining your personal brand helps you determine your needs and identify who is most likely able to fulfill them.

Chapter 15 shows you how you can nurture your network to build the support that you need in solidifying your personal brand.

Focusing Your Energy

You are probably as crazy busy as everyone else is. A benefit of having a personal brand is that when you have a clear understanding of who you are, what you do best, who you want to work with, and how you want to use your talents, you also know what you *don't* want in your life.

TIP

Using your personal brand like a filter allows you to more easily say yes to the right opportunities and say no to the wrong opportunities. You know what is "on brand" and what is "off brand" for you. Branding gives you clarity so that you can focus your energy on what's truly important to you.

Letting Yourself Be Lazy

A personal brand helps you avoid the need to reinvent yourself and the tools you use in your professional life. After you pinpoint your expertise, your goal is to use it over and over so that you reap maximum benefits from it. (Perhaps you write an article that is then broken down into blog posts and later becomes the subject of a presentation to a professional association.) After you craft a personal branding statement (a concise expression of who you are and what you offer to your target audience; see Chapter 7), you want to use it in every communication you create.

The beauty of personal branding is that while it's never static (you always want to learn and grow), it thrives on consistency. And consistency requires you to use key pieces of your branding puzzle again and again even as your personal brand evolves. So do your tough work up front and reap the rewards down the road. And remind yourself that it's sometimes good to be lazy!

Chapter 18

Ten Ways You Can Sink Your Brand

In This Chapter

- Ignoring the branding fundamentals
- Displaying behavior that tarnishes your brand

Your personal brand is more fragile than you may imagine. You need to be vigilant in maintaining the standards that you've set for your brand. All it takes is one major mistake, especially one that you handle poorly, and all that you've built will vanish. This chapter offers some cautions and tips so you can avoid a brand breakdown.

Letting It Go Stale: Taking Your Brand for Granted

Your personal brand, no matter how well crafted it is, is never "done." If you think that developing your personal brand is a one-time event, think again. Your personal brand can easily grow stale. What was once cutting edge can become routine. Staying on top of your brand is a way to set yourself apart from others in your market. If you ignore your brand, you may start looking just like everyone else and become the dreaded commodity.

TIP

Keep your brand fresh by continuing to grow and serve your target market. Yes, it's possible to stay on brand and grow your brand at the same time! Don't ever take your brand for granted.

Neglecting Consistency

Being inconsistent is a brand killer. People like to know what to expect; it gives them comfort and solidifies that they can count on you. In Chapter 3,

I talk about Lady Gaga, who has built her brand on the element of surprise. (Bubbles? Meat? What will she wear next?) Does her example contradict my point? No, because she is consistent in keeping you wondering. You can depend on her going to extremes to entertain her audience. But if someone like Diane Sawyer came out in similar attire, it would go against her brand.

You need to be consistent in your marketing materials, in how you dress, with what you say, and with how you behave. You need to maintain a brand identity and follow it steadily. Consistency is key so that people know what to expect from you and can trust what you stand for.

Speaking Before You Think

With branding, there's a certain irony: Your words alone can't build your brand; you need actions to back them up. But your words can most definitely undermine your brand all by themselves.

Remember Tony Hayward, the past CEO of BP Oil? After the Deepwater Horizon oil spill — the largest oil spill the United States had experienced — wreaked havoc on the Gulf Coast in 2010, Mr. Hayward tried to minimize the disaster and the environmental cost of the spill, denied any underwater oil eruptions, and looked increasingly arrogant. When he told reporters "I'd like my life back," he came across as selfish and completely out of touch with the devastation caused by the disaster. It seemed that everything Hayward said made the situation worse. The damage done to the environment was unbelievable, and the damage done to his brand was irreparable.

Most people won't ever have to deal with a situation as serious as the one Hayward faced, but at some point you'll undoubtedly need to explain why something went wrong or give an opinion about an issue. Be thoughtful in how you phrase your answers, and notice the impact your words have. Your words can support your brand or ruin it, so be careful in how you use them. (For more on this topic, see Chapters 3 and 16.)

Exhibiting Bad Behavior

Every time you're in public (whether at a professional event or at the drugstore), you represent your personal brand. Don't ever fool yourself into believing that how you behave matters only in the workplace.

I attended a conference where I witnessed one of the keynote speakers behave very badly. She was yelling at the hotel bellman and demanded a certain treatment from the hotel staff. I was appalled at this person's behavior, and when I realized that it was one of the people I was coming to see, I lost respect. I have never been able to listen to this person speak since that time without thinking of her demanding behavior that day in the hotel lobby. She has ruined her brand forever for me.

Be careful how you behave — even when you think no one is watching.

Being Unresponsive

Unresponsiveness reflects badly on your brand. It's especially dreadful in a business setting because your lack of response tells your clients that you don't respect them. Your behavior quickly becomes a known (negative) part of your brand: "That Bob, he never returns his calls."

Your personal brand is built around serving your target market. If you ignore them and don't respond to their needs, they won't recommend you to others. You may do excellent work, but if the customer doesn't get your full attention, your business will develop a reputation as one that doesn't care about the customer. To keep your brand sharp, respond!

Ignoring the Politics

Being a savvy personal brander means that you show an awareness that your colleagues don't: You notice your surroundings and have your antenna up for the nuances of behavior (in other words, the politics) that take place in your office. If you work in a company, part of your target audience is your boss and coworkers. You need to pay attention to the politics and understand how you need to adjust your brand to succeed inside your organization.

You don't want to offend anyone or step over the line, but don't be afraid to let the uniqueness of your brand show through. Chapter 16 describes how you can use your personal brand in the workplace. Watch the politics and pay attention!

Having an Unprofessional Online Image

You've worked hard to establish yourself as a solid professional. You dress the part, you put in extra hours, you produce stellar work, and then you blow it with your picture on Facebook behind a table lined with empty bottles of vodka (looking like you just drank every drop of it).

Getting crazy once in a while is okay, but you don't need to share that image with the world! You don't want your moment to be posted on the Internet for everyone to see for eternity. Monitor your online images and know that employers are watching. You don't want to work hard to build your reputation and have it ruined with a single picture.

Not Telling the Truth

Not long ago, a journalist who had fabricated stories (and hurt people with his untruths) made front-page news. He was banned from journalism and went to law school to become an attorney. The state bar of New York refused to admit him to practice in that state, so he moved to California to try to become a lawyer there. His reputation of lying followed him and has stuck as his brand. Even with testimony from his employer, psychiatrists, and other people promoting his character of reform and remorse, he cannot overcome the brand he has built as someone who cannot be trusted. The jury is still out on his license.

Always tell the truth. Being caught in a lie has sunk many a promising brand.

Being Inauthentic: Looking Like a Phony

True personal brands are based in authenticity. That means that you need to be you. If you're building your brand on what you think you *should* be instead of what you are, you'll most likely fail. You can't sustain phony forever. If you misrepresent your experience or skill set, you will be discovered. Don't call yourself an expert unless you are one. Build your brand from a position of strength, which means building it on truth.

I have watched people jump on the bandwagon of whatever is popular at the moment. To me, these people are phonies and just trying to capitalize on the latest trend. I can tell when a person's heart is not in her work and when a brand is built on a shaky foundation. An authentic personal brand is always built on the truth.

Losing Focus

Being scattered dilutes your brand. When you do too many things, you appear to lack focus, and people don't really understand what you stand for. I have seen websites where a person is promoting coaching services, interior design consultations, and contracting as an administrative assistant. Trying to represent yourself as appealing to everyone actually appeals to no one.

Know who you are and what you stand for. Identify the core of your work and be true to your brand. If you lose focus on who you are, who your target market is, and what you do best, no one else will be able to figure out your brand either. Stay focused and be on brand.

Chapter 19

Ten Ways to Demonstrate Your Brand

In This Chapter

- Letting the authentic you stand out
- Showcasing your best self online
- Building your brand every day

Everything that you do demonstrates your brand, from the way that you represent yourself online to how you treat people at the grocery store. Because a personal brand is built on your true self, you need to be aware that the totality of your actions makes up your brand. You're not just pretending when you are visible to your target audience. In this chapter, I describe ten ways that you can demonstrate your brand.

Being Authentic in All That You Do

Your personal brand is your legacy and your reputation. You must show your real self — not a fake version — to the world. Living authentically makes you memorable to others; they recall your actions, your expertise, and the emotional connections that you make. Your personal brand shows your authenticity from the inside out. What you are offering is your unique promise of value: something that only you can provide.

Part II of this book helps you identify your best self and guides you to articulate your authenticity in all that you are and all that you do.

Standing for Something

You want to use your talents and passions to become known for something special so that you can build a distinct personal brand. To be known for something, you need to figure out what you do well and then own it. You may become known for your personality, your community service, or your expertise. Whatever you want to be known for, you need to reveal your best attributes to build your personal brand.

Becoming known for something may include becoming knowledgeable about your chosen area of expertise. You want to find a niche and seek endorsements attesting to your expertise. Build relationships that support your personal brand. Chapter 6 helps you define that niche.

And finally, act with confidence in exhibiting your brand. Even if you don't yet feel confident, fake it until you believe it!

Having Consistency in Your Communications

When you're clear about your message, you want to deliver the message consistently no matter how you're communicating with your target audience. Every time you send your message, it needs to be perceived in the same way. The most important thing you can do is to be consistent in your message starting the first time you make contact with a potential employer, future customer, or other target audience member. Chapter 11 shows you how.

What you are wearing, the words you use, the tone of your voice, and the graphics, colors, or logos that you use are all ways that you can send a consistent message. Think about the message you're sending to your audience *before* you send it and be consistent in all that you do.

Building Character Online: Creating a Signature Look

Your social media sites often act as the hubs of your online identity, so make sure that they represent you well. Ask a friend to give you her first impression when she looks at your social media sites, and if it doesn't align with your personal brand, make the necessary changes. You want your online presence to communicate your brand and connect with your target audience. Use the logo, font(s), color(s), and images that speak to your brand and show who you are.

Your look online is as important as the look of the hard copy materials that you create. You want to carry a consistent theme from the printed materials through to your online visual identity. You want to apply your branded logo and colors to your e-mail signature, website or blog, social media sites, and any video that you add to your sites. (You can find lots of helpful suggestions related to visual identity in Chapter 13.)

Leveraging LinkedIn

You make a first impression online in much the same way as you do in person. Your success with social networking comes at the intersection where you're sharing the right information to the right people at the right time and on the right social media platform. LinkedIn helps you build effective business relationships based on nurturing the "know, like, and trust" factor. The first step is to get your LinkedIn presence moving in the right direction. Chapter 10 shows you how.

Going Viral on Twitter

Twitter is the great equalizer and a place where you can share your content expertise without being granted a PhD or holding a prestigious job title. If you're prolific enough and get enough followers who are interested in what you have to say, you can rise to the status of content expert rather quickly.

To build your presence on Twitter, you want to make sure that you're providing value to your target audience (your followers) by giving them links to articles, blogs, and websites that offer good, useful information. You can get a greater understanding of how to use Twitter to maximum effect in Chapter 10.

Facebooking the Right Friends

People form opinions about you and your reputation on Facebook just as they would in person: based on what others know about you, the way that you treat other people, the ways that you behave, information that you share, and who you hang out with. Chapter 10 fills you in on the details of using Facebook to enhance your personal brand.

Facebook is designed to share information and helps you tell your story in ways that connect, inform, and entertain. Facebook allows you to navigate the gentle balance of being social while also sharing enough of your personal brand to offer a satisfying taste of what others experience when they meet you in person.

But, as your mother always told you, be careful who you hang out with! Your community of choice makes an impression.

Marketing Your Materials and Business Cards

Your brand identity is carried through all the items that your target audience touches. It incorporates your logo, fonts, colors, and images into one look and feel. Each item should reinforce the unique promise of value that your brand stands for (see Chapter 7). You want to apply your brand look in everything that you do to create a set of coordinated materials.

If you want to increase the visibility of your personal brand, you need to use the visual elements that attract your target audience and be consistent with those elements. In Chapter 13, I offer specifics about how to select colors, fonts, and images that jibe with your brand and set you up for success.

Don't forget to pay attention to your business card as it may be the only visual tool that your target audience sees from you. Your card has one purpose — to get noticed by those receiving it. Your business card helps you stand out and be remembered by someone you just met.

Engaging in Community Involvement

Volunteering is one of the best ways to build your brand, widen your community, expand your network, and serve the greater good. How you volunteer your time, as well as which community you serve, becomes part of that brand.

You need to volunteer with the same standards as you would have in the workplace. You can damage your reputation and your brand by behaving badly as a volunteer with laziness, a complaining attitude, or poor follow-through. As a volunteer, you want to become known for your character, your good deeds, and/or the causes you support.

Highlighting Your Brand Daily

You can highlight your brand daily by living *on brand.* That means that you keep your level of self-awareness keen and continue to think about things that are on brand for you.

TIP

Sending a message online is an easy way to highlight your brand. Your brand attributes can guide you in how to communicate your personal brand online. The type of message you create clarifies and communicates what makes you special — what makes you different from other people. For example, if you're an avid reader, you can send book updates on Twitter. Your message should exhibit your personal qualities, your professional characteristics, and your style in how you apply those qualities to your work life. Make living your brand a daily practice.

Chapter 20

Ten Things You Can Do to Continue to Build Your Brand

In This Chapter

- Staying current to stay relevant
- Promising value with your brand
- Making your personal brand a Confidence Emitter

Building and maintaining your personal brand requires constant attention. You spend the most effort up front in the branding process, but in order to have an effective brand, it needs to evolve with you. In this chapter, I offer ten suggestions for ways to keep your brand moving forward.

Implementing Your Personal Brand Strategy Plan

Your personal brand strategy builds longevity into your brand. Setting a strategy means you are committed to your personal brand for the long haul. You create a personal strategic plan that accurately reflects who you are and what you can do. Setting the strategy is like setting any good set of goals: You first want to think about the big picture of what you hope to accomplish in communicating with your target audience.

Your big-picture vision helps you set an overall goal that is then best accomplished by filling in your plan with implementation details — the steps that will carry you toward your goal. By including details about the activities you want to use to promote your personal brand, you'll be more likely to follow through. (I show you how to turn your personal brand profile into a strategic plan in Chapter 7.)

Staying Relevant

Doing the personal branding process once and never looking back or reevaluating it are big mistakes. Crafting your brand is not a one-time process. People with strong personal brands continue to evolve by incorporating their new knowledge, changing business trends, or a change of target market into their brand.

In order to keep your personal brand relevant and progressing, you need to set goals and constantly work toward accomplishing them. The world is moving too fast to hang your reputation on a singular effort. Strong brands are always improving and making sure that they are significant to their target market.

Continuing to Evaluate the Competition

Your competition is not always who you think it might be. You need to constantly be looking at who else is serving your target audience and what new services or products he provides. Often, the greatest competition comes from the most unlikely sources, such as an online resource and not just other competitors in your town.

Set up RSS feeds on your known competitors and conduct regular Google searches in your area of expertise. Whenever possible, get direct feedback from your customers about who is trying to woo them away. Keep your finger on the pulse of what is happening in the market and know when you need to ramp up your visibility. Chapter 6 keys you in on the competition.

Producing Genuine Value

You can't maintain a strong reputation and therefore a strong brand unless you can deliver genuine value to the people you serve. You need to stay current in your area of expertise and continue to find ways to offer a great product or service to your target market.

Chapter 4 helps you identify what you have to offer and the value that you bring to your market. Chapter 8 guides you in telling your story so that your target audience is reminded about who you are and what you can deliver.

Working on High-Profile Projects

TIP

One of the best ways to get your personal brand noticed is to play a key role on a high visibility project. Volunteer for the projects that are important to your company or your client. Find extra projects that will allow you to be seen by the people you're trying to attract. Of course, you want to make sure that you do a stellar job and that the work you do enhances your brand and doesn't detract from it. Chapter 16 provides more workplace wisdom.

Setting New Goals

In a well-known Harvard Business School study, graduates of the MBA program were asked to set clear, written goals for their future and their plans for how to accomplish them. It turned out that only 3 percent of the graduates had written goals, 13 percent had goals that weren't written down, and 84 percent had no specific goals at all. Ten years later, these same students were studied. The researcher found that the students with goals, especially written goals, had far out-earned the students with no specific goals.

Chapter 4 gives the details of this study and offers you guidance in setting and achieving your own goals. People with strong brands are continually re-evaluating their goals and looking at what trends impact them. Set new goals regularly by reviewing smaller goals weekly and major goals at least once a year.

Aligning Your Time with Your Brand

When you have a personal brand, you're naturally more efficient. You know your purpose and are able to focus on the important on-brand activities. You have an easier time identifying an off-brand activity and eliminating the clutter that keeps you from being on-brand.

By extension, a brand helps you plan your time because you can align your activities with your personal brand strategy (see Chapter 7) and your communication plan (see Chapter 11). You learn to purge what no longer supports your unique promise of value. Aligning your time with your brand frees you from the things that you no longer want (or need) to do.

Keeping Up with Technology

This point is crucial: If you're computer illiterate, you're going to have a very tough time building a brand. You don't need to be a technical wizard to build and keep your brand, but you do need to know enough to hire the right people to help you communicate your brand online.

Chapter 10 provides a good basic overview of what you need to know to take and build your brand online. Working online can feel overwhelming if you haven't ventured into this world before, but have no fear: Many people make it their business to help you build your business online.

Nurturing Your Network

You won't keep your network for long if you ignore them. Chapter 15 is filled with ideas to honor your connections. Remember these tips to nurture your network:

- Make an effort to stay in touch by sending personal e-mails, going for coffee together, or speaking on the phone.
- Connect your contacts by sharing your connections with other people.
- Ask how you can help or be of service to your network contact.
- Let your network know about a valuable resource.
- Invite people in your network to attend events with you.
- Build your network by attending social events.
- Update your social media sites by staying current with posts on LinkedIn, Facebook, or Twitter.
- Send an online newsletter.

Be a Confidence Emitter

The *Confidence Emitter* is a brand persona on the 360Reach assessment (Reach Communications). A Confidence Emitter is comfortable in his own shoes and is self-assured. This person exudes confidence and gains the respect of those around him just from the way he exists in the world. He's happy with who he is and shows a great deal of self-awareness.

Ultimately, having a strong personal brand is hard unless you're a Confidence Emitter. Strong brands require a keen self-awareness. You need to be able to identify what is working and what needs improvement. You must also accept who you are. You, too, can be a Confidence Emitter and let the world know just how much you have to offer with your unique personal brand.

You can find out more about the 360Reach Assessment in Chapter 4 or online at `www.reachcc.com/360v5register`.

Index

• A •

• B •

• P •

• Q •

• R •

• S •

• Y •